The Darkest Hour!

Ann is trembling. A hand flies to her mouth and she bites one finger.

Then her screams come. One long shriek.

I am near the head of the stairs when I hear a door burst open, then footsteps coming.

"What's the matter with you two?" the president's mother snaps . . . "Please, can't you keep quiet? I've never heard such commotion. Do you want to disturb Mr. Kennedy," Mrs. Kennedy says, then turns and leaves. After a few steps, she snaps over her shoulder: "And someone tell Ann to turn that television off."

"Mrs. Kennedy, the president has been shot," I tell her.

Rose Kennedy staggers. Her upper body sways.

She steadies. "Is he dead?"

TORN LACE CURTAIN

FRANK SAUNDERS
with JAMES SOUTHWOOD

PINNACLE BOOKS **NEW YORK**

TORN LACE CURTAIN

Copyright © 1982 by Frank Saunders

A Pinnacle Books edition, published by special arrangement with Holt, Rinehart and Winston

First printing, February 1984

ISBN: 0-523-42121-4

Can. ISBN: 0-523-43094-9

Cover photo by Wide World Photos

Printed in the United States of America

PINNACLE BOOKS, INC.
1430 Broadway
New York, New York 10018

9 8 7 6 5 4 3 2 1

My eternal thanks to
Loretta M. Gorington
(now Mrs. Gordon B. Murphy)
7th Grade, Williard School
"Turn of River"

TORN LACE CURTAIN

PART ONE

1

I came back to their houses, to the compound at Hyannis Port, in the spring of 1980, ten years and a few months after my boss Joseph P. Kennedy died and his widow made good her threat to fire me. Rose Kennedy thereby kept a promise she had repeated many times, usually when I least expected it, during the eight years Mr. Kennedy was confined to his wheelchair, crippled and speechless from a stroke.

Standing again on the veranda of the big house that crisp and windy March afternoon, I thought back to the day I left the Kennedys. The decision to dismiss me as chauffeur had seemed petty of Mrs. Kennedy, especially considering the many times I had saved her husband's life. Whenever that alarm bell hooked up at my place at Hyannis Port or Palm Beach went off in the night, it always made me think that I was back in the navy. It was a connection I could never shake in those drowsy waking seconds before I remembered that the alarm was a signal; the boss was having an attack and would need oxygen, and off I'd run to help save his life. I never got used to that damn bell, although I got used to Rose Kennedy telling me that when the Ambassador died, the family would no longer be able to keep me on.

I couldn't really blame Mrs. Kennedy for her attitude, not when considering all she had been through. After all, I was the one who'd had to tell her that her son the president had been shot in Dallas. I understood what she'd gone through, all right. But why did she have to lie about my termination? If she thought that made it easier on me, it didn't. All she had to do was tell me the truth, that she wanted to be alone. I would have understood.

Instead she said the Kennedys could no longer afford to keep me on. That's what Rose Kennedy, matriarch of one of the wealthiest families in America, said to me. The Kennedys did not have enough money to keep a chauffeur!

Saying it, she had been unable to look me in the eye that final day. She knew I had loved Joe Kennedy. And she had memories of her own to wrestle with, such as what happened in Palm Beach when the boss had his stroke. If she could not face the truth and couldn't rid herself of all her torment, at least she could rid herself of a prime witness. So maybe her letting me go was understandable, even with the lie. The one thing I could not forgive her was that she never thanked me.

Maybe it just wasn't in her nature. I was hired help, after all, not family. But Frank Saunders was different from the rest of the help. I had been given the seal of approval by the Ambassador. I had been her husband's man. I had spent more time with Mr. Kennedy during my ten eventful years with the family than had all his children. Not only that, I had spent more time with Mrs. Kennedy than she'd spent with her husband.

In the first weeks after my boss's death, stories circulated about how, before he died, Mr. Kennedy dipped into his millions and took care of the household staff. His Park Avenue, New York, office arranged it all, the story went. Friends of mine read it in the newspapers and believed that Ambassador Kennedy must have made sure the chauffeur was left well fixed. Here I was, in desperate need of a job, and no one took me seriously. When I told my friends that it was just another Kennedy story, they smiled at me. It was only after I told them what had really happened that they knew I was telling the truth, but having to do that even with a few close friends upset me because it meant revealing a few secrets I had vowed not to tell.

I had made a promise to myself, that I would keep my silence about my years with the Kennedys until I knew that

4

anything I might say could not hurt Rose Kennedy. Time and time again Mrs. Kennedy had told me that her own memoirs would never be published while she was alive. She went back on her word, bringing out her book in 1974, four years after I left. Then came another reason to wait, when Ted Kennedy ran for the presidency in 1980; I did not want anyone accusing me of telling stories behind his back that might be used to embarrass him. But today Rose Kennedy cannot be hurt by anything I say. She is safely beyond that. I knew this for certain when I met her again during the summer of 1980. She had found by then the serenity she deserved.

There were no Kennedys around that March afternoon. I was there because the family needed a part-time security guard for the weekends. I welcomed the job. I could use the extra money, and being back there again, and alone, I could confront my memories directly.

Rose Kennedy was wintering at Palm Beach then. She didn't know that I had come back to work for the family. But then it was not something that any of the family needed to be consulted about. The New York office had simply put me back on the payroll.

I looked in on Mr. Kennedy's house. The place had hardly changed. A new coat of paint in some of the rooms, new carpeting in her bedroom. His room was exactly as it had been all the time I was there. Currier and Ives prints of the four seasons—original ones, I am sure—on the wall behind his bed. Not a big room and not very fancy, never the kind of place where you felt afraid to sit down on a chair. But then neither of them had been ones for expensive furniture or constantly changing decorations. It was a place to be used and lived in—a large beach house, really—and it was good to see that it had not changed.

The movie theater in the cellar was worn and in need of some paint. The grandchildren had taken their toll. That first time I went back into the cement-block projection booth I was chased out by memories.

Showing the movies was an extra job I had to do for the Kennedys, one that I got to like and was paid a bit extra for.

The cellar projection room is like a cement-block jail cell. It has a steel door and a narrow observation window in the blocks between the projectors. Some people get claustrophobic in a small room, but I was used to tight quarters on ships in the navy, so it never bothered me. In fact, it was a good place to hide. With the steel door shut and the projector going, you couldn't hear much. At the Saturday matinees for the grandchildren, I let them scream and yell.

Through the slit I had a limited view of the theater. I peered through it now as I had a thousand times before, craning so that I could see all the seats. I closed my eyes and tried to picture the Kennedys.

They were all there, laughing. I imagined that they were waiting for me to start the movie. All of a sudden, as though an invisible hand had turned on the projector, the reels began to turn. Black-and-white images flickered on the screen, blurred and jerky. I blinked my eyes and focused and saw President Kennedy sitting in an open car. The president was in Dallas.

I quickly pulled away from the observation window and hit my head on the naked light bulb hanging on a cord. I thought I heard the snap of film breaking and the reels whirring wildly. It was over. The theater was empty.

Then I saw the shadow of a man. Mr. Kennedy, the old man, alone in the theater, sitting in his wheelchair in the same place I always put him. He turned his head and looked back at me. His blue eyes were drowning in fear, and he opened his mouth and started to scream.

I fled from the cellar, haunted by what had happened in the theater. I understood, all right. Did they think we really fooled Mr. Kennedy that terrible day his son was murdered in Dallas? The memory of that day and the charade we played on Mr. Kennedy choked me.

When I was at the compound those Saturdays in the spring of 1980, before the family returned for the summer, and before Rose Kennedy came up from Palm Beach, I never knew when a memory might come flying at me. There were some I did not want to provoke.

One day I went into the room where Mrs. Kennedy keeps her dolls, locked in glass cases. The room is next to the movie theater in the cellar. Perhaps movie theater and doll room adjoin each other by design. They were set up long before I came to work for the family in early 1961. Joseph Kennedy's passion was the movies; Rose Kennedy had her dolls. They had their separate rooms.

She was secretive about her dolls. Few people ever saw them. She had collected them since childhood. Whenever she went to a foreign country, she brought back a native-dressed doll. Her collection gave her great pleasure. For me, the dolls were a chore.

But now, as I looked at the painted faces of dozens of her dolls, they were old friends. I knew them all, so often had I taken the dolls out of their glass display cases, dusted them. I remember painting the shelves once and how she'd never thanked me. I could not find any new dolls. None had been added since I was at the Kennedy place. But then, she seldom traveled after her husband died.

There she was.

The Rose Doll. The doll's painted face unblemished, her milk-white complexion highlighted by a blood-red satin and silk gown and a single alluring red rose set in her black hair above her left cheek. There is a blush of rouge on her cheeks. The doll's unblinking dark eyes are untroubled, placid, as if she knows she is safe behind glass. On her rosy lips is the frozen trace of a coy smile.

All those years I could never tell if it was the start of a smile, or the end of one. Her smile puzzles me still.

The Rose Doll's white face, without a line, a wrinkle, a crease, is surrounded by a black lace mantilla, a doll-sized black veil just like her mistress's veils—the ones she wore to the funerals of her sons and husband.

The Rose Doll is Rose Fitzgerald Kennedy's fantasy of herself.

In the glassed-in section right next to the doll are Mrs. Kennedy's Japanese and Oriental dolls. Next to the ornate Orientals, on the bottom row, is the cardinal and his friend the monsignor. The standing priest dolls are almost two feet tall. In real life, Mrs. Kennedy never liked to be too far from the church.

I looked at the Rose Doll for a long time. Had I put her

7

in that case that way more than ten years ago? The faint smile seemed to be mocking me, as if she read my thoughts. Not a hair out of place. So perfect. Her dress just so.

The Rose Doll's dress was as carefully arranged as Mrs. Kennedy's dress the day Barbara Walters came to interview her. Her face was as white as chalk, like the Rose Doll's. Mrs. Kennedy had on a special makeup for the bright camera lights. Mrs. Kennedy was very good. She survived the ordeal unflustered. Barbara Walters had pried into Mrs. Kennedy's soul with simpering questions about her courage, her struggle to be brave and to set an example, and when she thought she had Mrs. Kennedy off-guard, she sniped at her with loaded questions.

Other women have suffered the loss of children, other wives have had to care for invalid husbands. Like them, Mrs. Kennedy had her crosses to bear, and she dealt with her grief in her own way. She cried behind closed doors, and in places the television cameras never went.

But they would not leave her alone. They created an image of Mrs. Kennedy as they created an image of all the Kennedys. But she was the one who had nothing to gain from any of it. She was a wife and mother of nine children; she had nothing to win and everything to lose. I don't know why she gave that interview to Barbara Walters. I guess she thought it was expected of her, that it was her duty.

In the end, the Kennedys were trapped in that public image they helped shape. They could hide only in their own houses. And that is where I came to know them, where they felt safe and where they could be themselves.

Mrs. Kennedy's escape was to her dolls, or the attic, or her faith, or long walks alone on the beach at Hyannis Port. I would see her, at summer's end, walking the hard sand along the tide line. She wore a black wool coat most times and a kerchief when the wind was up. With her collar raised and her kerchief peaked, she looked like a tiny shorebird.

She played golf. The golf course is nearby at both Hyannis Port and Palm Beach. She was a solitary golfer and played in the afternoons, after her nap. Her husband had been a morning golfer. Often she would play the same

8

hole over and over. She golfed for the exercise, not for the game.

Frequently she needed to be alone. It was a contradiction. She accepted and enjoyed praise, but she hated to be in the public eye. Driving her somewhere, I'd tell her that the reporters and television people would be waiting for her. "Frank, take me in the back way," she'd say. "I don't want them to see me." And in the rearview mirror I would catch her checking her hair and making sure her lipstick was right.

She was shy; yet she was determined to be on the best-dressed-women list with daughter-in-law Jacqueline, and she had trunks of dresses shipped back from Paris. She drove her maid frantic trying on dresses. Mrs. Kennedy always took the money and time to dress well, but she was not a spendthrift when it came to running the household.

Perhaps she secretly envied Jacqueline Kennedy's extravagant spending sprees, although I doubt she could understand them. She was afraid to spend her husband's money, and I suspect she never really knew how much he had. Or maybe it was her frugal nature. There was something else too; she was still living in the twenties when it came to how much things cost.

She could put down a dime for a one-dollar magazine and know she would get away with it, but usually when she acted like that she was a million miles off, thinking about other things. That's the way she drove, too. Which was why Mr. Kennedy wanted her driven. The family was afraid of another bad accident, like the one I'd heard she'd had near the church in Hyannis years ago, in which a girl had supposedly been injured.

If she was tightfisted with money, she could be generous with her feelings. She told me often to enjoy life when I was young, and there was a kind of melancholy in her voice when she said it. She never stood on ceremony with her chauffeur, for which I was grateful. As the years went by, after the assassinations, she lived more and more in her memories, back to when she was young and they were all together.

The attic of the Hyannis Port house was where she stored her memories. She took me up there with her at

9

least once every year while she rummaged through old family belongings. She inventoried them each time. She knew what was there, but she had a compulsion to make those pilgrimages to the attic. I came to understand how important that ritual was for her.

But the attic was empty in the spring of 1980, one warm Saturday when I snuck back up the stairs outside her bedroom. Empty except for three big cardboard boxes that I did not recognize. The old steamer trunks, the furniture, the boxes filled with old photographs, and the brown paper package—all gone. Some of the attic things had been cleaned out during my last two years and sent to John Kennedy's birthplace in Brookline. Others, I guess, went to the JFK Library.

I wondered what was in the three boxes, and I knelt on the rough wood floor to find out. They were crammed with letters. I thumbed through a few, and as soon as I saw what they were I left the attic. In the boxes were tens of thousands of letters of condolence from Americans on the death of John F. Kennedy. Perhaps they are still there.

I'll tell you this: there are strong presences in that house. I am not a superstitious person, but if the spirit of John Kennedy is anywhere, it is in his father's house.

What did all those people with their microphones and cameras and notebooks know about the Kennedys as a family? They were onlookers who saw what they wanted and what the Kennedys let them see. They never looked in the rearview mirror to see the anguish creeping into the corners of Mrs. Kennedy's eyes as we drove to morning mass.

The Kennedys were stage actors as far as they were concerned, and they actually believed the script. The journalists dubbed John Kennedy's White House "Camelot." They were the ones who created the "compound." We never called the place that, not in the beginning, not until it became such a frequent catchword that even the Kennedys used it.

And that's the way it happened in other ways, too. The Kennedys—some of them—believed the myths. America's royal family. King, queen, dowager, princesses, and princes.

That's where the family missed the old man. He would have told them how to cut through all the crap, or how to handle all the noise, if only he'd been able to talk. He was the master, the Chief, the brains. Mr. Kennedy knew it had changed from his day, when you slipped a newspaperman a sawbuck and bought his pen; now you have to give an exclusive interview and, instead of cash, slip him a smile. They were all there on the Kennedy lawns for the press parties, on the take for a smile from any Kennedy.

Like the son of a bitch who stuck his camera in Mrs. Kennedy's face inside Saint Francis Xavier Church the morning after her son died in Dallas. Like the one trying to crawl over the stockade fence at the president's house that same morning, when I gave the prearranged signal that Mr. Kennedy had been told the president was dead.

They stood outside in the cold. They never got inside. They never saw the light in the attic where she would go when she couldn't sleep. The press parties had always ended by then.

I never asked to be part of the family's secrets, but like them I couldn't escape either. I was Mr. Kennedy's man. I drove the car. I showed the movies. I picked up the mail and the food. I had the keys to the gas pump. I cleaned their swimming pools, did painting and odd jobs. I carried Eunice Kennedy down the stairs when she was pregnant and rushed her to the hospital. I drove Joan Kennedy to the hospital for Patrick. I put up their Christmas trees and took them down again. And I was the one they called on Christmas Eve to put the toys together. I washed and exercised Mr. Kennedy. It was my door Ted Kennedy knocked on when he had the accident in Palm Beach. It was at my place in Palm Beach where young Joe Kennedy wanted to stay when he visited. I was the one Jacqueline Kennedy asked to help her out of the water after she'd water-skied at Hyannis Port. I went running when the alarm went off in Mr. Kennedy's room. And I was the man the secret service agents sent into John Kennedy's house alone before we knew for certain he was dead in Dallas.

I did the best I could. Mr. Kennedy understood that I

had a pact with him. The Chief knew I would not leave him. Rose Kennedy knew it too.

So what did the Kennedy chroniclers know of the truth? When it turned bittersweet, when the Kennedys became the family that Americans were supposed to imitate when it came to grieving and the two assassinations became tragic dramas on national television, these mythmakers talked about a mysterious curse on the Kennedys.

They never discovered the true curse.

The unspoken tragedy in that house was that Joseph Kennedy and Rose Kennedy, father and mother, husband and wife, could not share the burden of grief. They were unable to comfort each other.

That was the Kennedy curse, and it marked the whole family.

It got worse after Robert Kennedy's murder. She had to fight harder to hold herself together. A woman in her seventies can take just so much.

But at least she had daily mass and her rosary beads. The Chief had to sit in his wheelchair and watch the funerals of two sons on the television screen. I was with him in his bedroom at Hyannis Port for Robert Kennedy's funeral. They said he couldn't control his tears because of the stroke. Couldn't they understand that he cried because another son had died? They stole his sorrow from him.

It killed him. His heart stoppages got more frequent, and then there was Chappaquiddick, and five months later Mr. Kennedy was dead.

In his lifetime, Joseph Kennedy and Rose Kennedy lost three of their four sons and two of their five daughters. They also lost each other.

Alone in the Hyannis Port house on a Saturday in the spring of 1980, I went to the wall outside the study and looked at the gallery of photographs. I remembered doing the very same thing the night I waited alone to meet the president for the first time. These photos were private to the family then. Since, a few have become famous and are etched in the memory of many Americans, as familiar as pictures in their own family album.

Three of the children I never met.

Joseph P. Kennedy, Jr., handsome, smiling, and so confident. The eldest son who had boasted he would be the first Catholic in the White House. The bomber he was flying on a secret mission exploded mysteriously over the English coast at the end of World War II.

Daughter Kathleen Kennedy stood in a Red Cross uniform, wearing that Kennedy smile. The second oldest girl, she had married a young English nobleman outside of the Catholic church. Her husband was killed fighting in Normandy two weeks after her brother had died. Then, four years later, as she was flying to meet the family in southern France, her plane crashed and Kathleen was killed.

And Rosemary, their first daughter. In the childhood pictures she seemed the prettiest of the girls. When Mrs. Kennedy came back from her visits with Rosemary in the home for the mentally handicapped, where Rosemary had been since her teens, Mrs. Kennedy would say nothing. Usually she went alone, sometimes she visited with one of her other daughters.

All I knew about Joe, Jr., Kathleen, and Rosemary— beyond my impressions of those photographs—had come from the Kennedy help. Wilbert Marsh, the gardener, and his sister Evelyn Jones, one of Mrs. Kennedy's maids, practically came with the house; in fact, they had been with the family since Joseph Kennedy bought the place. Wilbert and his sister were totally devoted to the family.

It was a hot and humid August afternoon in 1944, in Wilbert's recollection, when priests came up the veranda to tell Mr. Kennedy that his oldest son had been killed in the war. John Kennedy was at Hyannis Port recuperating from the wounds he suffered a year earlier when PT 109 was cut in half by a Japanese cruiser in the South Pacific. Robert Kennedy was home on leave from navy ROTC at Harvard. Even Kathleen had come home to Hyannis Port, returned from the bombing in London. All the family was there that day.

Mr. Kennedy went into his bedroom and stayed for days. The sound of classical music seeped from the open bedroom window, facing the bay, for the remainder of that summer. Wilbert listened to that somber music as he tended the flowers around the front of the house. Mrs. Kennedy wore a brave face, the gardener said, for the other children.

How was I to know, listening to Wilbert Marsh's story about the priests coming up the veranda steps that long-ago afternoon, that I would be the one, nearly nineteen years later, who would go up the back stairs to tell Mrs. Kennedy that the president had been shot?

She intrudes on me every so often even now. Her voice is shrill. "Frank! Frank! The pool is dirty, Frank!" In my dreams, I've learned not to argue with Mrs. Kennedy. She comes on me without warning. It is never in a dream about the Kennedys that she appears. On the front of her dress are pieces of notepaper she wears fastened with safety pins. The dream is always the same. As soon as I tell her, "Yes, Mrs. Kennedy, I'll clean the pool right away," she tears a note from her dress, crumples it, and disappears.

There are so many memories. One day I was in the kitchen when I heard the clatter of a helicopter. The whirlybird seemed to be coming down right through the roof, and I ran out onto the front veranda as the helicopter's shadow skittered across the lawn like a giant crab. All those happy Fridays when the president came home, dropping into the compound by helicopter, rushed to mind. I lingered on the veranda remembering them.

Friends have asked me how it is that I can remember so much from my days with the Kennedys, so many little things. The question is no mystery to me. Whenever someone wants to know, I always ask them if they remember the afternoon of November 22, 1963.

Everyone remembers that.

Then I answer. If you never had a childhood family of your own, neither would you ever forget your days with the Kennedys.

2

The Kennedys are the only family I ever got close to, ever saw the inside of. Growing up in a Catholic welfare home in Stamford, Connecticut, I never knew my father. I didn't even know his name. Saunders was my mother's name. I was thirteen when I met my mother.

The first thing in my life I can remember was when I was four and they took me from one orphanage and sent me to another. They said I was a Catholic and that I shouldn't stay in the first place any longer because it was Protestant. I was confused and frightened. I thought I belonged in the first place.

The new place was on High Ridge Road and was run by the Hermans. She was a big, warm-hearted Irish-American. Her husband was Dutch and very strict. All around were his birds—golden pheasants and ringnecks he raised for dog field trials. I had to feed his birds. There were chickens and geese in the coop behind the house. He had a kennel of fancy dogs and, before school, I had to feed them and clean the shit out of the pens. I can remember cold winter mornings and the ice in the dogs' dishes and banging them on the side of the wire pens to get the ice out. All the children had to work, but I was there longer and had to do bigger jobs the older I got.

Foster children and orphans came and went. Sometimes their parents put them in the Hermans' with the help of the church, and when the parents straightened out their problems or could afford to raise their children, they took them back. The orphans got adopted. This was during the Great Depression, and Christmas morning there were no toys. One time I got an orange. The Hermans did their best.

We could take one bath a week, on Saturday nights. I shoveled coal for the steam furnace and Saturday nights stoked the coal high. Sometimes when I was in the tub Mrs. Herman would come in. She hiked her skirt and squatted. I was old enough to be embarrassed. I turned away and closed my eyes, but I could hear her toilet noises and smell the stench she left. She spoiled my bath when she did that.

One day when I was thirteen Margaret Herman said, "Francis, your mother is here." I didn't know whether to cry or run. I had never thought about a mother or a father. The Hermans had become my mother and father. But I met the woman and I felt no emotion. I had accepted that I was an orphan.

My mother would come around every so often after that, a few times a year. She said not one word about my father. Later I learned that I had a half brother, and one time when she brought him I saw that he looked nothing like me. Sometimes I wished that she had never come at all.

It cost five dollars a week to keep a child at the Hermans', and my mother was always behind on the payments. I worked summers at a dog kennel in Stamford to pay my way.

I went to the Willard School. My friends called me Curly because of my hair. I was editor of the school newspaper and I did the illustrations in the paper and the yearbook. I was a good artist. Loretta Mildred Gorington was my seventh-grade teacher, and she took an interest in me. As soon as I turned seventeen I joined the navy because I knew I had to be on my own. I remember the day of my leaving—January 13, 1944. The steam from the locomotive filled the railroad station as if a great cloud had fallen. Out of it walked Loretta Mildred Gorington. She had come to see me off, to say good-bye and good luck. I have never forgotten that cold day at the train station or her simple act of generosity and love. It was the first time anyone had ever done anything for me.

16

By the time I got to the Pacific the war was ending. The navy was good for me because nobody cared who you were or where you came from, only what you did and how well you did it. I never felt homesick. I was glad to be out of the orphanage and on my own. By the time I was twenty I'd seen a big chunk of the world. Japan, Panama. For a while I thought that maybe I'd found a home in the navy, but it didn't turn out that way. In a sense it reminded me of the Hermans', the way nothing seemed permanent. New ports, new duty, new friends. So I got out after four years and went back to Connecticut, and with money I'd saved over my hitch I paid the Hermans the room-and-board money I owed, money that my mother had never seemed to be able to pay for my keep.

I got a job with a furniture company. Then Korea heated up and I went back in the navy as a cook on the USS *Missouri*, and was on the "Big Mo" through most of Korea. I took the exam for chief petty officer, but by then I'd pretty well made up my mind that the navy was not for me. I think I probably passed the exam, but I never waited to find out. As soon as I got out of the navy I headed for Boston.

I kicked around, then took a job as an apprentice chef at the Wayside Inn outside of Boston. There I met Betty and we got married. Her family lived in the city, and suburban Somerville seemed like a good place to settle. Our son Bruce was born in 1952. The chef's job at the inn was a lot of work and not much money. When my wife's brother-in-law said he could get me a job running a parking lot, I decided to take it, especially after he told me that there was extra money to be made running a numbers book on the side. It sounded good to me.

The parking lot I went to was at the corner of Stuart and Washington streets in downtown Boston. I liked the job and the place right away.

My world in Boston bore no relation to that of the Kennedys. It was peopled by prostitutes, pimps, derelicts, mob guys, bartenders, striptease dancers, hustlers, drug dealers, gamblers, loan sharks, cops, and sleazy businessmen. It was a zoo, but it was entertaining.

17

The parking lot was next to the old Metropolitan Theater. And, through the grimy windows of my little office, I could watch an unending parade of screwy characters. It was always show time. Most afternoons there was a special show: across the street, high up in an apartment building, two young ladies did a little strip dance for anyone who cared to watch. It helped to pass the time.

Boston had squeezed it all into one neighborhood and called it the Combat Zone. It was a kind of mini-Times Square. The place was smaller back then in the fifties. Most of the street people were my friends and for the most part they were good and decent. We watched out for one another. There were very few secrets.

Following work at the parking lot I would go off to drink at Pat Lynch's Dirty Dozen, at Moakley's, Soto's Lounge, or around the corner on Stuart Street at Jake Wirth's, where there was dark beer, good German food, and sawdust on the floor. At these bars there were legends and gossip about Joseph P. Kennedy. During the 1960 presidential campaign the Kennedy stories flowed as freely as the beer. Joe Kennedy was a ruthless son of a bitch who turned his back on his people. He had been corrupted by Harvard. Or . . . he was the salt of the earth, a fighter who had taken on the Yankees on their own turf and won, a great father who would put the first Irish Catholic in the White House.

The stories depended upon who was doing the talking and who the listening. One story stuck in my mind, a story I found out later happened to be true. Before he was appointed ambassador to the Court of Saint James's by his friend President Franklin Delano Roosevelt, Joe Kennedy used his political friendship with Roosevelt to good advantage. Prohibition was about to end and Joe Kennedy knew it, so he went to England with Roosevelt's son Jimmy and, using that influence, brought back the franchise to import Dewars and Haig and Haig Scotch and Gordon's gin. Then the Kennedy liquor business began importing the Scotch and gin for medicinal purposes. It was all very legal. When Prohibition ended, the Kennedy warehouses were filled with real Scotch. It was a bonanza.

Listening to that tale of wheeling and dealing, I was

struck by the notion that Joe Kennedy would be right at home in the Combat Zone. He sounded like a pretty sharp hustler.

Of course every man with a Joe Kennedy story swore he either knew the Ambassador personally or had been there when the story had happened. But there was one man who really did know Joseph Kennedy. Johnny Ford had been working for him for a long time, running the Joseph P. Kennedy movie-theater chain from a second-floor office in the Metropolitan Theater next to my parking lot, where he usually parked his black Lincoln.

One day in early 1961, Johnny Ford asked me, "Have you ever thought of doing something else with your life?" I had known Mr. Ford for six years. Usually he stayed in his office for a few hours every day, and I would put his big car in a special place so he could get out when he wanted. He was a good tipper, but he never played a number with me.

"Why do you ask, Mr. Ford?" I said. He knew I was always looking for an opportunity. I'd had the parking-lot job since I got out of the navy except one time when I'd left for a few months and sold aluminum storm windows. Mr. Ford had let me do his house.

"Mr. Kennedy is looking for a new chauffeur and I thought you might be interested," he said.

I laughed. "I don't know a thing about chauffeuring."

"There's more to it than chauffeuring, Frank. He needs a man he can trust. I've known you for a long time and I think you'd be good for the job." Then he gave me a sales pitch, touting the Kennedy job as an easy way to live like a millionaire without being one. The Kennedy chauffeur had his own place at Hyannis Port for the summer and his own place at Palm Beach for the winter. It was a front-row seat—the driver's seat—in a rich and famous family. "You'll work for Mr. Kennedy. Who knows where the job might lead?"

Johnny Ford knew I was open to a good offer. What he didn't know was that Deputy Commander John Slattery of the Boston police had begun putting heat on bookmakers and that everybody was running scared. No one knew how long the crackdown was going to last. "Let me think about it, Mr. Ford," I said.

All I really knew about Johnny Ford beyond his working for Mr. Kennedy was that he had been part of the old Irish Mafia, a crew of Boston Irishmen Mr. Kennedy took to Hollywood with him in the twenties, when he got involved in the movie business as a financier. Edward Moore, Mr. Kennedy's longtime personal secretary and friend, for whom his youngest son was named, was in that crew. Ford and Moore and others of these Irishers did very well in Hollywood. I had read once that Mr. Kennedy thought the Hollywood moguls were a bunch of "pants pressers" and that he was going to show them a trick or two. I guess he did.

Johnny Ford told me often how he would go to the wall for his boss. He said Joe Kennedy was the smartest and toughest man he knew.

If Mr. Kennedy likes you, John Ford said, he'll do anything for you. But if you cross him you are in big trouble. He told me this during the fall campaign, and as the campaign heated up, Johnny Ford smiled more and more. "Frank, it all comes down to this," he said one time, beaming. "Jack has Joe for his father. Have you ever heard about Nixon's father?" Nixon never had a chance, Johnny Ford had said from the beginning. Joe Kennedy was calling in his favors.

I liked talking with John Ford about the election because he had good insights. He knew I was a Kennedy supporter and was doing campaign work handing out leaflets and things like that, and I never asked him about the gossip I had heard about his boss.

After a few days thinking about the job offer, I asked Mr. Ford what I would have to do. The police crackdown had convinced me.

"Just fill out an application. Of course, the secret service will have to run an investigation on you. But that's all there is to it, Frank. Mr. Kennedy has pretty much given me carte blanche on this."

The way I sized it up was that Johnny Ford was telling me he'd swing the job my way. All I could think about, standing there in the parking lot talking with him, was that if the secret service learned about my bookmaking, I might be in big trouble. "Put me in for it," I said, hoping my two tours in the navy would count for something.

The Kennedy job paid $100 a week, and places at Hyannis Port and Palm Beach went with it. But it wasn't the money that appealed to me, it was the Kennedys. The base pay at the parking lot plus tips and the money I made booking numbers added up to a lot more than the Kennedy salary, yet a job with the president's family seemed to have a brighter and more interesting future. The more I thought about it, the more I liked the sound of it. Mr. Kennedy's chauffeur. When I applied for the job, John Kennedy had been in the White House only a few weeks and the newspapers and the television were filled with the Kennedy family. The world that the Kennedys moved in seemed intriguing, a world I knew only from having read the novels of John O'Hara and F. Scott Fitzgerald.

Booking numbers in the parking lot had been a perfect setup, but my heart was no longer in it. It was a cash business, an extra service I provided my customers. Park your car and play numbers at the same time. I ran a small book. Most of my players were nickel-and-dimers. Everyone in the Combat Zone either played a number or booked. People handed me their tickets and cash; I was always walking around with tickets and receipts and cash, and I would stash the number slips in trunks of customers' cars. I kept the keys, knowing which regulars would be at the lot all day. The car trunks were as safe as a bank.

My deal then was that I kept half the take but handled the payoffs out of my pocket. If somebody hit big, the central numbers bank would give you a loan at a low interest. No one ever hit me that big. Each day I called in my list. A lot of it was repeat business and most of the people who bet with me had a set number. The central bank was always moving and the phone number kept changing, but the voices remained familiar. All I did was call and give them my book number—"This is number twenty-three"—and then read off my list. It was easy, and it did not take very much time.

But I was getting tired of the Combat Zone. As I thought about the glamorous world of the Kennedys, the street scene around me seemed suddenly tawdry. The bars, sex movies, dance halls, dirty-book stores had once been clustered and famous Scollay Square, but urban renewal and the politicians in the late fifties began pushing them out and they relocated in this section of downtown Boston around Stuart and Tremont and lower Washington Street. So this new Combat Zone was young in 1960, but it was getting old for me when I told Johnny Ford I wanted the Kennedy job. Nothing I saw walking the streets in the Combat Zone came close to the pictures of Jacqueline Kennedy.

I had waited a few weeks but heard nothing from Johnny Ford, and I never brought the subject up, figuring it was not my place. When I'd spot a real chauffeur with the suit and boots going up to the Kennedy office in the Metropolitan for an interview, it seemed I was kidding myself that I had a chance for the job.

The suspense got to me. "What's happening with the chauffeur's job?" I asked Mr. Ford finally.

"What's your views about it now that you've had time to think it over?" Mr. Ford asked.

"I think it would be a real challenge," I said.

"The job's yours."

I was stunned. I couldn't believe that I was actually going to be the Kennedy chauffeur. "What do I do now, Mr. Ford?" I asked.

"Wait," he said.

"How long?"

"Oh, I'll put you on the payroll right away. But until Mr. Kennedy needs you, you'll just have to wait."

The Kennedy office bought me a pair of chauffeur's suits, a hat, a dozen white shirts, and a couple of narrow black ties. Each day I went up to the Kennedy theater office, and I waited. "Take the rest of the day off," Mr. Ford would say. It became a routine.

John Kennedy had been president for less than two months, and his parents were in Palm Beach. Then they were in the south of France. The office had no idea when my new boss would be back. There were stories in the Boston papers that the president's father was deliberately staying away from his son. The Boston press liked to call Mr. Kennedy "Ambassador" from the days at the start of World War II when he was U.S. ambassador to Great Britain, and the stories claimed that Ambassador Kennedy did not want anyone accusing him of influencing his son's politics. I was getting tired of reading about the family in the newspapers. I wanted to meet the man I was supposed to be working for.

One day Johnny Ford said it might be a good idea if I took a ride to Hyannis Port. I jumped at it; anything to break the monotony. I had scouted every shortcut to Rose Kennedy's brother's house in Dorchester—a house where, in true Boston Irish tradition, her mother also lived—until I could find it blindfolded. Each time I checked out the Fitzgerald house—dressed in the black chauffeur suit—I felt as if I were casing out a Brink's heist. Other times, friends would see me in my Chevy with the hat and the suit and ask me what I was doing. Driving ghosts around Boston was getting under my skin.

"You know how to get to Hyannis Port?" Johnny Ford asked. I told him not to worry. "I'll find it!" I said excitedly. I couldn't wait to see the Kennedy place and the chauffeur's own quarters.

Anyone could have driven into the place as easily as I did that sunny spring day. An unguarded sentry box not much bigger than a telephone booth stood at the entrance to a macadam road that went to the beach. The white paint on the sentry box was fresh. As I drove by I could see that the wood inside was new and not weathered. My instructions were to take a hard left after the sentry box, before the road to the beach curved sharply right.

I turned in. The road was hard-packed gravel, and I came to a second empty sentry box, also new. I drove the convertible slowly so I could take a careful look at the white summer houses. About a dozen, counting rooftops. I did not know which were Kennedys', and some were bigger than others, but I would have taken any one of them. It was a pretty place and very private. Right now it was deserted.

The place smelled good. The wind made an eerie moaning as it buffeted the colony of waterfront houses. There were no tall trees that I could see, just hedges, so I was unable to gauge the force of the wind. But I knew it must be fierce because I could feel wind coming through where the cloth top joined the window molding. A big window at the front of a gambrel-roofed white house facing the bay shook when the wind caught it. I watched the sun shivering on the glass. There appeared to be a fire in the house, as the sun's reflection flashed on the window. The house belonged to Robert Kennedy, but I didn't know that then.

Halfway up the narrow dirt road, I stopped. Even though I was on the Kennedy payroll, I felt like an intruder.

I watched the waves on Lewis Bay for a long time. Then a lone seagull dropped down suddenly and seemed to be attacking my car. The gull's cawing was a laughing cry, and for an instant I wondered if the seabird was an omen. Was it laughing at me for wanting to be part of the Kennedy family?

The dirt road ended at a cul-de-sac in front of a big white house. I figured it must be Mr. Kennedy's. The front lawn slopes gently toward the beach and, where the lawn ends, there is a stretch of eel grass, then sand dunes with taller beach grass. The dunes then were waist high.

The flagpole in the driveway turnaround was not flying a flag that day, and its halyards, tied at the base of the pole, slapped in the wind. Beyond, I could see a rock breakwater.

I did not drive into the cul-de-sac but went down the driveway at the side of the house to where there is a good-sized parking area and, at the far end, a garage with four big double doors painted green.

I parked the Chevy in the middle of the parking area, alongside some hedges. From behind the big house an older man wearing work clothes hailed me. "Can I help you?" he asked, the wind carrying his voice as he walked toward me.

"I'm Frank Saunders," I said, walking to meet him. "I'm the new chauffeur."

I saw him smile and we were close enough now to shake hands. I guessed he was in his fifties. He had white hair and a reddish face, and I could not tell if his face was ruddy from the wind or was always like this.

"Been expecting you," he said. He seemed shy. I turned from his eyes and looked around.

"This is it, then? This is the Kennedy place?"

"Yup. This is it. I'm Wilbert. Wilbert Marsh, the gardener."

"Mr. Ford said you'd be here. He said you would show me around. It's looking good, Wilbert. The place, I mean."

The hedges behind the big house had been trimmed and a pile of clippings had been raked. There was fresh soil along the side of the house and some yellow and purple flowers. The gardener saw me looking at the flowers.

"Mrs. Kennedy loves her flowers," he said.

"These will be gone by when she gets back, won't they?"

I hoped the gardener at least might know just when Mr. and Mrs. Kennedy would end their vacation and return to Hyannis Port.

"There'll be other flowers," the gardener said. "Down for good, are you, Frank?"

"No. I just wanted to see the place, see where I'll be living."

"Mr. Ford hired you for him? You known Mr. Ford long?"

"Yes. For quite some time. I ran a parking lot near his office and Mr. Ford kept his car with me and we got to know each other fairly well."

"How old are you, Frank?"

We were walking toward the big house. "Thirty-four," I said.

"Young fella."

"Young enough."

"You married, Frank?"

"Yes. One son. He's ten."

"They'll be livin' with you, I suppose?"

"Yes."

"Done any chauffeurin'?"

"None that I can count."

"The chauffeurin's the easy part."

We were at the front of the house now, near the flagpole, and he kept his eyes on the house, studying it like a house painter who had been asked to give an estimate for painting the place. The house is very long, with a veranda that runs the length of the main section. The place reminded me of those old ocean-front hotels, except it is smaller than a big hotel, though still very big for a house.

"This here's Mr. Kennedy's house. Got fifteen or so rooms and seven bathrooms and the kitchen and a room for the help, for television-watching and resting, and a movie theater in the cellar. Mr. Ford, he told you about the movie theater in the cellar?"

Mr. Ford had told me a lot of things, and vaguely I recalled his mentioning the movie theater. At least it did not seem unusual that Mr. Kennedy, who ran a chain of movie theaters and had been a moneyman in Hollywood, would have a private theater. "I guess he did," I said.

The gardener did not take his eyes from the front of the house. "I think one of the things you'll be doing around here, Frank, is showing the movies."

"That's fine with me."

The gardener nodded and smiled.

"This one was the Malcolm cottage before Mr. Kennedy bought it. They first come to the Port in 'twenty-five, I think it was, about the time he was in the motion picture business anyway, and they rented this one."

"You call that a cottage?"

" 'Course Mr. Kennedy added on to it after he bought the place in 'twenty-seven, I think it was. Just about doubled it, I suppose."

"Have you worked with the family long, Wilbert?"

"Long enough. Thirty years or so."

"That's a long time," I said.

"Yup," he said. He motioned to the house with the big front window that had caught my eye on my way into the place, when the wind had shaken the glass. "That house there belongs to Robert." It was large too, set at an angle to the big house and almost as close to the beach. We were walking toward Attorney General Robert Kennedy's house and were in the driveway beside the big house again. The wind had died.

"He has a nice view," I said. "How do you like working for the Kennedys?" Wilbert did not answer. He kept walking. He stopped in the driveway. "There," he said, and pointed between Mr. Kennedy's house and Robert Kennedy's house, "over those hedges there, out to the street by the tree line there, you see it? That's the president's house. See it?"

"Yes." I could see the top of the house. I guessed the building was a hundred yards away. "The president doesn't have the view his father or brother has, does he?"

"Don't make no difference," the gardener said. "They's others 'round here. Mrs. Lawford, that's the daughter married to the actor, well, she don't have a place of her own. Edward Kennedy's got a place over to Squaw Island there." Wilbert looked down the narrow dirt road. "Over that way, some. Can't see it from here anyhow. He rents it."

I caught Wilbert's eye. "You like working for them?"

"Got a sister who works here too, Evelyn Jones. She's a maid. You'll be meeting her eventually, I imagine. She's been with the family long time herself." Wilbert dug at the gravel with his shoe.

"There isn't very much around here, is there," I said. "I mean stores."

"Nope, Just houses and people with money and some natives." He smiled.

While we talked I scanned the Kennedy place, looking for a small house or a cottage. I noticed a building behind the president's house. It had a flatter roof than the surrounding houses. And beyond Robert Kennedy's house there was also a cluster of buildings. Maybe my little house was over there.

"I suppose you'd like to see where you'll be living, Frank?" the gardener said, reading my mind.

I did not have time enough to say yes before Wilbert announced: "There." He was looking straight ahead. There was no doubt what he was staring at; it was the garage, all right.

"The garage?" I said.

He heard the skepticism in my voice and glanced at me. "The garage is on the bottom. There's an apartment up above. Have a look you want to."

I had not noticed the dormer above the garage doors until now. The building was big enough, but it had never

27

dawned on me that the man who drives the car for a rich family would sleep with the car.

I followed the gardener upstairs.

After he opened the door to the chauffeur's place I closed my eyes. I was heartsick. The place smelled bad. The linoleum was faded and cracked and very old. The furniture was castaways, hand-me-downs, and worse. One stuffed chair had a broken spring and the upholstery was torn. The kitchen table had been put together from furniture parts. I tested the kitchen table and it felt shaky. The place was filthy dirty.

"Dave made that himself," the gardener said. He sounded boastful.

I knew that Dave Degnin was the former Kennedy chauffeur. Dave had been with the family for a very long time. I had not met Dave, but now I wished that I had.

The old stove was fueled by kerosene and there was a long twisted copper tube running from the stove to an oil drum. The place was damp and you could smell the kerosene. The refrigerator was also very old and had a coil on top, covered with a greasy layer of dust. I was getting mad, angry with myself for taking Johnny Ford's word that the chauffeur's place was real nice. I was thinking of my apartment in a pleasant large house back in Somerville and the big double French doors and the nice furnishings and how friendly I was with my landlord.

"The hell with this!" I said.

I went into the bedroom. "To hell with this!" I repeated.

Wilbert's ruddy face flushed and veins on his cheeks were the color of a beet. He did not say anything for some time, while I walked around the apartment. Then he pointed out, "It has a good view. From the windows here you can see the water." He said it "wah-tah."

"John Ford said the place was real nice. Was he lying to me?"

The gardener was silent.

"I'm not going to live here, Wilbert. My wife would take one look at this dump and she'd leave me."

I was laughing, and I could tell that the gardener did not know what to make of me. "You live on the grounds, Wilbert?"

28

"Hell no!" he said.

"Let's see the cars," I said.

The Kennedy cars had been in the garage long enough for a coat of powdery dust to settle on them. There was a four-door white Cadillac that was about a 1954 or 1955 model, with long thin tail fins and a severe wraparound windshield. There was a white Valiant sedan, a Nash Rambler station wagon, and a big Lincoln convertible. The Cadillac was the oldest, and the Lincoln was the best car in the garage.

"The Cadillac belongs to Mr. Kennedy," Wilbert said.

"Who owns the Lincoln?"

"Ann Gargan. Mr. Kennedy's niece. She's with them in Europe."

"That's a nice car," I said.

"Mrs. Kennedy has that white one." The Valiant was the economy model.

"Do they take these cars to Florida in the winter?"

"Oh sure. The chauffeur has to see to all that."

The Cadillac was not in the best shape. Beneath the dust I could feel a rough finish. It had not been polished in a long time and seemed very faded, with a good number of nicks and scratches. The Valiant was cleaner but its paint was bleached from the sun. "The salt air is rough on cars," I said. "The Florida sun can ruin the finish."

I looked at the Valiant, studying it the same way Wilbert had studied the front of Mr. Kennedy's house, and stayed silent a long time, long enough so you could notice how quiet it was in the big garage. It was a spartan car and had no extras. I cupped my hand to my forehead and leaned against the window and read the mileage. The car had not been driven much.

"Did Mrs. Kennedy buy this car in Florida?"

"Tell you the truth, I don't know," Wilbert said quickly.

I looked at the car. "The car doesn't have a heater," I said.

"That so?"

The gardener came over and cupped his hand to his forehead to peer inside the Valiant. "No need for a heater down to Florida." He-tah, he said.

I laughed, and my laughter, loud as it was, echoed in

the big garage. Wilbert appeared to think I was laughing at his Cape Cod wit, but I was laughing about the apartment above and myself for wanting the Kennedy job so badly that I had gone into it with blinders on. I was laughing too about the mother of the president of the United States, the wife of a very rich man, with a car without a heater. And I was thinking how cheap the family must be.

"How did it go, Frank?" John Ford asked from behind his desk as I walked into his office. He gave me a funny look, realizing I was mad.

"Not too good," I said.

"Oh? What's wrong?" He pushed the papers aside and looked at me.

"I don't think you've been in the chauffeur's place for a while, Mr. Ford." I had decided to give him the benefit of the doubt. He didn't respond. "Because you never would have said that it was real nice, because it isn't. To be very blunt about it, I just cannot live there, not like that. It's in a terrible mess, Mr. Ford."

"Oh, Frank. I am sorry. I really am."

"My wife wouldn't live in a place like that. And I wouldn't ask her to. I just cannot live there like that. With the salary I'm getting I don't think I could afford to rent the kind of place I would want."

"Oh, no. No! They want the man right there, Frank. Here's what we'll do. Now you be a little patient. If the place is as bad as you say, and I'm sure it must be, then I am certain, Frank, absolutely certain, that Mr. Kennedy will take care of everything just as soon as he gets back."

"Can I have your word on that?"

"Absolutely, Frank. If Mr. Kennedy agrees that the place needs some fixing up, why I am sure he would not want anyone who works for him to be unhappy. And I have told them you are a very good man and they would not want to lose a good man over something like this, something that can be fixed."

Wilbert didn't live on the grounds, so at first I had the compound to myself. John Ford had told me I could take the president's little guest house for now, until the garage apartment could be fixed up. Mr. Kennedy's staff came up from Palm Beach. Matilda, a pleasant, heavy-set Norwegian, and Dora Lawrence, Mrs. Kennedy's personal maid, moved into the big house. There was a young Finnish girl with them who was the upstairs maid, but I don't remember her name, and I hardly ever saw her in the few years she was with the family. The third maid was Wilbert's sister, Evelyn Jones, who came in with her brother for day work.

There wasn't much for any of us to do with no Kennedys at Hyannis Port. The staff tried their best to make me feel at home, but with a slightly cool edge. I suppose they saw me as having some kind of special in with the Kennedys to rate the guest house, after I'd flatly refused to live where the former chauffeur had been quartered. None of them talked much about the famous Kennedys, except to say that I'd see it all for myself as soon as the family started coming in to Hyannis Port. They asked me when my wife and son would be moving in, and I told them that I wasn't bringing my family until the garage was fixed up. And that apparently was going to have to be put on the back burner until Joseph P. Kennedy returned from the south of France. What I didn't tell the other help was that I wasn't taking any chances moving my family into a new place until I was certain that I was going to stay on. If Mr. Kennedy decided that fixing up the garage for a new man was too much, I was ready to pack up and leave.

I asked Wilbert when the Kennedys would start arriving. "As soon as school gets out. Ethel will be the first," the gardener said.

Actually, Robert Kennedy's wife came to Hyannis Port a few days early that year because a big Memorial Day weekend was planned, with both Joseph Kennedy and the president due to arrive.

3

"Yes, Mrs. Kennedy."

"You won't be late, Frank?"

"No, Mrs. Kennedy."

"Mr. Kennedy demands punctuality. Do you understand?"

Ethel Kennedy's rigamarole had become ridiculous. What did she think we were doing, rehearsing for a high-school play? As she went through her lines with me again, I wondered if she was more nervous about her father-in-law's return home from the Riviera than I was. By now I knew her routine by heart. She was a fiery and energetic woman, and she was becoming a pain. I had no trouble with orders, having taken them all my life—tell me what you want and tell me once—but there was something unsettling about the manner in which she gave me instructions. Some kind of superior attitude? She was my age, I guessed. Finally I must have shown my feelings because the last time she repeated his arrival time she gave me a funny look.

"I'll be there, Mrs. Kennedy," I assured her politely.

Every time I'd crossed paths with Ethel Kennedy since her arrival at Hyannis Port she'd mentioned her father-in-law's return. Each time I'd told her that all I needed to know was the time and place and I'd be there waiting. But she kept on telling me that she was waiting to hear from Mr. Kennedy's New York office, with the main question being whether he'd be coming in to the local airport or Boston.

It would be Barnstable Municipal Airport, Ethel finally told me. She'd gotten the word from New York that he was on his way the next day. The airport was only five miles away, and I figured it would be a piece of cake meeting my new boss. I could be there in ten minutes.

In fact, I was so anxious to meet Mr. Kennedy that I planned to be waiting at the airport well ahead of time. I had even scouted the airport, clocked the mileage. I had sat in his Cadillac in the garage, in the backseat, and pretended I was Mr. Kennedy. The car was as clean as I could get it. I found myself carrying on a conversation in my mind with Mr. Kennedy. On his payroll all this time while they were in Florida and then the Riviera, I was feeling guilty about being his chauffeur when I had no one to drive, working for a man I'd never met. So I looked forward to my baptism behind the wheel. In my imagined conversations in his car, Mr. Kennedy and I got along fine.

The day before he was to arrive, after the staff meal at noon in the big house, I had ironed my spare chauffeur's suit. The next morning, I polished my shoes until they had a spit shine. My chauffeur's suit was spotless. Inch by inch I inspected it for lint before the mirror in the guest house, and went over it with a brush. I noticed red blotches on my neck from the second shaving. The starched white shirt collar was irritating. I tried different angles with the chauffeur's cap, each time rubbing fingerprints off the glistening black patent-leather visor. None seemed right. The man in the mirror looked more like a doorman at a second-rate hotel than a chauffeur.

I was ready to go. I leaned toward the mirror again and straightened my narrow black tie. A shape moving in the driveway caught my eye. A strange car had pulled in and was stopping at the side of Mr. Kennedy's house. A man in a black coat stumbled out of the car, his face hidden from me by a bunch of flowers. He stood still in the driveway, surveying the place like he owned it.

He did own it! Damn, it was Mr. Kennedy!

'Even from this distance he resembled the Joseph P. Kennedy in photographs.

I took a deep breath and tried to be calm. Then I shot from the guest house, door banging open and slamming behind me, as though someone had yelled fire.

I forced myself to walk slowly and steadily down the driveway. Obviously there had been a mistake. Maybe this gentleman was Mr. Kennedy's brother . . . if he had a brother.

"Where the hell were you!" Joseph P. Kennedy bellowed. His shout raced up the driveway, funneled between the side of the house and a wall of hedges. I felt it blow by me and echo off the front of the garage. It filled the place.

My mouth froze open. There was nothing to say.

He fixed his cold blue eyes on me and stared me down, until I thought I felt blisters rising on my face.

The flowers I could see were roses, red roses. He clutched the bouquet to his chest, and the closer I got the tighter he clutched them. With each step the rose bouquet crawled up his chest. I was close enough to see the color in his face slowly deepening almost to the shade of the flowers, now thrust up against his chin.

He stood his ground and sneered. "Where the hell were you?" he repeated as I came within range. This time he expected an answer. I had none for him. Waxed paper around the roses crinkled as he squeezed their stems. It was then I noticed he had a young woman with him. He turned from her and stormed into his house.

She was ordinary-looking, with black hair. There was something about her face, the way her features were arranged, that faintly resembled the Kennedys in the photographs on the wall inside the house. She was in her early twenties. I had a feeling that she was aloof—cold—as if, even though she had been standing next to Mr. Kennedy as he scolded me, she was really very far away. She gave me a quick disapproving look, then followed Mr. Kennedy into the house.

I had heard stories about her that made her mysterious. Ann Gargan had been in a convent with a nursing order of nuns when she contracted a terrible illness. She was going to die, the Kennedy staff said. Her uncle ordered the best medical care for her, and she was taken from the convent. She began a miraculous recovery and had come to work for Mr. Kennedy. She was a daughter of one of Rose Kennedy's sisters. Mr. Kennedy did not particuarly like his wife's side of the family, but in Ann Gargan's case he made an exception. In turn, she was devoted to her uncle, who had now become her vocation. Her bedroom was near his. She was his companion.

She was something else as well. Ann Gargan was his chauffeur. She drove him everywhere. He did not need me as his chauffeur, but it would take me time to understand all this.

My stomach was heavier than their suitcases. I carried the luggage up to his bedroom. Mr. Kennedy's reputation for toughness had intimidated me. By the time I left his bedroom I could see no other alternative for him except to fire me for my mistake. Well, not my mistake really, nor even Ethel Kennedy's. Ethel had given me the arrival time that somebody in Mr. Kennedy's New York office had passed on to her. And then, as I found out later, the plane had gotten to Cape Cod much sooner than was expected. But I figured it would be futile to tell that to a man who didn't like excuses.

Later that day, Mr. Kennedy asked me to polish his riding boots. There was no mention of my having missed the plane, but I could tell he was treating me stiffly. While putting his riding boots back in the closet, I was suddenly struck by a beautiful woman's face—a blonde's—in the framed photograph on his night table. It was the only picture in the room. I wondered why I had not noticed it before. It was a dated photograph and her hair was in an out-of-fashion style. She had perfect full lips and deep eyes.

I had heard gossip in Boston about Mr. Kennedy and Gloria Swanson. There was supposed to have been more to their relationship than his financial support. But the woman in the photograph was not Gloria Swanson. Yet she was familiar. She looked like a movie star. Where had I seen the face before? So familiar, but I could not place her. I was afraid of getting caught in his room staring at her, so I left. But she stayed in my mind, reminding me of those nameless movie stars I used to find under celluloid in a brand-new wallet.

The night after my blunder with Mr. Kennedy, I was sitting with him in the long room at the front of the big house awaiting another arrival.

It was a bad night for the president's homecoming. The weather was foul and so, too, was his father's mood. Joseph Patrick Kennedy's anger steamed from him like from a boiling kettle. "God damn it! He's the president of the United States! You'd think he could at least order somebody to make a telephone call and tell his family what goddam time he'll be home—wouldn't you, Frank—God damn it!"

"Yes, sir, Mr. Kennedy." My reply was a whisper. I coughed, trying to raise my courage. "It's the weather, Mr. Kennedy. His plane's been delayed," I offered in a raised voice.

"The weather be damned! He's the president. I came all the way back here from France just to see him. . . ." As his voice trailed off, he waved his arms in disgust.

We waited alone in the dim half-light, and I could hear him seething. He jerked his head to look at me, and his round black-rimmed glasses flashed. His blue eyes were on fire, simmering. I couldn't look him straight in the eye.

I was dying for a cigarette. I felt nearly sick. What was I doing in this house? What kind of man was Joseph Kennedy, anyway? Which of the stories back in Boston was I supposed to believe? I didn't belong here. These people were rich and famous, and what did I know about the way they lived? If the cream rug at my feet was mine, I'd throw it in the dump. In the daylight I had noticed the worn spots and the streaks where the sun had faded it. If I was to ask the president's father now whether Oriental rugs were worth more if they were threadbare, what would he say? Would he tell me it was a valuable antique? I had assumed that Joseph P. Kennedy was a very wealthy man. Instead I was seeing things that made me suspicious. This Kennedy job had been crazy from the start. To escape his stare, I traced with downcast eyes the filigree pattern on the rug.

My chauffeur's uniform was new and stiff, and I was afraid to move, even to cross my legs. If I could have, I would have crawled right under that rug and hid.

And no one had warned me about his eyes. I feel them accusing me, like yesterday afternoon when he found his new chauffeur gaping at him like an idiot in the driveway. Each time he speaks I wince, expecting him to fire me.

I stay silent.

Outside, a pelting rain slants against long sea-facing windows. The big house is quiet as a tomb. There is a steady tempo in the rain that drums against the glass like anxious fingers killing time. The president's father is losing his patience.

"The hell with him," he hisses. "I'm going to bed."

I come to my feet obediently, so quickly I startle him. The heavy cloth of my uniform sounds as if it is tearing as I stand. "Would you like me to wake you, sir, when the president arrives?"

He smiles weakly. "Yes," he says thoughtfully. He pauses as though he is going to give me further instructions, but says nothing, then turns and walks to the stairs.

My question echoes in my ears. When the president arrives? Did I really say that?

I follow the president's father as he climbs the narrow front stairs, his left hand grasping the banister, and I stand there at the foot of the stairs listening to him pad along the upstairs corridor to his bedroom at the far end of the house. I am still standing there, rigidly at attention, when I hear the muffled slam of a door.

"When the president arrives," I repeat under my breath. It's just like the movies!

I go back to the front room and sit in Mr. Kennedy's chair. You're wrong, I say to myself. This isn't anything like the movies! For one thing, the Kennedy Cadillac is white, not black. For another, it's ready for the junkyard! And for a third, in the movies they never show where the chauffeur lives. Now I know why.

Where is everybody?

The president is coming home for the first time since his

inauguration four months ago in the snow, coming home to celebrate his forty-fourth birthday, and neither his wife nor his mother is here. Where did Robert and Edward Kennedy go? To bed at their own houses? So the only one to greet the president at the front door is a chauffeur he's never met? What kind of a family is this, anyway?

And where is the secret service?

At least I'll have a story to tell back at the bar at Jake Wirth's in Boston after Joseph Kennedy fires me. The more I think about it, the more resigned I become.

Maybe I should just leave now. Then I won't have to have it out with him about the chauffeur's quarters. But no, I think, it's just as well to stay. Have a little fun instead. When the president arrives, open the door for him and yell into the half-dark and empty house: "Ladies and gentlemen, the president of the United States! Everyone up for the president!"

I catch myself smiling at my reflection in the window. On the rain-dappled glass my face is a scrambled puzzle. The reflection of the USS *Joseph P. Kennedy, Jr.* seems very real, and I turn to look at the oil painting of the destroyer that was named for Mr. Kennedy's oldest son. In the painting the *Kennedy* is steaming fast in a turn. I wanted to say something about the painting to Mr. Kennedy, to make conversation, but I had been warned never to mention his dead son. The *Kennedy* is the centerpiece of the room, there on the wood paneling above the fireplace. It's a fitting place for the painting—facing the sea.

I can't sit still, so I walk to the wall outside a small study, and again I stare at the gallery of family photographs clustered there. Joseph P. Kennedy, Jr., with his brothers and sisters. All the children. Father and mother. Churchill. Roosevelt.

During the past few weeks, while waiting for the family to come to Hyannis Port, I have often stood before this wall of photographs, hoping to find in them answers to all the questions I have about this family I've come to work for. But the photographs give up no secrets. Mr. Kennedy does not seem much older today than when he wore the tall hat and black coat as U.S. ambassador to the Court of

Saint James's. How proud Mrs. Kennedy must be of all those children, posed around her in the family photograph.

The sharp ring of a telephone jarred me out of my daydream. I was in a panic as I searched for the telephone. There it was, just outside the study, and I grabbed it. I brought the receiver up and hesitated, realizing that I hadn't the slightest idea what to say.

"Mr. Kennedy's residence," I announced after a long pause.

"Tell him I'll see him in the morning," Mr. Kennedy ordered. Then the line went dead.

There was a shuddering beneath me, and for an instant I thought it was my knees. Somewhere in the cellar, the oil burner had just come on. I welcomed the noise. By my watch it was a few minutes after eleven o'clock; not very late, but then the cook had told me that Mr. Kennedy was an early-to-bed, early-to-rise man.

Craving that cigarette, I went out the front door onto the veranda. The rain was blowing in from the ocean, driving in sheets onto the long front porch, and I stood with my back against the wood-shingled wall of the house so it could not reach me. Sometimes when the wind gusted, the rain came almost level across the porch, forcing me back inside the house. The warmth of the house was tempting, but each time I took refuge inside I decided quickly to move back out—to be standing on the porch when John F. Kennedy came home to Hyannis Port for his first time as president.

A foghorn kept sounding in the blackness of Lewis Bay. I struck a match for another cigarette and the damp sulfur fizzled, then caught flame. The foghorn was constant, its baying wind-blown so I could not tell exactly where it was. I timed my breathing to it, and the cigarette tasted good. The house is a hundred yards from the beach, but in the dark I could not see the water. Between gusts of wind and rain I listened to the waves lapping the beach.

From my vantage point on the veranda I would be able to see the lights of the president's entourage as soon as they turned in to the long driveway. I estimated two minutes, once I saw the lights, before they would reach the house. As the time passed, I tapped the steel tip of an umbrella on the wood floor. Finally, I saw them coming.

Headlight beams flooded the road. One car had a red light on its roof. Flicking on the overhead veranda light, I glanced at my watch. A few minutes past one. I opened the umbrella. The cars were coming very fast, and their headlights bounced in the blackness. The standing water in the ruts of the road splashed high around the lead car, and the spray spumed up onto the fronts of the cars trailing. There were four altogether.

I moved quickly down the veranda steps and stood at the edge of the curved driveway, the umbrella like a black mushroom above my head. Momentarily blinded from the headlights as the cars swung into the drive, I stepped back. The cars stopped simultaneously and doors burst open. Men in business suits and raincoats were everywhere.

No one said anything to me.

One car had lurched to a stop in front of me and was still rocking as I reached for the handle of the rear door. Before I could open it, a man with eyeglasses pushed the door against me and sprang from the car. A light went on in the rear of the car. John Kennedy squinted at the sudden light. His face looked tired.

Someone opened the opposite door, and out of it the president stepped slowly and walked around the back of the car. A burst of wind lifted the umbrella as I went to where the president stood. He was bent forward slightly and was pressing the palms of both hands to his back, at his waist. He straightened as I thrust the umbrella over his head.

"Welcome home, Mr. President," I said. "I'm Frank Saunders, your father's new chauffeur." My greeting was blown away in the wind, and I was sure he had not heard me.

He was wearing a gray felt hat. Seemingly distracted by the men talking around him, he paused for a second, then started for the veranda steps. I walked behind him with the umbrella.

"Frank. Glad to meet you," the president said without turning to look.

He halted suddenly at the edge of the light that spilled

down from the veranda and glanced up toward his father's darkened bedroom. Now in the light, I could plainly see his face. He was smiling.

As he strode up the veranda steps I tried to keep the umbrella over him, but it was awkward because he was taller and took the steps quickly.

"Grab the luggage!" someone shouted.

The downstairs guest bedroom had been prepared for the president. As I entered it, lugging suitcases, I thought I heard someone say, "Send in the broads."

The man with the eyeglasses, whose hurried exit from the car had pushed me back, was talking with the president. They had taken off their overcoats.

I put the suitcases where I thought they should go and was leaving the room when, on impulse, I asked, "Is there anything I can get you, Mr. President?"

His friend with the glasses was bouncing up and down on the bed making strange noises, acting like a child.

"Fine. Fine," the president said. He was looking at his friend. "Keep it down, Lem," he said.

"Let's wake him up!" his friend said, still bouncing on the bed.

"Is my father asleep, Frank? It is Frank?"

"Yes, Mr. President. Yes."

"Wake him up, Frank," the man on the bed said.

I looked at the president. "He said to tell you that he'll see you in the morning, sir."

As the president nodded, his smile widened. "Frank!" he said suddenly. "How about a glass of milk! And don't mind Lem, Frank," nodding to the guy on the bed. "He thinks he's still in prep school."

"Yeah? Well, who's asking for milk?" this Lem said.

I went for the milk.

When the light went on inside the double refrigerator, three dozen lobsters stirred. Joseph Kennedy had a big day planned the next day for his son, with a cruise on his yacht, *Marlin*. The refrigerator, an oversized restaurant type, was so jammed with food I could have used a shoehorn to get the milk out.

I turned with the bottle in my hand to find the president standing in the kitchen in his shorts.

41

"It's good to be home, Frank," he said with a broad grin. I smiled too, realizing that he had somehow been freed of the burden of the presidency the moment he had walked through the front door of the old familiar house. The disaster of the Bay of Pigs invasion in Cuba had been six weeks before and was still a hot topic in the newspapers. John Kennedy was taking the flak for the military adventure of some anti-Castro Cuban patriots that had been planned by the Eisenhower administration. But those problems belonged in the White House. Here, I could tell, he felt at home, and that made me feel comfortable with him.

"So what do you think of Hyannis Port?" he asked.

I told the president that I thought it was a beautiful spot, and we spent a few minutes talking about the place. I neglected to mention the chauffeur's quarters. He absent-mindedly massaged his back, which he had strained at a tree-planting ceremony in Canada a few days before. I remembered that from the papers, and then I caught a glimpse of the vicious scar above his waist. I was stunned. His was no cheap Purple Heart.

I felt self-conscious watching him sip milk.

"Are you Catholic, Frank?" he asked. His question came so quickly that I was taken aback.

"Yes," I said as I watched him walk slowly around the big unattractive gray kitchen.

"Good! Good, Frank. You'll be driving my mother to church. You'll be in a constant state of grace, Frank," the president said.

Then, favoring his back, he sauntered out of the kitchen to the guest bedroom and his friend, who, I learned the next day, was Kirk Lemoyne Billings, an old crony from prep-school days.

In the kitchen I let the excitement drain from me. How many people could claim to have seen the president in his underwear? And moments after meeting him? It was a good story for telling at the bar. The house was as quiet as it had been before he arrived. Where did all the secret service go? I wanted to laugh out loud, but was afraid to. John Kennedy wears navy-issue shorts! I knew navy issue when I saw it, and those shorts were navy issue, all right.

* * *

The president stayed inside his father's house most of the next day. The weather was raw and overcast and there was a stiff wind, so the cruise on the *Marlin* was scrubbed. I hung around the house in case I was needed, but no one went anywhere.

When it brightened, the president came out of the house and sat on the front lawn and read. He kept a wool Notre Dame blanket wrapped around him because his back was still bothering him. He sat on the lawn alone until the photographers came; from what I could tell he had come out for the photographers, not because he wanted to be out there. As he returned to the house, he seemed in some discomfort. His doctor Janet Travell was there. They were concerned about the president's back because he was scheduled to visit France and meet President Charles de Gaulle, right after this reunion with his father.

Everyone was talking about the upcoming trip to France, President Kennedy's first real state visit. Even the maids were talking about it, but their concern was not so much an interest in global politics as in house rivalry. In the dayroom behind the kitchen one of the maids mentioned what an interesting coincidence it was that John Kennedy's mother Rose just happened to be in Paris and would meet her son and Jacqueline there. There was speculation as to which Kennedy lady would steal the spotlight. That kind of household gossip made me uncomfortable, but I listened because it was one way to learn about the family, though I planned to take it all with a grain of salt. The maids and the cook agreed that Rose Kennedy was planning to remain in France for the summer as a gesture toward her daughter-in-law—to allow Jacqueline to have the Kennedy place all to herself.

I hadn't heard any such thing, not from Johnny Ford or any member of the family. But as far as the help was concerned, Rose Kennedy's absence was a bonus. "Count your blessings, Frank," one of the maids said. I kept silent. Besides, I was still not certain how much longer I'd have the chauffeur job. I'd had trouble falling asleep the night before, still thinking about the incident in the driveway with Mr. Kennedy and how I was sure I had lost the Kennedy job just as it was beginning. I figured Mr. Kennedy would wait until this Memorial Day weekend reunion with his son was over and then put the kibosh on me.

Then there was some talk about my having stayed up until after one to meet the president. I made the mistake of asking who this friend Lem Billings was. "Oh, him! He's always here," Dora Lawrence said. "I think he sleeps with Jack more than Jacqueline does," she said.

This was all so new to me, I did not know what the maid was talking about. And evidently I showed it. The maid laughed, a kind of half laugh. "President Kennedy doesn't like to sleep alone, Frank. Lem Billings is an old school chum, and he's always with him," she said.

The next night—I think it was the next night—I found an excuse to go over to the house. I figured there was a dinner party going on, because no one was around outside. All the downstairs lights were on, and I walked across the front lawn close to the veranda. Suddenly a beautiful young blonde appeared alone at one of the picture windows. Self-conscious, I turned away thinking that she was looking at me, but then realized that she could not see me from inside. So in the darkness I watched her. Her face was expressionless. She pressed against the window, and I noticed after a long while that Joan Kennedy was beginning to show her pregnancy. I was near enough to hear laughter in the house, and evidently whatever was going on in there meant nothing to Joan Kennedy. After she turned away from the window I did too, and walked back to the guest house.

The president went up to Boston for a big political birthday party, driven by the secret service, and then in a few days he was in Paris with his wife. His mother was there also, but there was no doubt who was the center of attraction. The French people went wild over America's First Lady; as her husband quipped, "I'm the man who accompanied Jacqueline Kennedy to Paris."

His father stayed on at Hyannis Port, and the confrontation over the airport incident that I had been expecting never happened. Not one more word was said about my absence that morning.

Feeling surer of myself now, there was something I had

44

to get straightened out with my new boss if I was going to stay on the job. One time when I was a boy back at the orphanage, there had been a fire and it had gutted the upstairs of the house. It had taken months to fix the place. In the meantime I lived in a filthy chicken coop behind the house. We tried to clean it up as best we could, but the stench was soaked into the wood and there were lice all over the place. I never forgot living in that rotten chicken coop, and while the room over the Kennedy garage wasn't that bad, it was a disgracefully filthy place for anybody to have to live in. I thought I had blanked out the nightmare of living in the chicken coop, but it came back that night the president returned home.

There was something else about it too, something unsettling. When Wilbert Marsh had seen how I reacted to the chauffeur's place, he'd been shocked. Apparently, you just didn't complain openly with the Kennedys, not if you wanted to keep your job.

Still, John Ford had just about promised that Mr. Kennedy would do something about the place once its condition was brought to his attention. And if growing up without a father and mother had taught me one thing, it was that I had to look out for myself because nobody else would.

My opportunity came a few days after the Memorial Day weekend. The big house was virtually empty, and Joseph Kennedy was himself about to leave.

"Frank, there's a couple of things I'd like to get straight with you," he said. "All I ask is that somebody who works for me does the best they can. If they do the best they can, if they try their best, that's all I ask. That is what I expect of my children, and it is what I expect from those who are with us."

The president's father spoke quickly. His voice was strong and he sounded younger than seventy. His days at Harvard and the places he'd been since he left Boston had dulled his accent. He kept his eyes on me while he spoke, and I understood then what the expression *eyes like daggers* meant. The most powerful physical thing about him was his blue eyes. He knew how to use a silent stare better than any man I ever met. He had the presence of a stage actor with those eyes, and his round black-rimmed glasses only served to set them off, to frame them.

"Johnny Ford has been with me a long time. I trust him." For the first time he smiled. I noticed that his face was peppered with freckles, even the top of his head where he had gone bald. There was still some red in his white hair, at the temples. He was trim, and that was the way he talked: trimly.

I nodded.

"Now I'm returning to France with Ann, to rejoin Mrs. Kennedy. We'll be there most of the summer, so you'll have to feel your way on the job. Don't let any of these bozos push you around."

He seemed satisfied with that, as if he had nothing more to tell me, not even how to tie my tie or how to polish the car.

"Mr. Kennedy. I wonder if I could have a few minutes of your time?"

He looked puzzled. "Yes, why yes. . . . What is it about, Frank?"

"I'd like to show you something, sir." I thought I detected a slight impatience, so I said, "My quarters. When you have a chance. . . ."

"Let's go," he snapped.

He led me out of his house to the garage. I opened the door to the chauffeur's apartment.

I said nothing. He surveyed the kitchen, then walked to the living room at the front of the apartment. It took him about five seconds. "Fix it up, Frank," he said. "Fix it the way you want it. Talk to Johnny Ford about how to send the bills to my office."

There was a trace of anger in his voice, but I knew it wasn't directed at me. I think he was embarrassed that Dave Degnin had lived in squalor all those years without ever having said anything to his boss about it.

4

Then everything quieted down again. Ethel remained in her house next to Mr. Kennedy's, but she was the only member of the family to stay after the Memorial Day reunion.

Carpenters and painters came right in and started sprucing up the garage apartment. It took only a couple of weeks for them to refurbish the place. I got new furniture and appliances and sent the bill to Mr. Kennedy's office.

Not only were there carpenters and workmen at the garage, there were crews all over the compound. John Kennedy had always come home to Hyannis Port for long weekends when he was a congressman and senator, and now that he was the president he was going to continue weekending on Cape Cod.

The anticipation grew circuslike. Workmen scurried over the Kennedy lawns. Carpenters constructed a helicopter landing pad at the front of Mr. Kennedy's house, off the cul-de-sac; they tore out a bank of hedges to do it. The secret service hauled in a house trailer and set it up behind the president's house, for a command post. The sentry boxes were guarded. In the cellar of the big house, telephone company technicians wired in a manned communications room complete with the red phone to the Soviet Union. The triangle of houses—Mr. Kennedy's, Robert's, and the president's—was alive, and dogs and cats, it seemed, were everywhere. The goats belonging to Robert Kennedy's children were always getting loose, and often I had to chase them out of neighbor J.D. Evans's flower garden. Beyond the Kennedy hedges and fences, Hyannis Port was crowded with tourists. The neighbors were issued little yellow stickers for their car windshields so they could get through the security checkpoints. I was under a deadline to get the chauffeur's apartment refurbished because important guests and celebrities would need the president's guest house.

The weather got nicer, and the days seemed to race by. Wilbert Marsh was teaching me how to operate the thirty-year-old dual arc-light projectors in the basement movie room. They were bastards to keep synchronized. The old gardener boasted about how Mr. Kennedy's theater had been the first private one in the East. Ambassador Kennedy absolutely loves the movies, Wilbert said, and I got the hint: it would be smart for his new chauffeur to love showing the movies.

Wilbert did not like showing the films. The projectors were tricky, and staying up late at night made it harder on him. He had over two acres of lawn to mow, flowers to take care of, and a mile of hedges to trim and prune. He loved gardening and he was very good at it. But Wilbert Marsh would do anything the Kennedys asked. His sister Evelyn Jones, one of Mrs. Kennedy's maids, was the same. If Wilbert had ever lost the Kennedy job, he would not have known what to do with himself.

So Wilbert had been showing the movies because it was expected of him in the absence of a chauffeur. But he also liked the extra money. Five dollars a film, he told me, as if he thought this was like stealing from the Kennedys.

"For Chrissake, Wilbert," I said, "that's slave labor. The movie's supposed to start at nine and nobody's ever there on time. They start coming in, what—around ten if you're lucky?—and we're up till one or two in the morning rewinding the reels. It comes out to maybe a dollar an hour. What kind of money is that?"

Wilbert flushed. Then he grew determined. "The chauffeur's expected to show the movies," he reminded me with as much firmness as he could.

"Okay, Wilbert," I said with a laugh, "but we're going

48

to have to do something about the short money we're getting. We are going to have to raise the price."

Now the gardener was nonplussed. "Oh, I don't know about that, Frank."

I smiled at him.

"How are we going to do it?" he asked.

"I'm going to tell them that people will think they are cheapskates paying only five dollars a movie."

The gardener said, "I don't want anything to do with it. Don't get me into this."

It was the same when I had asked for his help fixing up the apartment by advising me on a good local carpenter and where I could order appliances. He nearly fainted when I told him what kind of stove I was going to get. Wilbert suggested a smaller one. "It's not your money I'm spending," I said. "It's the Kennedys'."

"But Mr. Kennedy might get upset," Wilbert said sheepishly.

"Mr. Kennedy told me to fix up the place to my liking and I'm going to do exactly as he said." I smiled.

It never changed with Wilbert over the years. He was so devoted to the Kennedys that he spent their money on gardening supplies, fertilizer, bulbs, and seeds as if it was his own. But it was more than a native frugality; he was afraid of the Kennedys and afraid to stand up and tell them what he wanted. It was the kind of allegiance the family had come to expect from all their help.

The world of servants was something new to me. In the beginning I tried telling myself that it was like being back in the navy and that my captain was Mr. Kennedy. But it wasn't anything like that. There were lines of command in the navy—you knew what was expected of you; you had a certain job and you did it. The Kennedys expected their help to do anything they asked. Mrs. Kennedy especially wanted the help to react in a way that might best be described as subservient. I made every effort to stay clear of the petty intrigues her maids were always caught up in, but it was not easy. There was a lot of backstabbing among the staff, and if Mrs. Kennedy complained about something, often the person responsible for the mistake would try to blame someone else behind that person's

49

back. A new chauffeur was a good scapegoat. But I was blissfully unaware of all that my first summer.

My refusal to live in the chauffeur's quarters until it was cleaned up had thrown the staff for a loop. It made them uncomfortable thinking that the new man had made a demand on the Kennedys and had actually gotten his way. At the start, the maids were running me ragged with endless errands. A couple of them even decided to make me their personal chauffeur and had me picking them up and driving them to work and home again.

Dora Lawrence was Mrs. Kennedy's personal maid and went with her from Hyannis Port to Palm Beach. Evelyn Jones worked for Mrs. Kennedy at the Cape. And there was a lot of other part-time help. Mrs. Kennedy often had trouble getting and keeping maids. She had six personal secretaries in the ten years I was with the family.

In Dora and Evelyn Mrs. Kennedy had two hardworking faithful maids. The Kennedy cook Matilda was an even-tempered Norwegian stalwart, and I often wondered if Rose Kennedy appreciated her. She was an excellent cook and went about her business in a straightforward way that I liked. She did her job well and never let Mrs. Kennedy get under her skin. Or at least, she never showed it. One day soon after we met, Matilda asked, "Frank, have you been in service before?"

"Sure," I said. "Two tours in the navy."

She laughed. "Not that service. In service. You know, in service to other people. Have you ever worked for other people before?"

When I told her no, she seemed sympathetic, motherly. "Let me give you some advice, Frank," the cook said. "Keep the ears and eyes open and your mouth shut. Take nothing in a personal way. Never let your heart believe that the people you work for love you, and never think that you are part of the family. Because, if you do, your heart will be broken."

It was good advice. I should have taken it.

It was final now. Rose Kennedy was staying in France until the fall. The staff greeted the news as if they had been given a raise. "She cannot stand all this fuss and all these people. She likes it quiet, Frank. You remember that!'' Evelyn Jones said.

It was fine with me. I still thought I was Mr. Kennedy's new chauffeur. I had no reason to suspect that Ann Gargan was Mr. Kennedy's favorite in that job. But the rest of the staff knew that I would belong to Madame, as they liked to call Rose Kennedy, for with a man of her own on the staff to take her back and forth from church and run errands for her and carry messages to her children's houses, Mr. Kennedy would be assured of her staying out of his way.

5

I settled in. There was no routine. Spur-of-the-moment errands and sudden crises were so frequent at the Kennedys' then that if there was any certainty about my job, it was simply that I could never guess what might happen. Scheduling my day was as futile as forecasting the quick squalls that came off Lewis Bay without even the warning of a darkening sky. As it would turn out, that first summer was a paid vacation before Rose Kennedy returned and I became her chauffeur, her beck-and-call companion, subjecting myself to her habits and whims.

But the first summer spoiled me. I was footloose in a fairy tale. President Kennedy had me chauffeuring friends and politicians. The white Caddy was waved right through the gates of Otis Air Force Base, in Falmouth, twenty-five miles away, and when the young MPs snapped a salute I felt important. The Otis runs were usually weekend jobs. I made a lot of trips, but I cannot remember the names of the men I drove. They were important men, I guess—most of them, anyway—but I don't remember hearing anything important in the Caddy. Nobody mentioned any plans to invade Cuba, or anything like that.

There was hardly any other chauffeuring, but there was always somebody wanting something—the secret service needed a favor; Matilda needed groceries; the maids needed help; Wilbert could use an extra hand. Or Robert Kennedy's dogs might be loose again, bothering the neighbors. "Get the dogs, Frank!" Ethel would yell.

There were new movies to pick up at the Hyannis theater and reels to bring back. There was mail to get. There seemed like a million things to do, and all of them had to be done instantly.

One day I got a call that a Kennedy car was out of gas in Hyannis. The telephoner demanded a can of gas, and I had the keys to the Kennedy gas pump. When I heard directions to where the car was stranded, I wondered if the secret service was playing a joke. How could anyone be out of gas at a gas station? I arrived within minutes. A shouting match was going on. I cannot recall who had been driving the car, but the passengers were a crew of Kennedy children. They had teamed up against the station owner. They were yelling at him that they were *The Kennedys!,* and the garage man was yelling back that he knew damn well they were the Kennedys and that was why he wasn't letting them charge gasoline, because the Kennedys were notorious for not paying bills on time. I think I prevented a donnybrook.

Another time there was a frantic search at the president's house. The president needed a belt, and there wasn't one in his house that anyone could find. His valet must have been away at the time. Secret service agents had been scrambled. Then I was summoned. And so, while John Kennedy held up his trousers with his hands, I sped off to Puritan's, a clothing store in downtown Hyannis, and sped back with a fistful of belts, for him to take his pick. If I had needed a police escort, I could have requested one; it was a national emergency.

Once Mr. Kennedy called me from their villa at Antibes, on the French Riviera, with some little errand. "Mrs. Kennedy is looking forward to meeting you when she returns," he added. "I won't stand her up, sir," I promised, and the president's father laughed. It was the only time I heard from him that June.

I drove the maids around, chauffeured them in Mr. Kennedy's car. They loved it. Occasionally there were solo trips to Boston to pick up meat at a butcher the Kennedys used. As petty as some of my chores were, it was exciting just being inside the Kennedy place. And there was fun.

They were all there by now. The Kennedys. The Shrivers. The Smiths. Pat Lawford came to Hyannis Port after her daughter Robin was born in early July, then visited her parents in the south of France. Her husband, Peter, the movie actor, may have been at Hyannis Port, but I don't remember meeting him until we got to Palm Beach after Thanksgiving.

All the grandchildren were at Hyannis Port. And their pets. And their toys.

The president and his immediate family took quiet cruises on his father's yacht *Marlin*, captained by Frank Wirtanen. A Finn from West Barnstable, on the north side of the Cape, Frank had come to the Kennedys with the boat. He was in the merchant marine during World War II, on the Murmansk run shuttling freighters through wolf packs of German U-boats. Captain Frank knew his stuff. We became friends.

The First Lady liked to get away from Hyannis Port, where she felt she was always on view. She would get Frank Wirtanen to take the *Marlin* across the bay to the sheltered waters of Chappaquiddick, a little island just off Edgartown, Martha's Vineyard, and there she would water-ski away from prying eyes.

Sooner or later, anyone connected with the Kennedys could be found at the Yachtsman, a waterfront hotel. Pearl Nelson, the president's buxom blond cook, spent off-duty hours at the bar. The Yachtsman was where the secret service agents stayed. It was also press headquarters. During the presidential campaign the previous summer, Boston reporter Loretta McLaughlin had steered Pierre Salinger, the Kennedy press secretary, to the Yachtsman when he was searching for a place where all the media people could be put up. Salinger worked out a deal with Ted Clifton, who owned the hotel with his father. Then the secret service took over part of it. So with all the agents and the press traveling with the president, the Yachtsman became a popular watering hole.

There was live entertainment at the Yachtsman—the

Compass Players, a young theater troupe. One of them, a struggling actor by the name of Alan Alda, used to do a friendly imitation of John F. Kennedy.

I went to the Yachtsman quite a bit. One night I spotted one of President Kennedy's secretaries at the bar. The president often hauled a pair of beautiful secretaries up to Hyannis Port. When I first noticed them I did not know they were his secretaries and asked the secret service who the two dynamite-looking girls were. "Secretaries," I was told. "I never see them taking dictation," I said. The agents shrugged off my curiosity with smiles.

They had special names for the two girls. They called them Fiddle and Faddle, and I didn't know if those were code names—like the code names just about everyone around the president had—or if they were nicknames.

At the Yachtsman that night I sidled up to one of them. The bar was jammed and the crowd was noisy. "Are you Fiddle?" I asked her.

"Do I what?" she squealed.

I nearly blew my drink through my nose, I wanted to laugh so badly. Then I asked again, "Are you Fiddle," adding, "or are you Faddle?"

"Drop dead," she said.

A roar went up along the bar from agents who had overheard us, and they began ribbing her so unmercifully that she left.

Many of the agents were my age and we became friends. When they were on duty they had to be so on guard, so under control, that when they were off duty they just had to let off steam. I sympathized with them. I felt the same.

There was an attempt to fit an agent's personality to his job. Those who didn't like children were not put on the Kennedy kiddy detail. There was one agent we all called "Mother," because he liked the children so much he spent all his time with them. Some agents not only lacked patience to work with the kiddy detail, they couldn't stomach any Kennedy. Usually these didn't stay long on the regular detail.

We had three or four full-time agents at Hyannis Port. Dozens more flew up with the president. The presidential detail was a rotating one and each agent had to spend time on it. Except for Mother, they bitched about being "baby-sitters." Even guarding the president was considered baby-sitting. They complained constantly about how they had college degrees and ended up baby-sitters. Chasing counter-feiters and running investigations was what they wanted to do. Then too, the married agents missed their families. One agent got so sick of the Kennedy detail he left the service and went into real estate. The last I heard, he was acting in television commercials.

Seen on the TV news, secret service agents lurk around the president with dark glasses and walkie-talkies, looking like clones. But they are individuals. I got to know most of them. Mugsy O'Leary, the president's driver, had a great sense of humor. Mugsy chauffeured for John Kennedy before the election, and the president had him appointed as an agent, against the wishes of the secret service. Mugsy became a favorite with the agents. And then there was Bill Greer, who was driving the car in Dallas the day the president was murdered. I heard that Bill never got over it.

Frank McDermott headed the detail and traveled up from Washington on Friday afternoons. Every Friday night Frank came over to my apartment and I cooked him lasagna. Frank looked forward to it.

So did Eddie Cross and Ed Sullivan, two local telephone company executives who ran the communications center. Sometimes the telephone men would take a break and come over for a cold beer. Between Frank McDermott and other agents, and Eddie Cross and Ed Sullivan, I had a pretty good spy network and kept on top of things at Hyannis Port. I had to spy out of self-defense because nobody was telling me what was going on, and I hate surprises. But the network didn't help much—the Kenne-dys were too unpredictable. Suddenly the agents would get word—say, Robert Kennedy was coming up at such and such a time—and all the timetables would get changed. It drove some agents crazy.

Even when they were off duty the agents had to be close by, and close to a telephone. Mildred's Chowder House was another favorite eating and drinking place. They were there so often that a special red phone was hooked up at

Mildred's. And when the agents weren't at the Yachtsman or Mildred's, they would be at Dick Halloran's place, Luigi's.

Because the agents had to fend for themselves, I organized weekly chicken dinners at Luigi's, and for $1.50 the agents had a feast. I set up the meal and sold the tickets, which I also made—hand-lettered, actually. My chicken dinners became popular and, in the three summers President Kennedy was at Hyannis Port, we had some good parties at Luigi's with the agents and the college girls who summer-waitressed there, attracted by the Kennedy magic. After those dinners, we'd sneak some of the girls into the Kennedy place so they could say they had been there.

Sometimes we'd borrow Ted's speedboat and run around the bay to Luigi's and walk in. I ran the boat aground on a mud flat one night and we were stranded for hours, until the tide rose. Another night, with some agents, I shoved off from the compound dock, but Ted or some other joker had pulled the ignition key and we drifted until we got a tow.

We used the speedboat because we figured that nobody could get a ticket for driving under the influence in a speedboat. There weren't any faster boats on Lewis Bay than Ted Kennedy's speedboat.

The Saturday afternoon movie matinee for the children was my purgatory, though it was heaven for the nannies and maids. My job was to round up the children and their friends, not always easy, get them into the theater, show the cartoon and movie, and then get them home again. Robert Kennedy's house was a few hundred feet from the big house, but sometimes the attorney general's children demanded to be driven, especially if their cousins who lived farther away were being driven in. There were seven of them at Robert's house that summer, and it was hard for me to tell them apart. I remember two Davids and two Marys. Robert and Ethel's crew included Kathleen, ten; Joseph P. II, eight; Robert Jr., seven; David Anthony, six; Mary, four; David LeMoyne, three; and Mary Kerry, one and a half. Pat Kennedy Lawford spent only a few weeks at Hyannis Port that summer, but I remember her children being there: Christopher, six; daughters Sydney, five, and Victoria, two and a half. Their third daughter, Robin, was born that summer. Eunice and Sargent Shriver, he being the head of the new Peace Corps, had Robert, seven; Maria, five; and Timmy, one and a half. Jean Kennedy and Stephen Smith, who worked for his father-in-law, as Sargent Shriver had, brought Stephen, four, and little William, who wasn't one that first summer, when they visited Hyannis Port.

The youngest Kennedy was John, Jr., six months. He usually napped while sister Caroline, three, and her cousins whooped it up at the movie. Ted and Joan Kennedy's only child that first summer was Kara, one.

There were so many children we eventually got a Volkswagen bus. They wanted to sit where they felt they should sit. "I'm a Kennedy! You're a Shriver! Kennedys are better than Shrivers. You sit there!" The yelling was deafening. Sometimes I'd lose my temper and stop the bus and threaten to toss the troublemaker out. Some of them were better behaved than others, but it seemed to me they all had a pretty good sense of who they were. They knew that they were special. It would have been impossible, with all the attention focused on Hyannis Port, all the hullabaloo and the helicopters coming and going, the secret service agents and all the tagalong reporters, for the children not to think they were special. In fact, it spoiled some of them. And it really made no difference whether they were Smiths, Shrivers, or Lawfords. They all thought of themselves as Joe and Rose's grandchildren.

Once in the theater, it made no difference to me how much noise they made. I was safe in the projection booth. The small movie theater was not plush. The seats were regular old movie seats that Joe Kennedy had pulled out of one of his theaters. An amateurish mural of a French landscape covered one wall. There was always the risk that one of the children would crown someone, but while there were fights there were no great catastrophes.

The first time I saw John "Jack" Dempsey I didn't know he was a cop. I just thought he was someone important because he acted important.

"Good to meet you, Frank," he said in that blustery cop way he had. "Welcome to the Kennedys. If there's anything I can do, why you just ask. I've known Joe Kennedy for a long time and we are very good friends."

If I went around the corner of the big house, there was Jack Dempsey. If Jacqueline Kennedy was water-skiing, there on the dock watching was Jack Dempsey. If I went into the kitchen to see Matilda, there was Jack. He was always around. Who the hell is this guy? I wondered.

I found out that Jack was Mr. Kennedy's "personal" cop. Jack was one of the first state troopers, a motorcycle cop, on Cape Cod. Either he assigned himself to the Kennedys, or Mr. Kennedy picked him to be the family cop; I never learned which. But Jack Dempsey was an example of just how smart Joe Kennedy was. Instead of worrying about his children getting into trouble, Joe Kennedy dug up a cop to shepherd the clan and take care of any little problem any of them might fall into. Jack had been with them for a long time.

His official job was liaison between the family and state police headquarters at 1010 Commonwealth Avenue, Boston. Jack considered himself a family friend. Jack ran errands for the Kennedys. In William Manchester's book, *The Death of a President*, I've been told, there is something about Jack Dempsey riding in the car with me when I went over to Otis to pick up Eunice and Ted a few hours after the president was murdered in Dallas. Jack may very well have been in the car, but I don't remember. Manchester interviewed Jack, I guess, but he never talked to me. Not that I would have told him what was going on at Hyannis Port at the time. It seemed too personal and bizarre then, and it took me a long time to sort it all out. I never read the book. I just wanted to forget.

Jack Dempsey was just like Lem Billings and Dave Powers, the Irishmen from the Charlestown section of Boston who had begun working for Jack Kennedy when he ran for Congress right after the war. The Kennedys liked having them around because they would do anything the family asked. If a Kennedy had ordered them to climb the flagpole, they would have. Powers and Billings were the official Kennedy court jesters, the butts of the jokes. Dave

Powers idolized President Kennedy so much he even talked like him. Today Dave runs the JFK Library in Dorchester. To their credit, Powers and Billings loved the Kennedy children and were like uncles to them. And Dave was a valuable political aide to the president.

And so I learned the players.

Johnny Ford stopped in one day to see how things were going. I noticed a funny look in his eyes. "Can I ask you a personal question, Frank?" he said.

For an instant I thought he had found out I had been a bookmaker. "Sure," I said.

"Do you have a drinking problem?" he asked, blushing.

I was furious. "Who told you that?" I asked.

Johnny Ford was a gentleman, and I knew he wouldn't tell.

"Did a maid say that?"

He gave me a halfhearted nod.

"That bitch," I said. "It was about nine o'clock at night, John, and I'd had a few. She calls me at my apartment and makes out that the world is coming to an end. You know what she wants? She wants me to come over and change a light bulb. A light bulb! Can you imagine? Am I supposed to change the light bulbs?"

Johnny Ford was smiling.

"I don't have much time to myself, you know? But I went over and changed the light bulb for her and she saw I'd had a few. 'Frank, are you drunk?' she says, and I tell her, 'No, I'm not drunk. Because if I was drunk I wouldn't be able to stand on this chair and change your goddam light bulb.' Tell you the truth, I think it was more than a light bulb she was looking for me to screw in."

Mr. Ford laughed. "You be careful, Frank," he said.

"What do I do about the money I lend them?"

"Who?"

"The president and his brother the attorney general."

Johnny Ford smiled knowingly.

"They hit me up for ten bucks and promise to pay me back, but I never see it."

"Keep track of it, Frank, and send it to Mr. Kennedy's office on Park Avenue. They'll reimburse you."

The Park Avenue office was very good about paying me back the money I loaned the Kennedys.

Shouts woke me, coming from the president's house. It was well after midnight.

I looked out the front window of the garage apartment. Nothing.

At the side window I noticed lights at the president's, but couldn't see which lights they were. There was no noise now, and I wondered if I had been dreaming.

I could not sleep. So I smoked a cigarette by the open screened window and watched moonlight shimmering on the water until I got sleepy. One of Robert Kennedy's dogs barked off and on.

The next morning I brought the president's mail into the secret service trailer where, every day, I helped the agents sift through it. There were boxes of it. "What the hell was going on last night?" I asked the duty agent.

He gave me a sick smile. "That stupid son of a bitch Lem Billings scaled the fence last night." The agent shut his eyes for a split second and shook his head. "Big joke. That jerk came this close to getting his ass shot off," the agent said, holding up a thumb and index finger two inches apart.

6

You could feel the suspense as hot as the midday sun those Friday afternoons. The president's helicopter is coming! No one had to say it. Tourists started coming into the small tree-lined lanes of Hyannis Port in the morning. By afternoon they had trespassed their way across neighboring lawns and lined fences around the Kennedy houses. But they were friendly, in a kind of festival atmosphere. When the Hyannis fire truck moved into position, the crowds started searching the sky, shading their eyes from the sun as they looked to the west toward Squaw Island and down Craigville Beach way. The secret service duty agents in the command trailer behind John Kennedy's house would get the call: the president had transferred from *Air Force One* at Otis. Then one of the agents would walk across the backyard to tell Jacqueline Kennedy that her husband was coming home.

When the people got a glimpse of the First Lady, either as she walked across Robert Kennedy's lawn or in front of Mr. Kennedy's house near the landing pad, cheers went up. Then, faintly, a far-off clacking in the sky would get louder and louder. The noise came like a giant drum beating. Beach sand swirled when the helicopter dropped down to the landing pad and the tall beach grass bent. He stepped out of the big helicopter, waving and smiling.

The blue presidential flag was hoisted at the compound. And for another weekend we were the center of the world.

She was an apparition. Her clothes stark white—cotton pants and a white sleeved shirt, white sandals, and big dark sunglasses. Jacqueline Kennedy had slid without a rustle through the hedges a few feet from me in the driveway, and I smelled the air turn sweet. How did she do that? She had startled me. I was polishing Mr. Kennedy's car when she appeared. I stopped, paralyzed. Before I could speak she smiled quickly and her lips formed "hello," but there was no word that I could hear.

"Hello, Mrs. Kennedy," I said, trying to look nonchalant. By then she had turned and was walking across the driveway toward the back door of Mr. Kennedy's house. Her sandals clacked. I watched her go through the door. Then I went back to polishing the car, but moving to a position from where I would be able to watch for her.

In a few minutes she came back out the same door. I pretended to polish the car, but I was watching her. She was untanned. In her hands she clutched a jar of something. Again the same smile, the same soundless "hello." She slid through the hedges at the corner of Robert Kennedy's yard and, through the hedges, I saw flashes of white as a hunter might when he flushes a white-tailed deer. She seemed to be gliding as she crossed the nearest corner of her brother-in-law's lawn, moving toward her house. I pushed back the hedges and peered through. There was only the empty swing set and toys of Robert Kennedy's children scattered about, and beyond that a high hedge wall on the other side of which I heard a young child laughing.

A few days later she did it again, suddenly appearing in the driveway. The ice-cream truck had stopped in its regular place in the driveway. Robert Kennedy's children had the ears of foxes and could hear the truck's bell wherever they were. I was trying to keep the children away from the truck, trying to get them in some sort of line. They were underfoot everywhere. In the commotion around the truck, with all the children yelling, I had not noticed Jacqueline Kennedy. She was there, with Caroline.

All the children—a dozen of them—were jumping and screaming and dripping ice cream on themselves. In their midst Jacqueline, behind sunglasses, smiled broadly. One of the girls had dropped a Popsicle and was crying. I calmed her. The other children scampered away.

Jacqueline handed me a chocolate-covered ice-cream stick. "This is for you," she said with a smile.

She bit into her ice cream carefully. "Aren't they good?" she asked in the same hushed voice and, without waiting for an answer, walked away.

Whenever I would see her, she was alone. Sometimes in the afternoons when the tide was right I would catch sight of her in a bathing suit walking down Mr. Kennedy's driveway to the beach. She wore a one-piece bathing suit with a flowery pattern. Watching her, I thought: I have seen better legs.

There was a gentle knock on my door. She came in the middle of the afternoon.

"Pardon me, Frank," Jacqueline said very softly, "but could you lend me a dollar?"

She stood just outside the door as I reached for my wallet. "Is one dollar enough?" I asked. Now, the surprise of finding her alone on my doorstep gone, I wondered, What the hell does she need with one dollar?

"One's fine," she said.

I handed her the dollar bill.

She plucked it from my hand gingerly.

"Thank you," she whispered.

Then she went down the stairs. I watched her moving cautiously, as if she were sneaking off someplace. I put it out of my mind, figuring she needed the dollar to buy her children ice cream.

It seemed as if everyone was shouting my name. "Frank. Frank Saunders. Frank! You're wanted front and center. Frank Saunders!"

The call was coming from the dock, being passed along up the compound. I started running across the front lawn, and they were still yelling for me. I ran through the beach sand.

It was a hot day.

There was a crowd on the dock. I think Jack Dempsey

was there. A lot of police, anyway—state police, Barnstable town cops, secret service. "Frank, you're wanted up front," one of them said.

Jacqueline Kennedy was in the water at the front of the dock. She was holding on with one arm. She had been water-skiing. Her head and shoulders bobbed out of the water. It was deep there, but not too deep. I saw her skis lying on the dock.

She looked up and smiled. "Frank, could you help me from the water?" she asked.

I had to get down on my knees to reach her with both hands. She took them, and I pulled. She came out of the water in a fluid motion as I pulled her in, and I felt her press against me.

Then someone handed her a towel and she wrapped herself in it. She told me, "Thank you."

As I walked away I noticed the men smiling. I tried not to smile, but by the time I reached the end of the dock and started across the soft sand I had a big grin on. By the time I got to the big house the front of my shirt where she had pressed against me had nearly dried. Jacqueline did not want any of those cops putting their hands on her, I decided. Her skin was ice-cold when I touched her. It must have been all the time she had been in the water that made her feel cold like that, I thought.

One day Jacqueline came up behind me quickly. "Oh, Frank! Get me out of here. It's driving me crazy."

I knew what she meant. "Where do you want to go?"

"Anyplace. Anyplace. Just out, out, out!"

I don't remember what car I took. Maybe it was her convertible. I remember the wind blowing her hair. The secret service didn't see us.

"It's like living in a fishbowl," she said. "But I'm inside and all the fish are outside. Oh, Frank, all those fishy eyes. I see them from upstairs. All those eyes just staring. It's so good to be out!"

We rode.

I stopped at a small shop and she poked around, looking at touristy glassware. She had a great time.

She was relaxed as we drove back to Hyannis Port. She

asked about my wife and son. She said that sometimes it just overwhelmed her—all the Kennedys and their foolish lawn games. She loved horseback riding and water-skiing because she could be alone. She said she didn't know how many more summers like this one she could take at Hyannis Port. The tall cedar fence at the front of the president's house helped, but she still knew that tourists were all standing behind it. She thought of playing some great trick on them.

She had a good tan by now. Her brief escape seemed to have done her good. It was exciting being alone with her. She seemed so warm, so friendly, that I knew Fritz the Kennedy masseur must have lied to me when he confided that Jacqueline had the coldest skin of any woman he'd ever touched.

Alone in the theater one night, waiting for them to come for the night movie, I screamed: "Screw this!"

I'd had it with the movies and the late-coming Kennedys and the no-show Kennedys. The evening movie was supposed to start at nine sharp. It never did that first summer. Someone was always calling the theater and telling either Wilbert or me to hold the movie until they got there. Often there would be two or three separate parties going on—either at the president's or at Robert Kennedy's or over on Squaw Island at Ted's house. The guests would show up late. Sometimes they never showed at all.

In the meantime the people who were at the theater of course grew impatient and wanted the film to start. "Mrs. Kennedy has asked me to wait," I would say, referring to the First Lady. That request was usually granted, as no one wanted to go against Jacqueline Kennedy's wishes. But a request to hold the movie until Ted and his friends got there was given less of a hearing. It was typical of the hierarchy in the family. Ted Kennedy could always be outvoted by either of his brothers—and any of his sisters, for that matter.

Not only did they rarely come on time, but then they would fight about what movie they wanted to see. I'd set up one movie, and then somebody else would want to see a different one and I would have to rewind the film and reload.

That night was one when *nobody* had come, and I had waited for over an hour for the president to send word what movie he wanted. There was a party going full-blast at his house. It looked like I would be twiddling my thumbs in the theater all night.

Determinedly I marched out of the house, up the driveway, through the hedges at the corner of Robert Kennedy's yard, across the lawn, across the president's backyard, and into his kitchen.

The house was jammed. The party was in full swing. Pearl Nelson was sweating in the kitchen making hors-d'oeuvres. Part-time maids were rushing in and out of the kitchen like through a revolving door.

I stood there fuming.

"Oh Frank! How nice to see you," Jacqueline Kennedy said with a big smile. She could tell I was mad. "Is there something you need?" she asked as she picked up a tray of frozen daiquiris.

"Mrs. Kennedy, I would like to see the president," I said, unmistakably like an order.

"I'll get him for you. Now you wait right here," she said, leaning closer and thrusting the tray of drinks at me so I had to take it. "Now you wait, Frank," she said, smiling, turning to leave. "Wait now," she repeated over her shoulder.

I waited. The iced glasses dripped and the slushy ice inside them melted. I set the tray down on a counter. It was humid in the house.

"What are these things?" I asked Pearl.

"Frozen daiquiris," the cook said.

"Well, I am about to have the first frozen daiquiri of my life," I announced, and downed one. The sweetness tasted good. It was cooling.

Jacqueline Kennedy did not return. I had another daiquiri. Then another. Then another. They were like liquid candy. I polished off the tray.

I don't remember what happened then. I woke up in my bed, still in my clothes, sometime before dawn, my head pounding.

7

Joe Kennedy returned to Hyannis Port like a hurricane. We charted his arrival anxiously and this time his chauffeur was on time, waiting. Mr. Kennedy was a stick of fused dynamite. Rested by his long vacation on thé Riviera, he was raring to go. The months away from his sons and his exile from the limelight had charged him, and I could see that he was happy to be home and even happier now that his place had become the summer White House. He strode around like an old stage actor who had finally landed that big role he had dreamed of. Mr. Kennedy loved being the father of America's youngest president, and he played it to the hilt. Now the Friday afternoon arrival of his son, the helicopter dropping on his front lawn as he stood proudly smiling from his veranda, seemed as if it was all just for him. He had returned with his niece Ann Gargan. Rose Kennedy had stayed behind at their rented Antibes villa.

He demanded to know right away who had stolen the dining-room table. His wife had ordered it sent out to the furniture refinisher, the staff informed him. Rose Kennedy had been afraid that her grandchildren might try dancing on it again while she was gone. Okay, now he remembered. So it was all right about the table, he'd just forgotten. He gave the grounds a quick once-over—the flowers, the lawn, the hedges—and gave Wilbert an approving wink.

I found myself summoned. "What about these repair

bills?" He motioned me to pull my chair closer in his house office, then questioned the bills item by item.

"Did you see them put in that part?" he asked.

"No, Mr. Kennedy. I left the car with them at the garage."

He narrowed his eyes suspiciously. "How do you know they really replaced this part, Frank?" he asked.

It was the garage the Kennedys always used, I explained. I was about to tell him that I'd assumed he must have trusted them when he interrupted me. "Don't trust anyone, Frank. Don't take anything on faith," he said.

Then he began giving me some advice. His manner was fatherly. "You know, I only made a dime on a dollar but the dimes add up, and if you pay attention to the dimes, Frank, well before you know it, you have a pile of dimes. And then more dimes."

"Yes, Mr. Kennedy," I said.

"Watch every dime, Frank."

"Yes sir."

"The dollars will take care of themselves."

"Yes sir."

"These car bills add up, you see?"

"The car is getting old, sir. I think it should be replaced," I said.

"Nothing wrong with that car! That car will last a long time. You just make sure that those guys do what they say they do and you stay there when they fix it and watch the bastards."

"Yes sir."

"Good, Frank. Did you get your place straightened out?"

"Yes."

"Everything satisfactory?"

I nodded.

"That's swell. You kept your eyes on them?"

"I did."

"That's the stuff."

The early morning was all mine at the compound, even after Mr. Kennedy got back. With the garage apartment fixed up, I had moved from the guest house. My wife and son had joined me, but I always woke before they did, usually before dawn, and sat by the window facing the bay, having a smoke as I waited for the sun. Then I would check if Robert Kennedy's dog was up yet. At night I dropped the tail gate of the station wagon parked in the lot in front of the garage for the Irish setter. The dog slept in the car. He belonged to Robert Kennedy, but he refused to stay in their yard. He followed me everywhere and Ethel didn't like it, as if I had purposefully stolen the dog's affection. She asked me why the setter never came home. I shrugged it off. So in the early quiet I would take a walk, and the setter would jump out of the station wagon and trail me back to Robert Kennedy's house.

After breakfast Mr. Kennedy would be out, in jodhpurs, for his horseback ride at the stable in nearby Osterville. After his morning gallop he played a round of golf. This was when I found out he did not need me for his chauffeur. He had Ann. She drove him in her Lincoln convertible. The story was that she had won the big car in a contest.

At first it made me uneasy that he did not use me. I felt cheated. But I had the job of polishing his boots. He wanted them shined every day and set back in his closet. And Mr. Kennedy had dozens of pairs of expensive shoes, some of them handmade in London. I shined those too, but he was more particular about his riding boots.

Whenever I brought the boots back to his room I felt alone with the mysterious blonde in the photograph on his bedside table. I learned not to look at the photograph, not even a glance, because every time I did she stayed in my mind and it drove me crazy wondering who she was. I sensed that it was not something I could ask Mr. Kennedy.

I was summoned again. "Frank, have you the keys to my liquor cabinet?" He had caught me at my apartment in the early evening just after I got back from Luigi's.

"No sir," I answered firmly into the phone.

"Well, come on over and help me open the damn thing, will you?"

Perfect timing! I had a glow on. As I thought about it, his questioning upset me. Why would I have the keys to his booze? Unless one of the maids had said something to him. The hell with it, I decided, as I strolled to the house.

Every time I have a few drinks, somebody wants me. If they expect me to be on call twenty-four hours, they'd better get used to it. I wondered what Mr. Kennedy would think, because I'd heard he was down on liquor.

He was on his hands and knees. "I can't get this thing open," he grunted. "Damn thing's locked or stuck or something."

I joined him on the floor. Our faces were a foot apart and he got a good whiff of me. "Are you sure you don't have the keys to my liquor?" he chuckled as he fixed those cold blue eyes on me. He made a show of sniffing at me, then recoiling from my breath.

I blew on the president's father. "That's not Kennedy liquor you're smelling, Mr. Kennedy."

We were like two dogs panting, and we couldn't stop laughing. "I'll pry it open," I said finally.

He was pleased. He had guests waiting.

He was not a patient man, not with the people who worked for him or with his family. Even his favorite niece jumped when he called or snapped his fingers.

"Ann! Come on, Annie! Let's go!" If he was waiting in the car and she was not there and he was ready to go, Mr. Kennedy would yell out for her. And if Ann was not there within seconds, he slid behind the wheel and drove off.

Ann was shy and, at first, standoffish toward me. It seemed her shyness came from her time in the convent school. Her brother Joey was altogether different—an extrovert. About Ted Kennedy's age, Joe Gargan had been Ted's boyhood friend and spent a great deal of time with the Kennedys. His mother, Rose Kennedy's sister Agnes, died when the Gargan children were young, and the Kennedys "adopted" them. But Joe Gargan always knew he was not a Kennedy. "I'm the poor cousin," he once said to me. When Ted went off to Harvard, Joey went to Notre Dame.

Ann Gargan loved her "Uncle Joe" and was devoted to him. Her only other interest seemed to be her dogs, which she kept at the big house. She always had more than one dog. Rose Kennedy would have preferred not having Ann's animals in their house, but Mrs. Kennedy knew how important the pets were to Ann, so she tolerated them. After Mr.

Kennedy's stroke, when Ann became his caretaker, Rose Kennedy's niece became indispensable to her. Anything the Kennedys ever gave Ann she paid back tenfold with her love for the president's father.

Ann intrigued me. I felt a kinship with her. She had lost her mother when she was a baby and lived away from her father. But I never told Ann how I grew up in an orphanage. In a sense, both of us shared a similar childhood loss, although there were big differences. While Ann worked for Mr. Kennedy, he was her uncle—her family. And family was everything to the Kennedys. Everything.

Watching Ann and Mr. Kennedy go off together that first summer—several times out in the evening for dinner—I naturally expected that it would become a threesome when Rose Kennedy returned, and that I would be their chauffeur. I was wrong.

"You'll be much busier when Mrs. Kennedy gets home, Frank," Mr. Kennedy said. "I don't want her to drive herself. I'm afraid she'll get into an accident and hurt herself, or someone else. She's absentminded in a car. Now she will want to drive to the golf course, and that's fine. But you'll be taking her everywhere else. Daily mass and everything like that."

"Of course, Mr. Kennedy." I smiled.

He smiled in agreement.

Ann looked as though she'd seen a ghost.

"Is anything the matter?" I asked.

"It's Uncle Joe. Oh, I'm so upset. He fell over a chair. He just . . . fell over the chair."

"Is he all right?"

"Oh, yes. I don't think it's serious. I mean, he didn't hurt himself."

"Don't worry, Ann. Those things happen. I fall over things every so often myself," I joked.

She smiled. "It's not that. It's that he will not, absolutely refuses, to take his pills. I get so mad, Frank. He knows he's supposed to take them but I catch him flushing them down the toilet."

Ann did not tell me what the pills were for, and I did not ask.

72

"Maybe you can stick them in his food."

She smiled sadly. "He's too smart for that."

"Mr. Kennedy looks like he's in great shape to me, I mean for his age. How old is he?"

"He'll be seventy-three in September. He is healthy, if only he'd take his pills."

The next time I saw Mr. Kennedy I studied him as we talked. He looked strong. The only place he showed his age was around his neck where his skin was wrinkly. He had a good lean body for his age.

I cannot recall how it started. Maybe my mentioning something about one of the neighbors. I remember telling him a lot of the neighbors were complaining about how Hyannis Port was being ruined by all the tourists. They'd talk about it at the post office and I'd hear the same thing around Hyannis.

"They can kiss my arse!" Joe Kennedy said. "Don't waste your time listening to any of it."

Then he laughed. He had good teeth for a man his age, I thought. He didn't smoke.

"You notice how Jack likes to stroll around and wave at them, say hello to them and smile at them? It's marvelous! Jack's rubbing their noses in it, Frank. It drives some of them crazy seeing the presidential flag flying here."

I recalled how the president, after landing in the helicopter, would walk over to the fences and yell friendly hellos at any neighbors he spotted.

"You know, years back we lived in Cohasset and I wanted to join a club there and those narrow-minded bigoted Republican sons of bitches banned me because I was an Irish Catholic and the son of a barkeeper. The hell with them! You can go to Harvard, and it doesn't mean a damn thing. The only thing these people understand is money."

The president's father seemed to be talking to himself.

"Money is the great equalizer in America. Money is all they really understand. But it's funny, because a lot of people who have the money don't really understand money. They don't know what you can do with money. I was determined to make so much money that none of my children would have to worry about it."

I was tempted to tell him that he'd be smart to part with some of it and buy a new car.

"Well, the neighbors better get used to having a Kennedy president at Hyannis Port, because by Christ I think there's going to be presidents here for a long long time."

Now that Mr. Kennedy was at Hyannis Port, the theater filled up. He hated wasting the night's movie on one or two viewers, and everyone knew it. John Kennedy genuinely liked movies, but I think he went as much to please his father as to entertain himself. Many nights he slept through the movie.

"Frank, what's this one about?" John Kennedy would sometimes ask me. I'd give him a brief outline of the plot, who the actors were, and anything about the film I was going to show that I thought might interest him.

When the movie was going and the reels were running smoothly, I'd come out of the booth and stand at the back of the small viewing room. The president, his head slumped, would be asleep. But as soon as the movie ended and the lights went on, John Kennedy would be telling his father what he liked and what he didn't like. Mr. Kennedy never caught on, as far as I know.

Of all the family, Joan Kennedy was the only one who ever took the time to thank me for the movie. Joan had no airs about her. She was naturally nice and polite. Before the film began, if she had time, she'd pop into the booth and say hello. As she was leaving, Joan would again stick her head in, with a smile. "Thank you, Frank," she would say softly.

I always appreciated her gesture. She was very important to me that first summer, because she made me feel human, as if I was more than hired help. All the times I saw her at her house, at parties at other houses, in the movie theater where there was always a pitcher of Bloody Marys, I never saw Ted Kennedy's wife with a drink in her hand. Not until after Mary Jo Kopechne died in Ted's car on Chappaquiddick did I see Joan Kennedy drinking.

The Kennedys and their guests weren't the only ones who took advantage of the private movie theater. One afternoon I was with three new Hyannis Port friends and their wives. The wives thought it would be fun to see a movie in Mr. Kennedy's theater. The guys were tired and a little hung over, and went home to bed. In the middle of the movie Mr. Kennedy walked in.

He took me aside. "Who are those women?"

"My sister-in-law and her friends." I lied.

"Mmmm," he said. As he was leaving, Mr. Kennedy said loudly, "Well, one of the ladies looks just like Jack Bell's wife!"

"Did he recognize me?" Jack Bell's wife asked. Jack was a local plumber.

I was alone in the garage, polishing a car out of the midday sun, when Mr. Kennedy walked in, leaning against one of the other cars, and watched me work. After a while he said, "If you ever want to invite some friends or your parents down for a visit, go ahead. You live here too, Frank."

"I don't have any parents, Mr. Kennedy," I said, still polishing.

"I'm sorry, Frank. But some close friends or relatives. . . ."

"I never had a father." I said it so abruptly that I stopped my polishing, and put the rag down on the hood. "I grew up in a foster home. I never knew who my real mother was until I was thirteen," I said with a faint laugh. I figured I owed him that much of an explanation.

"Is that so, Frank? It must have been tough on you. I'd like to hear about it, if you want to tell me."

Mr. Kennedy stayed leaning against the car, one hand holding the other crossed in front of him, never moving as I spoke.

I told him about living in the chicken coop after the fire. I told Mr. Kennedy all of it. I felt a little foolish after I did.

"What about your mother?"

"She died two years ago. No one got in touch with me to tell me she was sick. They called me in time for her funeral. Just in time."

"You've got a family now, Frank, as long as you want, as long as you're with us," Mr. Kennedy said.

He stood away from the car and stretched. Then he gave me a friendly punch. "Stick with me, Frank. I'll take good care of you."

8

There was always somebody famous wandering around the place. The Kennedys had a good sense of who was "in" and who was a rising star, so if you were a celebrity who interested them, or someone they wanted around, you got an invitation.

It worked that way with astronauts, entertainers, scientists, journalists, and athletes.

That first summer two entertainers seemed always to be at the place: Andy Williams and Judy Garland.

Andy Williams played a lot of tennis with the Kennedys, especially Ethel Kennedy. I would catch glimpses of him wandering in the backyard or on the court behind Mr. Kennedy's house. He was very pleasant and never caused any trouble . . . unlike Judy Garland.

Judy Garland seemed to spend more time at the Kennedys' than she did at her own house around the corner. She and her chubby little children—Liza Minnelli and Lorna Luft— had the run of the place. The children played with Robert Kennedy's kids, although Judy's were older. Liza was by then in her late teens.

Judy Garland had been a boyhood ideal of mine. The first time I saw her at the Kennedys' I was excited, but then she was there so often and became so familiar I didn't pay her much attention. She wandered, glass in hand, from one house to the other, in the triangle composed of Mr. Kennedy's house, Robert's house, and the president's.

She went to the evening movies at Mr. Kennedy's. By that time, she was usually sloshed, and while most of the time she was nice, one night she went crazy.

I cannot remember who else was there or what the movie was the night she went berserk. I was having trouble again with the old arc-light projectors. The film was fluttering and the soundtrack was out of sync. It happened quite often and never lasted too long, and usually the people watching the movie understood and were patient. Hell, it was no fun for the projectionist, either.

I was in the booth sweating, trying to get the film running right. At first I thought the screaming was part of the soundtrack, it was that loud. Then there were two soundtracks. One was Judy Garland.

"Heh, you stupid son of a bitch, can't you run that goddam projector?"

I looked through the tiny window. There was Judy staring back at me, yelling.

Her voice grew louder and her language got filthier. She hurled words at me I hadn't heard since I was in the navy. "You stupid bastard, if you can't run that fucking projector, we'll get someone who can. You goddam . . ."

I came out of the booth. The movie was still going and the others seemed oblivious to her antics, as if they were used to this. I tried to calm her, explaining that the projectors were old and that I would try to fix the machine as quickly as I could.

But she kept swearing at me. Her words got more slurred, but I understood what she was saying. She was putting together some very original hyphenated curses. At first it was even comical. But then as she kept it up, it got disgusting.

I retreated to the projection room, praying that I could get the trouble with the machine straightened out before my temper went.

Was this the sweet little Dorothy I remembered from *The Wizard of Oz?*

Then, suddenly, she was inside the booth. I had left the door open, and she was screaming at me again. For an instant I thought she was going to attack me, she was that wild. "You incompetent son of a bitch!" she yelled.

That did it. there was no need for this. I decided to get her out of the theater no matter what.

Drunk as she was, she must have realized that I was not going to let her stay, because she calmed down a little.

But I had had it. "Come on, Miss Garland! The movie's over!" I said. I put my arm under one of her elbows and began pushing her ahead of me, out of the booth. She grew angrier. She had on thick makeup and her lipstick was smudged. She was about five years older than I, but she looked older than that. She was not very big, and was trying to stop me by digging in her heels. But I kept up the bum's rush and in a few seconds we were out of the cellar and upstairs, at the back of the house.

She seemed to slump then, as if her tirade had drained her. I carried her to a couch in the living room and left her there.

The next morning shaving I discovered a long scratch across the base of my neck.

Strange business. . . . Years later I read someplace that Judy Garland's father—with whom she had a love-hate relationship—had been a movie projectionist. I had to wonder if Judy's problems with her father might have had something to do with the irrational way she had come at the Kennedy movie projectionist that night. It had been such a terrible rage. After John Kennedy was murdered, Judy never came back to Mr. Kennedy's house that I can remember.

It was strange the things you don't forget. There's another night that comes back to me whenever I let myself get lost in a Sinatra song.

Frank Sinatra was another frequent celebrity at Hyannis Port, and he was there that night, with a crowd of jet-setters and Beautiful People for a big party at Mr. Kennedy's. Snatches of music drifted through my window. It was far-off, almost inaudible music that seemed to wander about, as if someone was walking with a portable radio on the far side of Mr. Kennedy's lawn, near the beach. I remember a big white moth fluttering against my screen, and me blowing cigarette smoke through the screen at it, but it would not go away. Then the music faded.

Voices rose through the dark trees at the side of the big house like a flock of suddenly frightened pigeons.

Through the garage apartment window the moonlight was screened, shaded, and the bay was dead calm. A single tall sail moved slowly on the water, framed between Mr. Kennedy's and Robert Kennedy's houses. I imagined painting it. That scene—the moonlight shaded by the window screen and the sail glistening on the bay—reminded me of a silk print I had seen once in Japan in the navy, one night when we were out chasing whores.

The women they had trucked in that afternoon had looked like whores to me. The playboy Porfirio Rubirosa had come, and the maids were buzzing. But the star was Frank Sinatra. Maybe President Kennedy was returning a favor, because Sinatra had entertained at his inaugural. It was a safe bet that Judy Garland had wandered over from her house down by the yacht club.

It was a big bash, all right. I kept my eyes peeled, hoping to see something.

The sail moved out of my imagined painting.

Then I remembered Mr. Kennedy's riding boots, still there in my apartment. I grabbed the boots, walked across the parking area, and entered the house by the narrow back hallway that leads to the back stairs. I could hear party noises. There was enough spillover light to see.

I came on them, dark shapes in the hallway, and stopped in my tracks. She was giggling. Mr. Kennedy was pressing her against the wall. Then he stood away from her, his arms extended, hands against her breasts, fingers tickling. Her silhouette showed big tits.

I stayed motionless, cradling his riding boots like a baby at my chest.

He saw me first. "Frank!" he said lightly. "It's Frank, dear. My chauffeur."

She giggled.

I stepped closer and could see that her dress had a thick net top, and through the weave I saw her flesh.

"I have your riding boots, Mr. Kennedy," I said. I said it loudly, as if to assert my excuse for being there.

"My riding boots! Just in time!" The president's father laughed. The woman giggled.

Back at the garage apartment, I lit up a cigarette. Soon I was laughing out loud. I wondered again about that face in his bedroom. And then, for the first time, I thought about the one Kennedy woman I had yet to meet. I wondered what Rose Kennedy was doing alone at Antibes.

The next morning Mr. Kennedy told me that I would drive Frank Sinatra to Boston. It was Sunday and traffic off the Cape would be heavy.

"My pleasure, Frank," Frank Sinatra said, shaking my hand. "This is my buddy, the well-known internationally famous cock-hound Porfirio Rubirosa . . . and his lady."

The swarthy Rubirosa smiled. The woman giggled.

"Hello again," I said.

"Hey, what's going on here, chauffeur?" Sinatra joked. "You know the lady?" The singer's blue eyes sparkled. They were almost as blue as Mr. Kennedy's.

"I met the lady last night. Mr. Kennedy introduced us," I said, nodding at the lady in the net dress.

Sinatra sat in the passenger seat. In the rearview mirror I watched Rubirosa fondling the woman.

Over the Cape Cod Canal, I took a wrong turn and went twenty-five miles in a detour getting back on the road to Boston. But I didn't tell them.

It was hot. The air conditioning was broken and Sinatra was uncomfortable. Halfway to Boston, he said, "I could use a drink. You want a drink, Ruby? Yeah, Ruby wants a drink. You want a drink, bird? Yeah, she wants a drink. And, Frank, I know *you* want a drink! You know an out-of-the-way place we can have a drink?"

"We'll miss the plane," I said.

"Screw the plane," he said.

"I know just the place," I said.

The Hotel Bradford was right across the street from my old parking lot, and I knew that the lounge would be empty on a Sunday afternoon. The bartender was an old friend, and I told him to keep quiet. Every time Sinatra or Rubirosa ordered a drink they stuck a ten or a twenty in my hand. We drank alone for two hours. I was making a small fortune. Then Sinatra needed the men's room. At the Bradford bar you have to go out, past the newsstand in the lobby, then down a flight of stairs to the men's room.

Someone spotted him. The Bradford lounge fronts on the street, and a crowd gathered. By the time Sinatra wanted to leave, as we walked out, there were over two hundred people outside.

I heard someone yell: "Hey, it's Frank Saunders! And he's with Frank Sinatra!"

Cheers went up in the Combat Zone. I was in seventh heaven.

We tried to get a plane at Hanscom, a suburban airport, but the place was socked in. We were told we'd have to stay overnight in a motel, and I asked Sinatra to call Mr. Kennedy and explain.

"Hey, Dad! I'm taking your man Francis Joseph Saunders with me," I overheard Sinatra saying. "Your air-conditioner's on the fritz. Get a new car, will you, Joe! Don't be shanty Irish."

Sinatra took good care of me. And he told me to take good care of his pal Peter Lawford when he showed up, because the Kennedys, Sinatra said, were driving the English actor to drink. On the way back to Hyannis Port the next day I looked forward to meeting Peter Lawford. I wanted to ask him about those Lassie movies.

9

Ted floored the pedal, and the old white Caddy flew down the Mid-Cape. The front end shimmied, and the faster we went the worse it shook. It was late at night and we were heading home.

"The tires need balancing," Ted snapped, but I knew he was wrong, that it wasn't the tires. I kept quiet, and stiffened my legs and braced myself in the passenger seat.

He was in a good mood. He had just given a speech at Bedford, outside Boston, and the crowd had cheered the president's youngest brother. I thought the speech was terrible and hadn't understood a thing he said. When I drove him up, he came with a spare shirt that had crib notes for his speech printed in ball point on the starched white cuffs. He thought that was super. I thought it was a waste of a good shirt. Ted was an assistant district attorney in Boston's Suffolk County, but everyone knew he was already running for the Senate seat his brother had vacated when he won the presidency.

The Kennedys had it all arranged. Ted wouldn't be eligible until the following February, when he turned thirty, so the president appointed his old Harvard roommate and family friend, Ben Smith, to keep the seat warm. Then, when Ted was ready, they'd have the election.

I breathed a sigh of relief as we turned off the Mid-Cape and Ted slowed the Caddy.

He would drop me at the garage and take his father's car

home to Squaw Island, he said. It was fine with me. I was tired.

Standing in the driveway, I heard the rear tires kick up gravel as he headed for Squaw Island, a peninsula about a mile away.

Ted never made it home. On the road, the front-tire rods snapped and the Caddy swerved off the road. Ted had finished off the Caddy.

When I learned what happened I said a silent prayer, because if the tie rods had come loose while we were flying down the Mid-Cape we might have been killed.

I had warned Mr. Kennedy about the car. The next day he gave me an order. "I want a new car!"

"Yes sir," I said.

"You pick me a car," he said.

"Me?"

"You'll be driving it, so you pick it out."

"Okay!" I said excitedly.

"Now hold your horses. First, I want you to go around and get prices; do some hard shopping for the best deal and give me your recommendation. And, Frank, you let them know that it would be smart advertising for a car dealer to say he sold a car to the president's family," he said with a wink.

Mr. Kennedy's final choice was a big Chrysler. He got a good deal. I couldn't have been happier. The Chrysler was a beauty with all the options, and at the wheel of that big shiny new car I finally felt like a legitimate chauffeur.

It was around that time, close to the end of the summer, that I learned about the face in Mr. Kennedy's room. It was Marion Davies's, the movie star. Her photograph in the newspaper one morning stopped me. It was not the same one as the picture in Mr. Kennedy's room—in this one she was older—but it was her, all right. I recognized her right away. She had just died.

Marion Davies—movie actress; mistress of William Randolph Hearst, the newspaper magnate; queen of San Simeon, Hearst's California castle; blond comedienne of the twenties; the Marilyn Monroe of her day. I read on, but there was nothing about Joseph P. Kennedy. She had died of cancer.

He looked sad when I saw him.

I kept quiet.

A few days later I mentioned that I saw in the paper that Marion Davies had died. I just blurted it out, took a chance.

"She was a wonderful woman," he said. He had taken so much time to say it, I had thought he was going to let it slide. "She was a great friend. We stayed at her house the night Jack won the nomination in Los Angeles. She was a woman who understood men. She understood men who wanted great things."

Now I wished that I had not mentioned it to him, because Marion Davies's death seemed to pain him.

"She understood me," he said. He was looking at me, looking into my eyes with that way he had of making you wonder if he could see your soul.

But then Mr. Kennedy had someone to cheer him up. A few days later, Joan Kennedy gave birth to Edward Moore, Jr., Ted and Joan's first son.

10

Rose Kennedy's trunks full of new Paris dresses arrived ahead of her. The summer was over by the time she came home.

I think there was more fuss about her trunks coming than there was about her actual arrival. However she arrived, it certainly wasn't as dramatic as the day I'd met Mr. Kennedy. In fact, I can't remember whether I met her at the airport or if she found her own way home. All I recall is her shaking my hand and telling me to be at the front door at 6:30 the next morning to take her to mass.

Rose Kennedy had missed a good summer at Cape Cod. Everyone said it was one of the best in recent memory, sunnier and warmer than usual and without too much fog. But the natives denied that Kennedy luck had anything to do with the fine weather.

The fall is the best time on the Cape. I thought of those crisp mornings when I picked up the mail at the post office early, when there was still a thumbnail of frost in the corners of the small-paned windows of the Hyannis Port News. The year-rounders would come for their mail and the Boston papers, thanking God and each other that the tourists were gone. The rich summer residents were gone too, and after Thanksgiving the Kennedys would be fleeing south to Palm Beach, and then, at last, the village would be theirs again.

In the evenings I lit log fires in Mr. Kennedy's fireplace,

and I took night walks alone along the narrow streets and listened to the dry autumn leaves rustle and smelled the wood smoke.

She began at once attending morning mass, every morning. The mass was at seven, but she liked to be there early. Saint Francis Xavier in Hyannis was not much more than five minutes away, driving slowly. I was in the car in the turnaround at the front of the house just after six. She came out the front door. And that's the way it would be for the next eight years—with my having Thursdays off, but only after having brought her home from mass.

Saint Francis, with its white clapboards, is a countrylike church, plain and simple. Though not a practicing Catholic, I felt it was my duty to go in with Mrs. Kennedy.

As I dipped my fingers in the holy-water font I read the inscription on the brass plaque:

The Main Altar
presented by
Mr. and Mrs Joseph P. Kennedy
in Memory of their Son
Lt. Joseph Patrick Kennedy, Jr., U.S.N.R.
Killed in Action
August 12, 1944

From the rear of the car on our way home she explained the carved wooden altar: The U.S. Naval Air Force plane represented her son's. Saint George on one side and Joan of Arc on the other, both in military dress, symbolized the fact that her son's plane exploded between England and France. She was very proud of the altar, and I understood that it was not only God she honored at mass there; she went to honor her first son.

The next morning I sat in a pew near the rear of the church. She was up front. There were two hundred people in the church, many of them obviously there to see the president's mother, now that they'd heard she was back.

As the mass was being said, she stood up, walked out of her pew, and up the center aisle. I thought she was leaving. Heads turned, and all eyes were riveted on Mrs. Kennedy.

Then she turned into my pew, smiling her way past parishioners who had to lean back and turn their knees so she could thread her way past them.

"These are for you," she whispered in my ear, and handed me a set of rosary beads.

I smiled my "thank you." We were the center of attention.

"Are you all right?" she asked.

I nodded. I felt my neck getting warm.

Then everyone leaned back again, angling their bodies to let her out, and I watched all the heads follow her.

I daydreamed through the mass, wondering what might have been if Joe's plane had not blown up. Would he have been the first Kennedy president? The mass was coming to an end when I noticed her standing up again. Again she marched up the aisle, high heels clicking.

I muttered under my breath.

She came back into my pew, politely smiling her way in and out. She said she only wanted to make sure I was all right.

The next morning I made an excuse and told her there was an errand I had to run while she was at mass. From then on I made sure of other excuses, until she stopped asking if I was going in with her.

When Mrs. Kennedy returned from morning mass, Mr. Kennedy went horseback riding, then played golf. She spent those first weeks trying on new dresses, and she kept Dora and Evelyn and the other maids hopping. Dora said she was praying that Mrs. Kennedy would be named to the best-dressed list, figuring that she wouldn't give up until she was on it with her daughter-in-law Jacqueline.

After a light lunch, Mr. and Mrs. Kennedy would go into their separate bedrooms and nap. The house rule was for absolute silence. After her nap, Mrs. Kennedy would jump in her little white Valiant and drive herself to the nearby golf course, not crowded now that it was fall.

That Indian summer was perfect. Mrs. Kennedy liked to walk alone on the beach in front of their house, to the breakwater. She was the unchallenged mistress of the place, until the weekends when the president and Jacqueline returned and attention focused on the First Family. But as the weather turned we saw less and less of the helicopter on Fridays.

I saw less of Mr. Kennedy, as Mrs. Kennedy found errands for me to run. One day she was furious with me. "Where have you been? I've been looking all over for you. Where have you been!?" She spit it out.

I explained some errands the maids had me running, and that I had thought she would not need me until later in the day.

"I'll put a stop to this right now. My, yes!" she said. "You are *my* chauffeur. You are *not* their chauffeur. Oh, it's not your fault, Frank. You are not to blame. These . . . people!"

She called a staff meeting and laid down the law. Frank Saunders was *her* chauffeur, Mrs. Kennedy said sternly, and she wanted *her* chauffeur there whenever she or Mr. Kennedy needed him.

I stood by listening, a little swelled over my new stature. It was good finally to know just what my job was.

Then she sent word to her children that the chauffeur belonged to their parents, not to them. She wrote them notes. This was a quirk of Mrs. Kennedy's which I never understood. For example, Ethel Kennedy lived a couple hundred feet away, and Mrs. Kennedy would send her first daughter-in-law handwritten notes. If she happened to see the grandchildren's bikes out at night, she would send a complaining letter. I guess she thought the written word more impressive.

And she straightened out the nightly movie. "You begin the film at nine o'clock sharp, Frank," she said. "It is of no matter whether anyone is there or not. Do not wait for them. It is up to them to get there in time. I don't want you standing around all night because of inconsiderate people."

I beamed my approval.

Sometimes Mr. and Mrs. Kennedy breakfasted together, but that was rare. They almost always shared lunch. Mrs. Kennedy had a queasy stomach and she often ate the same lunch—boiled chicken, white meat only, plain with no salt, pepper, or dressing of any kind, between two crustless pieces of white bread; for dessert she liked a piece of angel-food cake, no frosting. As our employers munched their sparse sandwiches and salads, the staff sat down to a full-course dinner. Matilda cooked roasts at noon—with all the trimmings. One day beef, then pork, then lamb. The heavy midday meal made me sleepy, so while Mrs. Kennedy napped I took my own siesta. Afterward, if she wasn't golfing, I would either take her to the hairdresser or shopping.

There were few shoppers on Hyannis's Main Street this time of year. One afternoon as we walked along the sidewalk talking, she reined to a sudden halt. "Never call me Mrs. Kennedy in public!" she hissed. At first she had a look of disgust, as if I'd just shouted a filthy word, but then as she went on rebuking me on the sidewalk, she flashed smiles to passersby staring at us. "I don't want them to know who I am," she whispered sweetly. It was hard for me not to laugh. Who is she kidding? I thought. She was more recognizable in Hyannis than the First Lady.

Certainly all the shop ladies knew her, and because they did they were patient with her. She never seemed to know what she wanted. And then, after she'd finally decided, she'd never be sure of her choice. In the backseat on the way home she'd express doubts to me about whether she had bought the right pair of stockings. She was really thinking out loud to herself.

But I obeyed her and tried not to call her Mrs. Kennedy in public. Her secretary didn't want me to call her Mrs. Kennedy ever. One morning as I delivered the mail to this secretary, the first of six Mrs. Kennedy was to have in the years I was with her (I can only remember the names of two), I asked if she knew what Mrs. Kennedy's plans for the day were. "We do not call Mrs. Kennedy Mrs. Kennedy," she said sourly. "We call her *Madame!*" She had a way of pursing her lips when she spoke as if she'd just sucked a lemon. *"Ma . . . darm"* she repeated as if she were my kindergarten teacher. *"Ma . . . darm."*

"When Mrs. Kennedy calls me *Mis . . . ter* Saunders," I said in my best imitation of her accent, "then I shall call her *Ma . . . darm!*"

Mrs. Kennedy never asked me to call her Madame, but I would have if she had asked me personally.

She puzzled me. Her moods were as changeable as the weather, which in the late fall on Cape Cod is very changeable.

Mr. and Mrs. Kennedy did no entertaining. The only friend who visited Mrs. Kennedy was Mary Moore, the wife of Eddie Moore, who had been Mr. Kennedy's personal secretary. I drove Mary Moore over to the compound and took her home again.

Mrs. Kennedy was a recluse in her own house. In fact, she liked to be alone a great deal. But when she wanted someone around, she wanted them instantly. And that someone was often her new chauffeur.

"Is there anything wrong with Mr. Kennedy?" I asked her on our way back from mass.

"There's nothing wrong with Mr. Kennedy," she snapped.

"I mean his falls." Mr. Kennedy had tumbled from his horse. His toss had frightened Ann, but Mr. Kennedy had sloughed it off and gone out riding again the next day. Ann was naturally concerned. "Ann says he won't take his pills."

"Oh, pills! Mr. Kennedy is in wonderful condition for his age. Exercise and physical activity keeps you healthy. That's why I like to walk every day. And golf . . . golf is wonderful." After a minute she said, "Of course it is a little dangerous for a man his age to ride horses. But it is something he wants to do. And I cannot tell him what he should do and what he shouldn't do."

"Jesus, Ann, is Mrs. Kennedy all right?" I asked.

Ann looked at me dumbly.

"Her face!" I said. Afraid Mrs. Kennedy might overhear, I whispered. "It's all bandaged up! Did she fall down the stairs?"

Slowly a smile crept across Ann's face.

"Oh, you mean Aunt Rose's frownies."

"Her what?"

"Her frownies. They smooth her wrinkles."

I've got to get a good look at this, I said to myself. So I found something to ask Mrs. Kennedy about and went to see her. The frownies were brownish cloth bandages. She had them plastered to her forehead and stuck high on her cheeks, at her temples. Mrs. Kennedy knew I was staring at her.

"Frownies keep the wrinkles away, Frank." Her voice lilted. I figured, at seventy-one a woman could expect a few wrinkles. I wondered if the brown face bandages hurt when she peeled them off.

"Frank, I want you to go to the butcher's in Boston today for the meat," Mrs. Kennedy said. As she spoke, she grabbed a handwritten note she had pinned to her dress, ripped it off, and crumpled it. There were a half-dozen other notes fastened to her bodice. Then she marched off to the kitchen to deliver her next instructions to Matilda and tear that note from its safety pin.

11

She led me into the attic.

The door to the attic is a few steps from Mrs. Kennedy's bedroom, on the opposite side of the narrow second-floor hallway leading to Mr. Kennedy's bedroom at the far east end of the house.

"We must go to the attic at once!" Mrs. Kennedy had said. "I want you to help me inventory."

Although it was a cool autumn day, the sun beating down on the long roof had heated the big attic. I felt the dry heat hit me as soon as I started up behind her, as though summer too was stored in that attic. A naked light bulb dangled on its cord from the ridgeboards. She had flicked it on, but there are dormer windows in the attic and plenty of sunlight was streaming in. The place smelled of old wood.

"Oh my," Mrs. Kennedy sighed as she spun in a small circle. "Oh my!"

It is a big attic, running the full length of the house and over ten feet high at the roof peak. You can stand up most anywhere in it. I noticed a section of old roof shingles and could make out where the original house had ended and where they had added on and extended the roof line. Wilbert had been right. They had doubled the cottage.

Their attic looked like everyone's attic. Old furniture. Old trunks. Dry old cardboard boxes. Broken lamps. Clutter. At the east end, at a place just about midway between their bedrooms below, were two nice walk-in cedar clothes closets. I walked the length of the attic, down the center on the rough wood boards and, when I turned to come back, I could barely see Mrs. Kennedy's black hair above a stack of boxes which had been piled on an old wooden chair. She was tugging at them. "Frank! Help me," she said. "Frank! Please!"

I helped her set one of the boxes down, and as we moved it the dust flew off its top. In the slanting rays of sunlight the dust particles sparkled and swirled above her head like a halo. "Oh, yes. Yes. I know what these are," she said, attacking a pile of old photographs which were strewn in the box. "This is I," she announced, "with the king of England." I nodded and smiled recognition.

I left her flipping through the photographs and walked around, curious now. "Here is one of me with Lady Astor," she said. I kept looking. . . . An old wood cradle. Busted wicker lawn furniture. Old steamer trunks from the days of great liners. Junk. Treasures.

"Now that Jack is president I must be careful to save all this. It will be historically valuable someday, don't you think?" she asked as she feverishly rummaged through another box. She didn't need an answer from me.

"Yes, Mrs. Kennedy," I said.

The heat was suffocating. It was like an oven, and my nose was itching from the stirred-up dust. I wanted to open a window. When she had finished inspecting a box or trunk, she scribbled on it with a pencil. I shuffled boxes and moved furniture for her. We'd been at it for what seemed a good hour when I noticed a brown paper package nearly hidden where the roof sloped to the attic floor at the eave. I had to bend to reach it. "Do you want this, Mrs. Kennedy?" I asked when I had it in my hands, tilting it one side to the other for her to see. It was tied with hemp. The package felt soft. I shook it. Nothing rattled.

She stood ten feet away. "What's that?" she asked as she peered my way. I was in shadow, and the sunlight was in her eyes. She shaded them with her hands, but did not come nearer. "What do you have?"

I rested the bundle on a chest of drawers. The old stiff hemp had been tied in a bow. It pulled loose easily. I spread the paper back. Inside was white lace that had yellowed and, from the heft of it, I thought it might be an old wedding dress. I poked at the lace. It was brittle. My nose began to itch again.

"What is it?" she asked, but now she sounded disinterested. She was studying an old lamp.

The lace was folded in large squares. "It looks like old lace curtains," I said.

"Lace curtains?" she said finally. "Why would I keep old lace curtains?"

I had lifted the layers of lace now and saw that they were torn, perhaps frayed by age. "They're lace curtains, Mrs. Kennedy. And they're torn."

"Oh, Frank! Why would I keep an old torn lace curtain? Let me see." The tone of her voice was a bit angry, as if she would prove me wrong as soon as she inspected the forgotten package. I carried the bundle to her and she fingered the yellowed lace. I was fascinated at how small and fine-boned her hands were. The lace seemed to crumble when she poked it, the way old dry newspapers do. "They *are* lace curtains," she said quietly and stood back. "Oh my!"

She smiled slowly and a light filled her blue eyes—a look that a child has when discovering the presents under the Christmas tree. She remembered.

"They must be from Beals Street," she said. She looked at me, her eyes dancing. "Oh yes. Yes!" she said, and touched the lace curtains again, this time reverently. She looked up at me and realized I didn't know what she was talking about.

"Beals Street. In Brookline. Where we lived when President Kennedy was born. Oh yes! I'd forgotten, completely forgotten." She stroked the curtain and began laughing.

"We *were* lace-curtain Irish!"

Her laughter filled the attic. I was happy for her, seeing her like that. It was the first time I'd heard her really laugh. She looked at the package for a long time, then asked me to rewrap it. When I was done she wrote on it with her pencil.

I put the package back in the place where I had found it.

"Mrs. Kennedy, it's terribly hot up here. May we leave now?"

"Yes. Yes!" she said. There was still joy in her eyes and her cheeks were rosy, but I couldn't tell whether it was the heat in the attic or her childlike excitement that had flushed her face that way.

As she led me down the stairs she said, "Where is Joe? I must tell Joe about the lace curtain you found in our attic!"

Rose Kennedy handed me the cardinal gently, so she wouldn't crush the big doll's fancy silk cloak. At the same time she handed me the monsignor and started for the cellar with me close on her heels. Looking back to the kitchen, I saw Dora the maid cover her mouth with her hands to keep from laughing. "I want you to fit them into my display," Mrs. Kennedy said.

The doll room was windowless, a fifteen-by-twenty-foot room next to the movie theater. It was Mrs. Kennedy's own room.

"They are all my friends," she said of the dozens and dozens of dolls standing on shelves inside glass display cases against the walls. She told me that since she was a little girl she collected them in all the foreign countries she visited. One Japanese geisha, almost as tall as the two-foot priests, reminded me of a night on shore leave in Japan, but I didn't think that the president's mother would like to hear about that.

"They must be worth a lot of money, Mrs. Kennedy," I said.

"Oh, I don't think about that! I collect them because they help me remember where I've been."

The shelves were dusty and there was a yellowish film inside the glass. Some of the dolls looked a bit dingy. We had set the cardinal and the monsignor on the floor.

"If you like, Mrs. Kennedy, I can paint these shelves and the background. Dress it up a little, you know?"

She thought for a few seconds. "That would be nice, Frank."

"It will take me a few days."

"Fine."

96

"I'll have to do some rearranging."

"I want her in a prominent place," she said. She tapped the glass in front of a doll with a red rose in her black hair. "I want her to have a special place."

It was hard painting under the fluorescent lights, and it took me a week to finish her doll room. She looked in a few times but didn't stay long. She wanted to know where I got the paint and how much it cost. All the time the Rose Doll seemed to be staring at me. Finally I had to cover its face with a rag.

Mr. Kennedy came down when I was nearly done. "It looks swell, Frank. Mrs. Kennedy should be very pleased," he said, and patted me on the back.

When Mrs. Kennedy came in later she nodded silently. She nodded so many times that I thought she was counting to herself to make sure all her dolls were still there.

The clan gathered at Hyannis Port for Thanksgiving.

I was on the Kennedy family team for the football game against the secret service. We played on the lawn in front of the big house, and I made a good play. I don't remember the play itself, but I recall Mr. Kennedy watching from the window and cheering, both arms above his head, fists clenched. He made me feel great. The photographers were encouraged to take a lot of pictures, and the next day we were in all the newspapers.

12

Right after the holiday, Palm Beach was on everybody's mind.

The house at Hyannis Port and the one at Palm Beach are as different as the areas they are situated in. The big white house on Cape Cod is the one the Kennedys call home, although none of them was born there and none of the children went to school on the Cape. Mr. Kennedy bought the Hyannis Port house in 1927, after a few summers renting it, and it is the homestead because the family made it that. They all say that Hyannis Port is where they feel they belong.

I always felt the family fitted in better at Palm Beach, where people with a great deal of money spend a great deal of money and no one cares what the neighbors do. That is not the way it was at Hyannis Port. Some of the old Republicans at the Port actually believed Mr. Kennedy ordered his son to summer there as president just to infuriate them and ruin their summers with all the tourist traffic on the narrow lanes. I used to hear them grousing at the post office, but they were complaining to the wrong people because Bill and Mildred O'Neil, who ran the Hyannis News store and the post office, were Kennedy Democrats.

Besides, Hyannis Port was originally an upstart resort. The steel barons from Pittsburgh and the big store owners from the Midwest who built houses in the sleepy village at the turn of the century came there because they couldn't get into the socially acceptable places like Bar Harbor and Newport and Southampton where money alone was not enough to buy entrance.

Then these newcomers turned around and gave the cold shoulder to the Irish Catholic Kennedys from Boston. But Mr. Kennedy was used to it. It didn't faze him one bit. He had the house with the best water view. Eventually the neighbors came around. They tolerated the Kennedys. They had to. But I'm sure John Kennedy and all the Kennedys never forgot that in the 1960 election Richard M. Nixon beat him in Hyannis Port. This precinct, which includes the village, went 1,224 to 733 in Nixon's favor.

Unlike the Cape house, which has only one or two neighboring rivals, the Palm Beach house is not a particular standout in the midst of all the other mansions. With its Spanish tile roof and stucco façade and high cement walls, it is situated on North Ocean Boulevard, close to the beach.

We were always painting something at Palm Beach. The heavy stuffed furniture the Kennedys had there seemed to me more in tune with an English Victorian house than with a pseudo-Spanish Florida home. Mr. Kennedy bought the place a year or so after buying the Hyannis Port house. Each house had its own gardener.

Neither house was meant to be a showplace. They were homes, places where people lived. The Kennedys treated both places the way they did their cars. They needed them, they used them. There were more important things in life than houses and cars.

A Kennedy could get away with more at Palm Beach. So could the chauffeur. It was more relaxed. The living was higher there and there weren't as many people watching. Palm Beach was always a vacation; at least that's the way I tried to take the place. Mrs. Kennedy had me painting big flower pots and cement curbings, and there was the hedge over the arched doorway that always needed to be cut. But I liked Palm Beach. The only time I didn't like it was at Christmas. Whenever I had to set up their big tree in the high-ceilinged living room I got nostalgic for cold weather and the snow.

Not a bad setup Mr. Kennedy had given his family, was

it? A house on the beach on Cape Cod from late spring to Thanksgiving, and then a house on the beach at Palm Beach. After Joe Kennedy had the stroke, he and his wife gave up the yearly trip to the south of France.

Moving from house to house was something I dreaded. Not only did I have to get all the cars back and forth, I had to pack silverware and other household articles that Mrs. Kennedy took with her from place to place. I never understood why a family with all those millions had to live like ordinary people packing for a couple of weeks at the beach. If she had bought duplicates it would have saved us a lot of grief.

The front of Mrs. Kennedy's dress was a bulletin board of pinned-on notes for me. She had notes for all of us, all the things that had to be done to get ready. I had sold my own Chevy convertible so there was one less car to worry about. A new Cape Cod friend of mine was going to take one of the Kennedy cars down and then fly back, and I told him that the family would pay for his ticket back. But when I mentioned it to Mr. Kennedy he said, "No, Frank, that's not the way we do it. You have to take care of all of that. I'm not paying for extra people to take the cars down." So I made other arrangements. Every time I was set to move a car, Mrs. Kennedy came out with more household stuff she wanted to put in it. The only good thing I recall about that first move to Florida was my excitement about seeing Palm Beach.

Mr. Kennedy flew down in his plane the *Caroline* with Ann. It was not a very fast plane, and the pilot had joked with me, saying that I could probably drive to Palm Beach as fast as the *Caroline* could fly there. Mrs. Kennedy went her own way. Matilda and the maids, those who went to Palm Beach, went on their own. The old Kennedy chauffeur, Dave Degnin, did me a big favor by coming up from Florida, where he'd retired, to show me the way to Palm Beach.

When Dave saw how we'd fixed up the old apartment, his eyes got pretty big and he asked how I'd managed it. I told him that I let Mr. Kennedy know that I wanted it spruced up. Not wanting to hurt his feelings, I didn't tell him that I would have refused to live in the old apartment the way Dave had it. Then he said maybe I could also get Mr. Kennedy to do something about the chauffeur's place in Palm Beach, and hearing that kind of took the edge off my excitement about going south for the winter.

On the way down Dave told me how he'd left the Kennedy job heartbroken. He'd been with the family long enough to get a small pension from the Kennedys, but he had dreamed of driving John Kennedy to the armory in Hyannis to make his victory speech the morning after he won the election. Dave figured it would be the crowning glory of his years with the Kennedys. He was in the car ready to drive the president-elect when the secret service told him he couldn't because they wanted an agent driving him now. Dave said he couldn't understand it, they had only a few miles to go to the armory. But they made him get out of the car and Dave drove Joe Kennedy instead. After telling me that, Dave was silent for a long time, and then didn't talk much about the Kennedys. But by the time we got to Palm Beach Dave had come around and he gave me a few tips.

Palm Beach smelled of money. The people smelled of money. Maybe it was just the palm trees and the bright blue sky, blue the way it was on Cape Cod in the fall, and the big waterfront mansions painted in pastel colors. Whatever it was, it smelled rich. I had never seen so many expensive cars in one place before, and I was glad Mr. Kennedy had gotten rid of the old Caddy.

The Kennedy house on North Ocean Boulevard is a big L right on the water, and I could tell looking at it that the wind and salt water took their toll. There were splotches of mildewed paint and the roof tiles had fungus on them in places. The courtyard was a jungle. There is a swimming pool outside the living room, and a tennis court. On both sides of the yard and at the street front there are thick high concrete walls. The house has more privacy than the Hyannis Port house because of the high walls, but not as much land. You get to the ocean by walking down concrete steps and through a door in the retaining wall right on the beach. I heard that the house, located not far from the Palm Beach Country Club, was built in the twenties for one of the

Philadelphia Wanamakers and that Mr. Kennedy bought it in the depression for $100,000. There are better houses around it. The driveway curves into a courtyard at the front of the house and there is a very long archway leading to the front door. The archway gives the house its one real touch of style.

"What's all this?" Mrs. Kennedy wanted to know as soon as she saw the old furniture piled in the driveway.

"This is the stuff from my apartment that we are throwing out, Mrs. Kennedy," I said.

She inspected it. "Why, it looks perfectly all right to me. I don't see anything wrong with any of it."

"Mr. Kennedy thought that I should have new furniture," I said.

This time Mr. Kennedy had not even needed to look at the chauffeur's apartment. I had told him the place needed painting and that the furniture was shot, and he told me to go ahead and buy the furniture I needed and even recommended a good place to buy it: Burdine's. I told him that I would do the painting myself and he liked that.

Mrs. Kennedy continued to inspect the old stuffed furniture. Even out in the driveway, it still smelled of mildew, and most of it was worn out and broken.

"There's some usable pieces here," Mrs. Kennedy said.

"The Ambassador told me to get new furniture," I said.

"Well, if my husband says it is all right, then I suppose it is," she said. "But, Frank, inquire of the nuns first and ask if they could use any of this before you merely throw it away."

But even the nuns didn't want it. I had to have it carted off to the dump.

13

"Whose car is that?" President Kennedy shouted from behind the wheel of an open convertible. He had just pulled in the driveway.

"It's your father's new car, Mr. President," I yelled back.

"It looks sharp, Frank," the president said. He was closer now. Jacqueline was with him. There was another couple sitting in the back, and Jacqueline was talking to the woman. None of them paid any attention to the president when he hailed me.

I was hosing down the new Chrysler. The president walked over. "How long will it take to finish that, Frank?"

"Fifteen minutes or so."

"Listen, can you be down at the dock in fifteen minutes? We are going for a cruise on the *Honey Fitz* and I'd like you to come along." He touched my shoulder and smiled. "Can you do it?"

I left the Chrysler dripping wet in the driveway and ran off to change my clothes.

The *Honey Fitz* was moored at Mr. Kennedy's yacht club, a short drive away.

I stepped on board. "Frank. Here's Frank, Jacqueline. It's so good of you to come, Frank!" the president said. John Kennedy took my hand and shook it vigorously. "The special guest is aboard. We can shove off," he said loudly and commandingly.

I had expected a big crowd. I had even half expected that the president might have me working on the yacht, but the only guests on the *Honey Fitz* were the president and the First Lady and the woman and man I had seen with them in the car.

It was a bright, gorgeous day. The pink and pale blue and creamy white stucco mansions looked even richer viewing them in a long, passing row from the ocean. Down the beach the towers of the breakers stood like giant chalk cliffs. I saw a Coast Guard cutter moving toward the *Honey Fitz.* There seemed to be commotion all around, but on the presidential yacht's aft deck it was as quiet and shady as if we were in a grove of trees.

The man from the convertible smiled at me. "Stash," John Kennedy said, "I'd like you to meet a friend of ours, Frank Saunders. Frank, this is my brother-in-law, Stanislas Radziwill." The president smiled. *"Prince* Radziwill," he added. The man was a Polish-born nobleman, I learned later.

"Prince," I said, shaking his hand, "it's a pleasure. Frank Saunders." Prince grasped my hand for longer than I was used to. I thought he'd never let go.

"Lee, come meet Frank," the president said. The woman with Jacqueline Kennedy timed a wide smile with her turn, and walked across the deck. "So nice to meet you, Frank," Lee Radizwill gushed, and clasped the hand I had extended between both of hers and shook it slowly up and down.

I caught Jacqueline Kennedy and her husband looking at each other, both of them smiling broadly.

"Frank is very important to us," Jacqueline Kennedy said in that hushed way of hers.

We sat down in deck chairs. The president crossed his legs. He was wearing brown cotton trousers and had on old moccasins and no socks. The *Honey Fitz* was turning and the sun angled under the canopy; I noticed a glint of red in John Kennedy's tousled hair. He lit up a thin cigar.

"A vodka-tonic," I told a Filipino servant who had just come topside.

Everyone else relaxed, but I was still a bit nervous.

The vodka-tonic helped.

The Coast Guard cutter closed on the *Honey Fitz* and the president watched the cutter. We had outdistanced a small friendly flotilla of boats. Behind us the mansions of Palm Beach were by now very small.

"So, Frank, have you reached an agreement with my father?" the president asked.

"Ah . . . yes," I said.

"Frank is very close to my father," the president told his brother-in-law. Prince Radziwill nodded and smiled at me. John Kennedy took a deep breath, exhaled some cigar smoke, and stretched in the chair. "This is just great," he announced. He looked contemplatively at his thin cigar and asked, "Isn't this great, Jackie?"

The Filipino in a short white coat was back in front of me, refilling my glass. "Ice, Mr. Saunders?"

"Yes," I said, surprising myself with the authority in my voice. I remember Jacqueline Kennedy talking to her sister about the White House. She reeled off the names of all the rooms. I recall her listing colors and what she was going to do in this room and how she would furnish that room. I remember Lee Radziwill saying, "Oh, how I envy you." And kept on saying it.

"You were in the navy, Frank?" the president's voice interrupted. I thought, How does he know that? *Does* he know that? Did I tell him that, or had he read it in a secret service report on my background?

"Two tours. I was on the *Missouri* during Korea," I said.

"A battleship sailor!" The president was enthused. "A battleship man, Stash!" he repeated, but Prince Radziwill seemed preoccupied, even as he stared at me.

John Kennedy and I had a conversation about the *Missouri*, and we each guessed how many knots the cutter alongside was making.

"Frank, haven't we met before?" Prince Radziwill intruded.

"Yes, I'm sure we have," his wife joined in.

"No," I said slowly, as if I, too, was trying to recall, "I don't think so." Again the Filipino was refilling my glass. By now I was no longer nervous about the company I was keeping. "Perhaps we crossed paths," I offered

105

bravely, "but I'm sure we've never been introduced before today."

Jacqueline Kennedy and her husband were beaming at each other, happy as children with their little game, and I was not about to spoil it for them. Besides, I was having the time of my life. I eyed Prince Radziwill through my sunglasses, over the rim of my glass.

Suddenly the prince blurted, "Monte Carlo!"

I sipped my drink and shook my head no.

"Yes, Monte Carlo!" he persisted. "Last winter. I am certain of it." Palm Beach was out of sight now. The Coast Guard cutter still stalked us like a shark.

"Frank is a mystery man," John Kennedy helped.

There was a long pause while everyone drank. The prince had not given up. He tried Paris, Rome, Gstaad, Switzerland.

"What do you do, Frank?" Lee Radziwill asked. I stared blankly at her. She resembled her sister slightly, but only slightly; her skin was darker, I could tell, even with her deep tan. I was feeling the drinks now, having had five—five very tall ones.

"Princess," I began. The three of them looked at me as if I had said "princess" the wrong way. I started over again. "Mrs. Radziwill." Then I took a long sip from my sixth vodka-tonic. "I am a bookmaker!"

I watched with a deadpan expression as Lee Radziwill's mouth opened wide.

The president laughed first. It was a good laugh, a real laugh. The First Lady's laugh was more like one she might give a naughty child. It was manufactured—there just because her husband was also laughing. Then the prince joined in, and I laughed too. I was really laughing to myself, thinking about my days back in Boston in the Combat Zone and wondering what some of my old friends would do if they could see me now.

I don't remember the rest of the cruise, although I know it lasted a long time. I never turned away the Filipino with the drinks—I remember that—and I recall that Prince Radziwill soon gave up the guessing game. Once Lee Radziwill shot me a strange look. President Kennedy had whispered in her ear.

106

Whether the president or Jacqueline ever revealed my identity to the Radziwills, I never heard. I know they didn't while I was there. It had been the president's game and I had gone along. That cruise on the *Honey Fitz* was one of the great days of my life.

Afterward, sweating in the hot sun from the walk back to Mr. Kennedy's house, I went off and hid out of sight in the hedges and was very sick. My old navy ulcer was killing me.

14

It was six days till Christmas. When Mrs. Kennedy returned to the house around noon after mass and errands, she was told Mr. Kennedy was in bed.

This time Ann was really worried. She explained to her aunt what had happened on the golf course, trying hard to keep calm. Mr. Kennedy had gone faint while they were playing the back nine and had had to rest on a bench, Ann said. After that Uncle Joe had difficulty balancing himself. He walked like a drunk. She'd gotten him into the golf cart, then her car, and she had driven him right home. He seemed confused.

"Was he able to walk into the house?" Mrs. Kennedy asked.

"Yes," Ann said. "But I had to help him."

Mrs. Kennedy was silent.

"I'm afraid it could be something serious," Ann said.

"He needs rest," Mrs. Kennedy said.

I knew Ann was not an alarmist, but I could see that she was very tense. Mrs. Kennedy had to see it, too.

Ann told her that he had been stubborn and did not want to go to bed. "I think you should have a look at him, Aunt Rose," she said.

When Mrs. Kennedy came back from her husband's bedroom she said he would be fine. She said that he needed to rest and that there had been too much golf, too much exertion, too much excitement over the president's

108

visit and the coming Christmas. She was certain that he would feel better after a nap. Hadn't he always? She smiled at Ann, to reassure her.

That morning, as usual, I had taken Mrs. Kennedy to mass. Then she had errands to run, some Christmas shopping on Worth Avenue, so it was later than usual by the time I got her home. Her husband had meanwhile ridden to the airport with the president, who was returning to Washington. Caroline had gone with them, but she would be staying on with her grandfather; Jacqueline, Caroline, and little John Kennedy were all going to remain in Palm Beach until the president came home for Christmas, the First Family having taken over another seaside mansion for the holidays. So Ann drove Mr. Kennedy and his granddaughter back from the airport, before taking him to the golf course for their usual round of golf.

Later that morning I snuck into Mr. Kennedy's bedroom. "How you feeling, Chief? You feel all right?" I asked.

He made a noise in his throat indicating that he did. But he didn't sound all right. He didn't look all right either.

"He doesn't look too good to me," I told Ann. She gave me a quick sympathetic look and shook her head.

Neither his wife nor his niece wanted to call the doctor, I guessed.

Mrs. Kennedy looked in on her husband again after her lunch.

I was in and out of the house quite a few times during lunchtime, and when I inquired how the boss was doing I was told that, instead of snapping out of it, he was getting worse.

Mrs. Kennedy still planned to play golf that afternoon.

Finally they called for a doctor. The doctor came at once and they wasted no time. They put the president's father on a stretcher and wheeled him to an ambulance. Ann got in with him. As the ambulance pulled out into the boulevard its lights began flashing.

In the house the staff whispered that Mr. Kennedy had had a stroke. They were all shaken.

I went to Mrs. Kennedy and asked her when she wanted me to drive her to the hospital and if she was ready to go right then.

"There's nothing I can do except pray," Mrs. Kennedy said. Her face was pale. "He'll be all right. Ann's with him. He'll be fine, you'll see. I just cannot let this get me down. I must keep up my schedule. I have my routine. I'm going to play golf now, Frank," she said. "Yes, I will play."

She was still at the golf course when the hospital called the house. They wanted her at the hospital right away to sign papers, something about needing her permission if they had to operate.

I went after her in the Chrysler. The golf course is one-half mile from the house, so it didn't take long to get there. I didn't bother to ask—I just jumped in a golf cart and started it up, and took off across the course, and then I got to thinking that I should have driven the Chrysler onto the course because the golf cart wouldn't go fast enough. I was thinking something else too, that they should have called the doctor sooner.

I yelled at a group of golfers to get the hell out of the way, and as I went through them one of them looked at me as though I was crazy. The cart steered wildly and swerved on the slippery grass as I cut left and right over the fairways looking for her. By the time I found her alone I was not in a very good mood.

She seemed annoyed too. She hadn't seen me coming until I was right on her, and I guess it startled her. "Mrs. Kennedy, the hospital called and they want you to come," I said as soon as I was near enough.

"Oh, what is it?"

"It's the hospital."

"What can I do?"

"They need you to sign some papers."

"Oh, very well," she said. She asked me to put her clubs in the cart. I tossed them in the back.

Mrs. Kennedy was silent as I raced the little cart back to the clubhouse. It felt like I was driving one of those bumper cars in an amusement park, but I could see she wasn't at all amused.

"Slow down, Frank!" she said. I could feel the cart fishtailing.

In the Chrysler I asked if she wanted me to head right

for Saint Mary's. "Oh, no, Frank. I must go home first. He's had these before, you know. It's just a passing weakness. He will be all right."

I searched for her in the rearview mirror. She seemed very small in the big backseat. I eyed her for a split second in the mirror. "I hope so, Mrs. Kennedy."

"He'll be all right," she said, the way you do when you want something to turn out all right but you're not certain that it will.

"I am going to take a swim first, Frank," she said when we reached the house.

A swim?

"Mrs. Kennedy, the hospital did say they wanted you right away," I said.

"I am going to swim now, Frank," she said. "Yes, I will have a good swim. These people . . ."

"Do you want me to call the hospital?"

"No," she said. And she went up to change into her swimsuit.

I watched her in the pool. Mr. Kennedy had told me to keep an eye on her whenever she went swimming, just in case. She wore a bathing cap and swam hard from side to side at the shallow end of the pool. I tried to keep my observation casual, so that she would not think I was playing lifeguard. It looked to me like she was swimming hard to tire herself out. She is sure taking her sweet time, I was thinking.

I helped her from the pool. She toweled herself slowly. "Now I must have my shower," she said.

As I waited for her in the car I kept saying to myself, For Chrissake, come on! Come on! I was thinking that her husband could be dying. When a hospital calls like that it has to be bad. This wasn't Ann calling her to tell her that everything was all right; it was the doctors who wanted her.

"I don't know the way to Saint Mary's," I said as soon as she got into the car.

"I'll show you," she said.

As I wheeled the Chrysler out of the driveway my foot kicked the pedal, and in the rearview mirror I glimpsed her lurch back against the seat.

111

She told me we had to go across Lake Worth to West Palm Beach. "It isn't that far," she said.

Suddenly there were police at the intersections. Who had called them? The hospital? The secret service? I was speeding now, and the police waved me through. As I looked down the long, straight, wide road ahead to the bridge I saw the rotating lights on the police-car roofs flashing blue in the dusk. I didn't need Mrs. Kennedy's directions now because I could have found my way to the hospital by going from one flashing blue light to the next.

On the bridge I glanced again in the mirror. Her face was the face of a granite statue. The color had drained from it, and as we speeded toward the hospital I wondered if she was thinking what I was thinking: the police wouldn't be out like this unless it was bad.

She didn't wait for me to open the door. She strode into Saint Mary's ahead of me and a doctor met her. They went into a room and closed the door.

I wandered through the hospital corridors. When I got back to the room she was gone.

"Where's Mrs. Kennedy?" I asked a nurse. She saw the chauffeur's suit. "I'm Mrs. Kennedy's chauffeur," I said.

The nurse smiled. "I think Mrs. Kennedy is in the chapel."

"How is it with Mr. Kennedy?"

"Not good."

"How bad?" I asked.

"He's had a stroke."

"A bad stroke?"

"They're all bad."

"But this one?"

"If only we'd had him sooner. A lot of damage has been done."

"Will he make it?"

"They don't know. It's touch-and-go."

"Did the doctor tell that to Mrs. Kennedy? Did he tell her how serious it is?"

"I don't know," the nurse said. She smiled. "I really don't know. Please excuse me now."

I went looking for Ann.

All the rest is a blur. I was at the hospital for hours. Mrs. Kennedy stayed praying in the chapel for a long time. I don't remember what I said to Ann. The secret service came. The reporters were around. Someone told me that the president was flying back and that all the children had been notified and that I should stand by in case they needed me for airport runs. Maybe I went to the airport that night; I just don't remember. I do recall the doctors saying that this night would be the crisis and that if Mr. Kennedy made it through the night he had a good chance. The hospital issued a press release saying that the president's father was holding his own. His name was on the critical list but his condition was stable. But I talked to some of the doctors and nurses and the truth was that they didn't hold much hope he would live very long. They did not come right out and tell that to Mrs. Kennedy.

The telephone rang at my apartment Christmas Eve and I dreaded picking it up. Mr. Kennedy had developed pneumonia a few days before, and his throat had had to be cut open so they could put in a tube for him to breathe. So I figured the call, here on Christmas Eve, was bad news.

"Yes," I said.

"Frank, it's me, Pat."

"Oh, yes, Mrs. Lawford."

"Could you come over and light the fire?"

I heard my breathing in the receiver and had to wait a few seconds to control myself before I could answer. I wanted to explode. It had been a rough five days; rough on everyone. "It's all set, Mrs. Lawford," I said.

"What?"

"The logs are set to light. All you have to—"

"Can you come over right now?"

"Now listen, Mrs. Lawford. It is all set. There are newspapers under the kindling. You look and you'll see the crumpled newspapers. It's all set to go. I made it so anyone could light it. Just touch a match to the newspapers, you see?"

"Oh? Oh! You mean light the newspapers?"

"That's it. Like I said, just light the newspapers and you'll have a fire."

"All right," Pat Lawford said.

A few minutes later the telephone rang again. "Frank, come over now! We want a fire!" Pat Lawford said.

I cannot recall who was there, though I have an idea there were quite a few in the big living room. The tree lights were on, and it was the first time I had really seen the big tree at night. I had just gotten it up and decorated it when Mr. Kennedy had his stroke. It was the biggest and tallest Christmas tree I had ever seen in a house. The ceiling in the Palm Beach living room must be fifteen feet high, and the tree almost touched it. It was so tall that I had had to fasten a wire from the ceiling to the top of the tree, to keep it from toppling over. But it looked beautiful that night, and even though none of them could have felt very happy it sure looked and smelled like Christmas at the Kennedys'. All they needed to complete the mood was a roaring fire.

"You take the match like this!" I announced, and held up the matchbook for the gathering to see. "And you strike the match against the cover like this." The match lighted. "And you take the match like so and you light the fire by touching the match to the newspapers!"

I crouched and touched the match to the newspapers.

The crumpled balls of newspaper underneath the dry kindling caught, slowly at first, and then in a loud poof the papers burst all at once.

"And like magic," I called as the kindling crackled, "you have a fire!"

I waited a few more seconds until I was satisfied that the logs were going to catch, and then I walked out of the living room. I heard someone clapping behind me, but I never turned to see who it was.

I had taken a room at the hospital down the corridor from Mr. Kennedy's. Ann had the room next to her uncle. In the mornings I drove to the house and picked up Mrs. Kennedy and took her to mass, then drove her to the hospital, and then brought her home. Then I'd take her back to the hospital and I would wait. Some days she would make five or six visits. That's the way it was for the next month.

The stroke had been a bad one. How long had it been before the doctors got to him? Four hours? Maybe longer. A lot of damage had been done. His right side was paralyzed, and he might never be able to walk again. The doctors weren't so sure about his speech. They said it would take time. Of course he had the best care.

After the pneumonia left him, he started to gain. But we all knew that it had changed at the Kennedys'.

15

There was bad blood between Mr. Kennedy and his English son-in-law, the actor Peter Lawford. I never asked Peter Lawford what it was about, and he never came right out and told me, but I got the feeling that it had a lot to do with his being an actor. Anyway, Mr. Kennedy had been against the marriage, and with Peter Lawford realizing that his father-in-law was not too keen on him, he slept over in Mr. Kennedy's house as seldom as he could. Except for this period when Mr. Kennedy was still in the hospital.

I never understood why Mr. Kennedy did not like him because I thought Peter Lawford was a hell of a guy. For one thing, he was never too proud to have a drink with the Kennedy chauffeur.

"I feel like a drink," Peter Lawford said as soon as I met him at the West Palm Beach airport. Just the way he said it made me want to laugh. He had a way of arching those thick eyebrows and smiling like the cat that had swallowed the canary. I guess I saw his best side, but he sure made me feel good and could get me laughing like no one else. When I see him now on those television commercials he has me laughing again.

"I feel like a drink myself," I said.

We found a quiet bar.

"How's things at the castle, Frank? Is Queen Mother treating you properly?"

"Things are pretty depressing," I told him.

"They must be. Yes, I should think so. Then we should have another drink," the actor said.

"Mr. Lawford . . ."

"Peter, Peter," he said quickly.

"You know those old movies you were in with Lassie?" I said.

His eyebrows arched, and he had that smile again. Peter Lawford was around my age, and I remembered those Lassie movies he made after the war. They had made me cry. Lawford had played Lassie's young master in one of the movies, and the collie had followed him for days and days.

"Yes," he said, baiting me. "The original! The real Lassie!"

"Well, Peter, how did they train that dog? You know, to come to you like that?"

"Lassie was a vicious bastard! A bastard! You want to know how we did those scenes? I had raw meat stuck under my arms and under my shirt and rubbed on my face and stuck up my clyde, and that animal was trying to eat me alive! The bastard! What you saw on the screen, what you thought was the true love of an intelligent dog for his master wasn't that at all, Frank. No, it was animal hunger. The bastard was trying to eat me alive!"

He had acted it out. He had pretended to stick meat under his arms, under his shirt, under his pants, and he had me roaring and holding my stomach. Everyone in the place was laughing, too. They all recognized him as Peter Lawford.

"First little Dorothy in *The Wizard of Oz*," I said, when I had stopped laughing, "and now Lassie!"

"Dorothy?" he asked.

I told him how Judy Garland had attacked me.

"Isn't it terrible how precious little is as we see it; how it's all make-believe? I think we should have another drink," Peter Lawford said. ". . . So we can see the truth more clearly."

Peter Lawford was in and out of Palm Beach often those months. His wife, Patricia, had come down when her father collapsed, and she stuck with Mr. Kennedy. Pat was determined that, whenever her father opened his eyes at

117

the hospital, one of his children would be right there at his bedside, and usually it was she. She spent hour after hour with him after he came home, talking to him when no one knew yet if he could understand a word. She would stay in his room into the early morning.

Then, back at the house, she would get up in the late morning, and for breakfast would have a piece of toast and a full bottle of white wine. I had to make sure the wine cellar was stocked for her.

Her husband usually stayed with some Palm Beach friends, the McMahons. I used to go over there and wake him up, and then, after I brought Mrs. Kennedy back from mass, he and I would go down to one of the swanky bars for a Bloody Mary eye-opener.

I celebrated New Year's Eve with some of the secret service agents. Mrs. Kennedy had told me that she would not be going to early mass New Year's Day, so I took full advantage of the change of routine.

It was just after sunrise when the telephone started ringing. I was a little hung over, and the phone rang for a long time before I got to it. I just picked it up and didn't say anything.

"Frank! It's Mrs. Kennedy. I want the Christmas tree down!"

I was mumbling about it being very early.

"I want it taken down now, Frank! This instant!"

I woke up one of the secret service agents who had done less celebrating the night before than the others and told him that Mrs. Kennedy needed him. It was an order, I said. Then I got the stepladder so I could disconnect the wire from the ceiling to the tree.

"Do we have to take all these ornaments off this thing? All these lights?" the agent asked.

I was still half asleep—all I wanted to do was go back to bed—and Mrs. Kennedy had not put in an appearance.

"The hell with it," I said. "Let's just drag the damn thing out to the tennis court and leave it there. She'll forget all about it as soon as she sees it gone."

The agent proclaimed it a good idea.

I unfastened the ceiling wire. The big tree started tipping.

The agent shouted to warn me, and already I was shouting instructions at him as I clambered down the ladder. I jumped, and the tall stepladder crashed onto the red-tiled living-room floor. Looking back up, I saw the tree tilting badly. In fact I could hear the tree creaking over and the decorations and tinsel rattling and chiming.

"It's going over!" I yelled, and tried to grab the tree. But I couldn't get at the trunk to steady it because the branches were too long and prickly.

The agent and I stood back.

"Timber," I muttered.

Suddenly, Peter Lawford stumbled out of a little study off the room.

"What the hell's going on?" he asked, rubbing his eyes.

The big tree caught him coming down. Branches swept him back, scraping down his face and body. He staggered in surprise. The tree had not fallen flat, being so bushy at the bottom, but was listing like a beamy sailboat run high and dry on a sandbar. The dazed actor stood smiling. "This is a gas, man!" he said. He was fully dressed, and I figured that's how he must have fallen asleep, in his clothes. He looked the way I felt, which was pretty awful. A long strand of tinsel hung from one ear.

"You all right?" I laughed.

"Oh, yeah! Frank? Hey, Frank! Shall we have a Bloody Mary?"

"I'm working. I've got to get the tree out of the house," I said.

"I see," he said, groped his way out from under the fallen branches and tinsel, turned on his heels, and walked slowly back into the little study. "Happy New Year, gentlemen," he said.

Through the wide-open French doors we dragged the big tree, ornaments and all. Behind us we left a trail of tangled tinsel and busted decorations. We left the tree on the tennis court.

When I called her from my apartment, I said, "Mrs. Kennedy, I am reporting that the Christmas tree is now down."

I guess Dora and the other maids must have cleaned up the mess in the living room. Later, standing in the tennis court and taking the decorations off the tree, I felt somewhat bad, realizing that Mrs. Kennedy had probably wanted the tree out of the house because there wasn't much to be happy about that Christmas.

16

The boss came home in a wheelchair. That blue fire still flickered in his eyes, but not as brightly. The medical explanation was that blood had clotted in an artery in the brain and then hemorrhaged. So that's what the pills I never asked about and he never took were for. His right arm and leg were dead, paralyzed, and his speech had been impaired. I heard that word a lot in those weeks— "impaired." What did they mean by "impaired"? Hell, he'd *lost* it. The doctors ruled out surgery. Instead, they said it was up to him, that it was courage and determination he needed. That if he *wanted* it badly enough, and if he *fought* hard enough, he could come back.

Joe Kennedy was seventy-three years old, and telling someone that age that it is up to them, that it has to be a test of their own strength, is a goddam cruel thing. But doctors tell the family what it wants to hear, and there were those in that family who did not want to hear the truth about the sentence that he had been dealt, this man who was their "patriarch," as the newspapers now called him. There were a lot of white lies that winter.

His children showed him their love, and that more than anything else cheered him up. After Jacqueline left him his spirit would be high as a kite. Ted could make him laugh. The president kept asking him when he'd be up to a trip to the White House, and that made him feel important.

His children, when they left him, were mostly frustrated

121

and angry about what had happened. He had been so independent, so in control, always able to do just what he wanted to do. Seeing him in that wheelchair tore them apart. Robert Kennedy let his frustration out more than any of them. It wasn't that he loved his father more, it was that he was outraged that his father had been struck down like that. Bobby didn't want any bullshit from the doctors or anyone. He wanted the truth. Would he walk again? Would he be able to talk again?

We all wanted answers. At night I would go down to the *Marlin* and drink Mr. Kennedy's Scotch and talk with Captain Frank and we would wonder what would become of us.

Every morning I read Mr. Kennedy the sports pages. His friends came by. There was Morton Downey, the Irish tenor from the early days of television, who had a house on Squaw Island and also wintered at Palm Beach. Also Carroll Rosenbloom, the owner of the Baltimore Colts, who was about twenty years younger than the Ambassador. Flamboyant Joe Timilty, the old bachelor who was Boston police commissioner and a godfather of sorts to Joe, Jr., would drop by. The comic Joe E. Lewis visited quite a bit. I'd chauffeur Lewis up from the Miami Beach nightclub he was performing at, and he'd do his routine again for his pal Joe Kennedy. On the way back up, Joe E. always wanted to stop and have a drink before we got to Palm Beach.

But that was all. I was surprised that a man who had been so powerful and was so rich did not have more close friends. I guess it was as true for the president's father as for anyone that you find out who your real friends are when you are sick.

The doctors had a plan. Since money was no object for the Kennedys, as soon as he got some strength back Mr. Kennedy would begin an expensive rehabilitation program. Everyone held out hope that he would walk and talk again. In the meantime the family hired Rita Dallas, who'd been his nurse at Saint Mary's, to come in as the day nurse. Other nurses handled the night shift. An elevator was put in for the wheelchair. He should be exercised, the doctors said, so I took him down to the pool every day until they could hire a male aide. The doctors taught Ann and me to operate the oxygen equipment which was kept in his room. They wired up an alarm at my apartment with a button in Mr. Kennedy's house for the nurse to push when she needed help.

All this swirled around him as he sat in that wheelchair, soaking it all up with those cold blue eyes. His big word was "no." Only he did not speak it. He made a noise out of it. A long, loud no. NNNnnnooooo! Over and over again. Sometimes he could squeak a yes, and sometimes he'd use his good left hand and arm to make gestures and motion us. He tried to write with his left hand, to give us instructions and tell us what he wanted, but it frustrated him. I would see this look of fear creep into his eyes, and at times there would be something more fleeting in his eyes too—the look you can get from a wild caged animal. He was trapped, and he knew it.

He was at the mercy of three women: Mrs. Kennedy, Ann, and the nurse Rita Dallas. Each of them during those first few months thought she knew what was best for Mr. Kennedy.

Mr. Kennedy did not want his wife in his room. When she came in, he would attack her with that long, loud no and start flailing at her with his good left arm, swinging it like a sword, screaming at her.

"I'm going, dear! I'm going, dear!" Mrs. Kennedy would say. It shook her, I could tell. She pretended that being chased out of his room didn't bother her and that it was his illness that made him do it, but she knew it was more than that.

The bell went off like someone had snuck up while I was sleeping and fired a gun at my head. I ran over in my pajamas. He was having an attack, was choking and fighting for his breath. The night nurse had the oxygen out but she didn't know how to operate it. I slapped the mask to his face. He was kicking like a horse. I had it wide open. He came around and I stayed with him until the nurse thought it would be all right for me to leave. The next morning I told Rita Dallas what had happened. She told me not to tell Mrs. Kennedy because it would upset her unnecessarily.

Actually, Rose Kennedy seemed incapable of being upset.

"Enjoy life while you are young, Frank," she said one morning on our way back from mass. She was in a good mood.

"I try to, Mrs. Kennedy," I said.

"Oh, I really mean it, Frank. We waste so much time on things that aren't really important. And then we wish afterward that we had done what we wanted to. You really have to seize the moment! It's so true. Just look at it today; isn't it going to be another marvelous day, so bright and sunshiny? What a perfect day for golf!"

"Yes, Mrs. Kennedy," I said.

"Do you play golf, Frank?"

I told her that I had tried it a few times but wasn't very good.

"You must learn, Frank. It is a wonderful way to relax and exercise at the same time. Now, I have a good golf pro and he has helped me and I'm sure he can help you." She laughed. "What I will do is have him give you some lessons. I will pay for them, Frank. You should have some time for yourself. I think you'd love playing golf once you, you know, get into the swing of it!"

She had me laughing along with her. "I'll take you up on it," I said.

"Oh, that's wonderful, Frank!"

A few days later, while I was again painting the white clay flower pots that lined the driveway, she asked me if I'd done anything about her golf offer. I told her I'd set up a date with her golf pro.

"Wonderful!" she said. "Let me know about your progress." Then I went back to the pots. By the time we were ready to return to the Cape, I'd repainted those clay pots three times. She wanted them always pristine white.

17

Almost immediately after Mr. Kennedy's stroke, special preparations began for his return to Hyannis Port. A big hole was dug right behind the big house for a swimming pool, and Freddy Lawrence from Falmouth built it over the next several months. The pool was heated and enclosed, and they put in whirlpools and bubblers and a stainless-steel rail for Mr. Kennedy to grab with his good left hand. It is a big pool, holding fifty thousand gallons, and it takes a day and a half to fill it. The Kennedys didn't want to hire a pool-maintenance outfit, so eventually I got the job of taking care of it, which meant cleaning it every day, not such an easy task given the size of the pool. I cleaned it after we returned from mass and after I got the mail. The pool at Palm Beach, which I also cleaned, wasn't nearly as big.

One summer at Hyannis Port—I can't remember which one—Eunice Shriver called me, clearly out of sorts. "Frank! There's too much chlorine in the water!"

"What do you mean too much chlorine, Mrs. Shriver?" I'd put in the same amount I always had.

"It's too strong. Take some of it out!" she said.

Take some of it out?! She didn't know what she was talking about. Did she think I was going to spend a day and a half draining the pool and then another day and a half filling it again?

So I pumped more water in and let the fresh chlorine

burn off for a couple of hours. Then I called Mrs. Shriver and told her to try it now. She did and reported, "It's fine now, Frank."

I was wrong about Mr. Kennedy. I knew he was tough but I didn't know how strong-willed he was. He made progress at Palm Beach and he was taken that spring to the Institute of Rehabilitation Medicine in New York. Mrs. Kennedy, Ann, and Rita Dallas went with him. We heard later that he had struggled to stand for President Kennedy's visit. It was good news.

While he was gone and they were still building the swimming pool at Hyannis Port, an elevator was set up on the east end of Mr. Kennedy's house, with doors to his bedroom, the main floor, and the movie theater. And they wired an alarm bell in my garage apartment.

The First Family took over Morton Downey's house on secluded Squaw Island, and that summer there were a lot of trips to Newport and Jacqueline's family's place, Hammersmith Farm. The tourists had driven her out of Hyannis. But the helicopter still landed on the front lawn of the big house, and Mr. Kennedy rode down in the elevator in his wheelchair to greet his son, and we rolled him back again when it was time for the president to leave for the White House.

The helicopter landing had become a ritual, but the president's mother wanted to change it. She told her son not to stop and talk with tourists and the neighbors but to go right to his father as soon as he was out of the helicopter. But John Kennedy didn't always do what his mother asked or told him to do, and it infuriated her.

Not long after we returned to the Cape there was a big mess. Some anti-Kennedy southerners began the "Reverse Freedom Riders," an effort to embarrass the Kennedys for their strong civil-rights stand. The idea was that if the Kennedys were the champions of America's blacks, then the Kennedys should welcome them to Cape Cod. The anti-Kennedy people behind this little scheme were telling the blacks in the South that the Kennedys would get them all jobs and houses on the Cape. And up they came by the busload.

Of course Cape Codders didn't take this too well, and the Kennedys were caught in the middle. The town weekly, which had taken occasional punches at the Kennedys for "ruining" the Cape by attracting hordes of tourists, said the busloads of southern blacks were the President's fault. A *Barnstable Patriot* editorial said:

> Until President Kennedy, who professes a deep and abiding love for Cape Cod, and his brother, the Attorney General, who professes to be the champion of the Negro race, come out and make some effort in behalf of their professed loves, the Cape and its newest one-way guests are in the hapless position of being unable to solve the complex problem of what to do next.

That was the attitude the Kennedys frequently had to put up with from some of their neighbors. The bused blacks were bused again, this time to the barracks at Otis Air Force Base, until they could be moved off the Cape. Some of the families stayed and still live on the Cape, and in fact the Kennedys did find jobs for a couple of women Reverse Freedom Riders as part-time maids at Mr. Kennedy's house.

The Reverse Freedom Riders publicity stunt was a big story on the Cape, and it also got national attention. But the reporters never discovered the cruel hoax someone had played on a stout black lady from Mississippi who showed up one day at Mr. Kennedy's doorstep. She forced her way inside and I got the call to rush over and usher her out.

Rose Kennedy was nearly in hysterics. She had never met a woman like this, I guess, and didn't know what to do.

The woman was screaming at Mrs. Kennedy that folks back home promised her that the Kennedys had a job for her and had given her a one-way bus ticket to Hyannis. How she got through the police and the secret service no one knew, but by the time I got to the house nobody cared how she had slipped in; they wanted her sent back to Mississippi right away.

"Take her to the bus station!" Mrs. Kennedy kept telling me. The black lady was crying.

Then the president's mother gave the woman one of her best coats as a going-away present. The lady from Mississippi was of a size that would have made three Mrs. Kennedys. I managed to drive her to the bus station and gave her some money, and we never saw her again.

The big thing that summer of 1962 was Ted's campaign for U.S. Senate. It was like a tonic for Mr. Kennedy, doing more good than all the expensive physical therapy.

In the middle of the summer Ted made a speech in Worcester, and I drove his mother there for a public appearance. It was smart politics, bringing Rose Kennedy into it, and Jack Crimmins, the South Boston bachelor who was Ted's driver, treated me royally when we got up to Worcester. Anything I needed or wanted, Jack delivered.

"Us chauffeurs have to stick together," Jack said. Jack was a great organizer, and we got along well together. It's too bad Jack wasn't Ted's driver that night on Chappaquiddick.

Ted Kennedy couldn't rely on playing Joe College now that he was thirty. He was in a real fight. He was running for the party's nomination against Edward McCormack, who was nine years older, the attorney general of Massachusetts, an honors graduate of Annapolis, the nephew of the Speaker of the House, Congressman John W. McCormack, and the son of Knocko McCormack, a giant of a man who was a familiar figure on a big horse every Saint Patrick's Day in the South Boston parade. Eddie McCormack was a handsome blue-eyed blond with a smile to match any Kennedy smile.

I could tell the family knew they were in a fight, and at the meetings in the big house with Ted, Jack, Bobby, and top Kennedy campaign advisers, they let Ted know it. Ambassador Kennedy was brought down for some of the meetings, and the noises he could make and those hard looks he could still flash let Ted know that he was not to let the family down.

No one worked harder. John Kennedy was a tireless campaigner, but it would be impossible for anyone to work harder or longer than Ted did that summer. He had Jack Crimmins bleary-eyed from day after day of nonstop campaigning.

As the midsummer Democratic convention approached, the campaigning turned nasty. There was a debate in South Boston and Eddie McCormack scored heavily. Resentment about this Kennedy "dynasty" surfaced along with charges that Ted was riding his brothers' coattails. Ted had a slogan that he had borrowed from his brother John's earlier congressional campaigns—"He Can Do More for Massachusetts"—and some people read it as political blackmail.

Eddie McCormack, Knocko's boy, finally took off the gloves and went for the knockout. Up till then he had been sparring with Ted, just throwing jabs. But he landed a real good punch when he said that the office of U.S. senator "should be merited and not inherited." He slapped at the president's brother about his quick trip to Ireland, just when Ted announced his candidacy, as a cheap publicity stunt. Edward McCormack knew Edward Moore Kennedy's temper had a short fuse. Toward the end of one of their debates, McCormack said: "I ask, since the question of names and families has been injected, if his name was Edward Moore, with his qualifications—with your qualifications, Teddy—if it was Edward Moore, your candidacy would be a joke, but nobody's laughing because his name is not Edward Moore. It's Edward Moore Kennedy. . . ."

Ted certainly didn't laugh. Ted kept his cool. I guess he was too stunned to say or do anything. He told me later how close he had come to punching Eddie McCormack for what he took as an attack on Eddie Moore, his father's former personal secretary. He was more upset about the attack on the Moore name than he was at McCormack's calling his candidacy a joke. As it turned out, Eddie McCormack's tactic backfired, and Ted won the Democratic primary.

One of Ted's biggest assets, although she didn't get much credit in 1962, was Joan Kennedy. She did a good amount of quiet campaigning, and her sisters-in-law were jealous of her. I guess they envied her blond good looks. I saw all the Kennedy women often and up close, and Joan Kennedy was the best-looking of all, including Jacqueline.

But Joan didn't flaunt her natural beauty; she was prouder of her musical ability. But the Kennedys used to belittle her when she played the piano at the big house.

Some mornings I'd read the newspaper stories about Ted's campaign to Mr. Kennedy. He was interested in every tidbit and didn't miss a thing. If there was an article he didn't like, the Chief would start batting the air with his left arm. When he liked what he'd heard, he would flash a big smile. But it was a smile now twisted from the stroke.

One of the tragedies of his paralysis was that his grandchildren had become afraid of him—the old man with the twisted smile in the wheelchair . . . the noises he made trying to talk. Sometimes, when he'd reach out for one of his younger grandchildren with his good left arm, they'd cry and run away. Then Mr. Kennedy would cry. He had only wanted to hold the child.

He exercised every day in the pool. I had the job of caring for Mr. Kennedy on his aide's day off, which meant washing him in the bed, taking him for a swim, taking him downstairs for meals, taking him to the movie theater, and, every so often, wheeling him to the dock for a cruise on the *Marlin*.

When we were in the pool and Mr. Kennedy was holding onto the side rail, struggling to walk in the buoying water, I stood behind him and helped him. But he didn't want help. So I played a trick on him. With my right leg I would kick his right leg as I walked behind him in the water. Only he didn't know I was doing it. He thought he was doing it on his own.

I was in the pool with the Chief the day we heard the news that Marilyn Monroe had been found dead in California. I remember that a strange silence came over everybody who was there. I don't recall who else was in the pool, other than Mr. Kennedy, but there were several. It was such a curious reaction, I thought, and it stuck in my mind. Years later, when the rumors came out about Marilyn Monroe and John Kennedy, and then Robert Kennedy, I remembered the silence that August afternoon in the pool when we got the news that she had committed suicide.

Marlene Dietrich visited Mr. Kennedy. At Mrs. Kennedy's

request, I drove up to Framingham, where she was appearing at a supper club, chauffeured her to Hyannis Port, and took her back the same day. She stayed for an hour. She seemed sad on our way back and didn't say much, but she told me that Joe Kennedy was a good friend and she wondered if it might not have been better for him to have died than to have to spend the rest of his life crippled and unable to talk. "It is a cruel penance God has given him," the movie star said. Marlene Dietrich was wearing a blue denim jacket and blue denim trousers—a kind of working outfit. She was near sixty, and it was hard for me to take my eyes off her in the rearview mirror because I had never known a woman that age who looked so young.

I also drove astronaut John Glenn and his wife that summer. He was in the news for his pioneering ride in space, and the president invited him to Hyannis Port. I took the Glenns to Saint Andrew's, the stone Episcopal church on a hill overlooking Hyannis Port, for the Sunday service. When I asked if they wanted a ride back, they said that they would rather walk, since it didn't seem very far. John Glenn and his wife were the nicest people I ever drove for the Kennedys.

Glenn used to water-ski with Jacqueline a good deal, with me waiting at the dock to pull her out of the water, and it may have been on one of those occasions that I found Robert Kennedy jumping up and down on the dock and yelling at his wife. Ethel Kennedy was speeding off in a boat, and her husband was jumping like a child. "Ethel! Come back here! Ethel, don't leave me!" he yelled. I don't know if it was a game or if he was really mad at her, but I didn't stick around to find out. You didn't want to be around Robert Kennedy when he was in a bad mood.

There was the time, for instance, when he had to drive off somewhere and spotted me in the driveway. Robert Kennedy pounced on me like a tiger. "Give me the keys to my father's car," he ordered.

"I can't, Mr. Kennedy," I said.

"Come on, Frank, give me the keys to the car," he said. He waited. "I said, I want the keys." He was slowly burning. He glowered at me. It would have been easier for me to hand the keys to him, but I had my orders. "The keys!" he said, and stuck out his hand.

"Mr. Kennedy, you know what your mother's orders are. No one is to use that car," I said.

"It's my father's car and I want the keys. I need a car right now!"

"No," I said.

"I want the keys," he said. His voice was high now.

"If you want the keys, ask your mother," I said.

The attorney general made an exasperated noise, then walked off. He never came back for the car.

It was a mistake at the Kennedy place to leave your keys in your car. If one of the Kennedys needed a car they'd grab whatever was nearest, and you might not get it back until the next day. Ted and Bobby were the worst car thieves, but the president was pretty good at it himself. When it came to using Mr. Kennedy's car, I always figured it was better to have one of the sons mad at me than to have Rose Kennedy on me for disobeying her.

18

Tom Fitzgerald waved me in from the car where I'd been sitting for over an hour, waiting alone.

"Her nibs is taking her nap now," he said, meaning his sister Rose. "She'll be good for an hour," he added with a smile. Tom jabbed an index finger in the air, pointing to the upstairs of the tall wood-framed house in Dorchester where the president's mother was resting. "Let's have a jar now, Frank," he whispered.

We went into the old kitchen. Tom took out the whiskey and we drank from water glasses.

Mrs. Kennedy had come to her brother's house in that section of Boston for a visit with her mother, who was ninety-six. Mary Fitzgerald lived with Tom, her eldest son. The true tradition of the Boston Irish was for a widowed mother to live with her eldest daughter, but that wasn't the way it was with the Kennedys and the Fitzgeralds.

There were nice white lace curtains on the front windows, and I mentioned to Tom how neat and clean they looked. This Dorchester neighborhood was mostly Irish, then?

"Oh, sure," he said. "The Fitzgeralds were never shanty Irish. We were *born* lace-curtain. But of course one of us"—he winked and tossed his head quickly at the ceiling—"has gone beyond the rest and is Venetian-blind Irish now."

I laughed.

"It's an ahta-tude more than anything else, isn't it,

Frank? Don't you think it's an attitude?" Tom swallowed. "I think it is an attitude. And how you getting on with darhlin' Rose, Frank?" he asked.

"Fine. You know," I said.

"Let's have another," he said.

Tom Fitzgerald was built like a fireplug. He was five years younger than his sister Rose and resembled his father, John F. "Honey Fitz" Fitzgerald, in the photos I'd seen of the feisty former mayor of Boston. Tom had his father's looks, and his nephew the president had Tom's sense of humor and quick wit.

"How's himself?" he asked, inquiring of Mr. Kennedy.

I told Tom about his brother-in-law's struggle to overcome his paralysis. I told him about the workouts in the pool and how Mr. Kennedy would sometimes get so frustrated about not being able to talk that he cried. Tom winced as he listened, and I could tell that he felt genuinely sorry for Joe Kennedy.

"Of course, Joe talks to me now about as often as he did when he had the facility," Tom said.

I gathered that Mr. Kennedy was not particularly fond of some of his wife's relatives. You have to know the Boston Irish to understand how petty and backstabbing they can be with relatives. Rose Kennedy did not want the Fitzgeralds visiting her at the Hyannis Port house before Mr. Kennedy had the stroke, afraid that her husband might get mad, and now that he was in the wheelchair she was touchy about the in-laws coming from Dorchester lest Mr. Kennedy learn they were there and have *another* stroke. But she visited her mother and brother in Dorchester quite often. Sometimes she would bring old clothes and give them to the Fitzgeralds.

Tom Fitzgerald was a likable, decent, gentle man, and I enjoyed the times we spent drinking whiskey in the kitchen while Mrs. Kennedy took her nap before heading back to Cape Cod.

On our way back one summer afternoon she spotted a hitchhiker and told me to stop for "the young man."

"He looks like a bum to me, Mrs. Kennedy," I said.

"Oh, give him a lift, Frank," she said.

I stopped and motioned the kid to sit up front with me.

As he took in the chauffeur outfit, the well-dressed lady in the backseat, and felt the cool air-conditioned air, he said, "Oh, wow!

"You're going to the Cape?" he asked. "Oh, yeah! Wow! That's real good."

We headed for the Cape. The hitchhiker had a big smile. "A real limo, right?" he asked. I nodded. I kept glancing at him out of the corner of my eye. He was scruffy.

Then Mrs. Kennedy began playing "What's My Line?" with our rider.

"Guess who I am?" she asked. Mrs. Kennedy had a snappy, quick way of talking. She was always concerned about people speaking clearly.

The hitchhiker looked at me. He shrugged.

"Go ahead now. Guess who I am," she said.

He pulled himself up in the seat, looked at me again, then half turned so that he could get a good look at the lady in the backseat. "I don't know," he said.

"Oh, come on! You must know who I am," she said. She sounded as though she was enjoying the game. "Go on, guess," she taunted.

The hitchhiker had his arm over the back of his seat. He shot me a look of puzzlement.

"I really don't know who you are," he said after a few seconds looking at her. "Ma'am, I really don't."

"You must," she said.

"I really don't," he said.

"You really don't? Really?"

"No, lady."

"I am the president's mother!" she announced.

He looked over at me, but I was staring straight ahead at the road. Then he turned back to Mrs. Kennedy.

"The president of what?" he asked.

"The *president* . . . *of* . . . *the* . . . *United States*!"

There was a long pause. I glanced in the rearview mirror and saw her smiling, beaming.

135

Finally the hitchhiker said, ''No shit, lady!''

We drove in silence. I had to bite my lip to keep from laughing. She kept a scowl on her face for a long time after that.

19

Mr. Kennedy did not really settle in at Hyannis Port that first summer after his stroke until the Fourth of July weekend. I think that was when they brought him home for good. The Fourth was always a big event for the Kennedys and, in a sense, it was the official start of their season. By then the horses had been shipped up from Maryland and all the boats were in the water and their dogs had been flown in. I never knew exactly how many dogs the Kennedys had up with them, but it was never less than a dozen and more often around two dozen.

Mr. Kennedy started therapy in the new pool behind the house right away. The pool was enclosed and so was an entranceway connecting it to the house. Of course we had christened the pool ourselves while the boss was still in New York, and we'd been having wild poolside parties at night crowded with secret service, town cops, and college-girl summer waitresses. I'm sure Mrs. Kennedy never knew about our parties, and you can bet I enjoyed myself when she was visiting her husband at the rehabilitation center.

It worked out fine with the elevator. Because his bedroom was on the east end of the house they were able to build the elevator shaft up the outside of the building and cut a door into the end wall of his bedroom. The elevator opened conveniently six feet from his bed. There was another door into the living room, and the elevator went down to the basement and opened in the movie theater. A few rows of seats had to be taken out to make space for the ramp to the elevator but, all in all, it was a good arrangement. I thought, It's damn nice to have the money to afford all this.

The way Mr. Kennedy's bedroom was decorated it could have been a woman's bedroom. The wallpaper had a flowery pattern and the furniture was painted white. There were framed prints and a painting on the wall. The furniture didn't look very valuable to me, just ordinary. But the room was airy and bright and pleasant. He got the early morning sun, and then, when the sun moved to the front of the house, Mr. Kennedy got that from the room's other exposure. He had sunlight all day in that room, and he even had the best of the sunset.

There was nothing personal around, nothing special. It seemed as sparse as a guest bedroom. He had his clothes and shoes, and a TV. It had been the same before the stroke, except for the picture of Marion Davies. But now the photo was gone. I don't know who took it and I don't know what became of it. One day I just noticed she was gone.

Once, reading the sports section of the morning paper to him, I glanced up to see his closet door open and his polished riding boots—all those expensive, handmade English boots—standing on the floor in plain view. The sight of that row of boots, polished and ready to go like that, could be painful for him, I thought. So I moved the boots out of sight, back in the closet, when I got the chance and he wasn't looking.

Although I doubted he'd ever walk again, I thought maybe he'd be able to get some of his speech back. When he came home from therapy he had several words he could say that you could understand. But his big word was no. For a while, he would say both yes and no, but then he used yes less and less, and finally the only word he'd say was no. He said no even when he meant yes. He sounded it in different ways, and we learned to figure out what the various intonations meant. Usually when he spoke softly, you could figure he meant yes. It was always a good idea, however, to search his eyes to be certain.

The doctors tried to get him to learn to write with his left hand, but that was too tough for him. When he tried to scribble on a piece of paper he'd lose his temper and throw the paper away, and then he'd start in with the long no. Doctors visited him regularly at Hyannis Port, but as I think back it seems to me that they were there more to make the family feel it was doing everything it could than to help him. He soon gave up trying to write with his good hand.

But he sure knew how to use his good left in other ways. He hit with it and he gestured with it. One hot day I pushed him in the wheelchair across the lawn—the wheel rims sinking in so that it was hard going—down toward the dock where Captain Frank had the *Marlin* waiting. But when we were almost there Mr. Kennedy started screaming, "Nooooo! Nooooo!" and was tossing his left arm around to give directions. I didn't know what was wrong. I asked him, but he just kept swatting the air with his left arm and yelling nooooos. Then I realized what it was. It was the wind that was bothering him. He was afraid of the wind. So I pushed him back. I told Ann not to schedule a cruise for him when there was any wind at all, because it seemed he hated the wind.

Ann said he had always hated the wind. She told me that there had been times, when the wind was blowing hard and a big storm seemed to be coming up, or when the forecast predicted high winds lasting for a few days, Mr. Kennedy flew off in the *Caroline,* away from Hyannis Port. The wind made him feel lonely, Ann told me; when it moaned and whined around the big house, it stirred up old Irish folk stories for Mr. Kennedy about the banshee wailing. The banshee wail meant death was coming.

The wind was the only thing Mr. Kennedy was afraid of.

Mr. Kennedy got moodier. One day he swung at me with his cane.

He kept the wooden cane with him in the wheelchair,

139

when there was still hope of his walking again. I cannot recall what provoked him to swing at me. Probably something childish. It was usually some little thing that set him off, like angling him into some spot in his bedroom where he didn't want to be.

Anyway, he missed.

I told him that he must have had a good swing when he played ball for Harvard because he still had a smooth follow-through. He liked hearing that, and he laughed for a long time. He even pretended he was waiting for the ball to come over the plate. He gripped the cane at the bottom with his good left hand so tightly that the hooked handle quivered above his head while he hunched over in the wheelchair in a batter's pose.

He was making noises in his throat urging me to throw an imaginary ball, then jerked his head for me to pitch to him. The top of the cane he cradled in the crook of his right shoulder. He wanted to grab the cane with his dead right hand, to hold it like a genuine baseball bat, but of course he couldn't.

He stayed bent over for a few minutes, and I could tell from his eyes that he was thinking about his paralyzed right side. He took his eyes from me and stared at his dead hand. Then he stopped laughing, and the cane dropped. It was sad to see, but at least he still had fight.

He still had his curiosity too. He loved to follow sports, and I would read the sports pages to him in the morning after I had brought Mrs. Kennedy home from mass. He became more interested in the scores of games than in the stock-market quotations. Soon Mr. Kennedy and I were betting dimes on games. He enjoyed it, especially as I made sure he won. He was still interested in dimes, so I'd kid him. "Well, there's another dime to pile up, Chief." I don't think he ever caught on how I made sure that he would never end up losing, not with a few tricks I could still call up from my bookmaking days.

Sometimes I'd fold the newspaper back so he could hold it with his good hand while resting the paper on his lap to read the news for himself. But he tired easily, and sooner or later I'd have to read it to him.

I think he liked having the company, but there were other times when he wanted only to sit by the big bedroom windows and watch the water. From his room he could watch Jacqueline and the rest of them water-skiing. There were always boats going by, and from one window he had a view down to the breakwater along the beach where Mrs. Kennedy liked to take long walks. With its panoramic view the room was a good place from which to watch the helicopter. But Mr. Kennedy preferred to be down on the veranda for the president's landings and takeoffs.

I learned to watch Mr. Kennedy's eyes because they tipped you off to what he was thinking. And I always did what I thought he wanted. If we were in the basement watching a movie and he didn't want to stay any longer, I'd turn off the projectors and take him right back up the elevator to his room. I never argued with him, even when he was trying his damnedest to let me know he was ready for a battle. I was a good actor with him, and would not let him think that I might know better than he what was right for him. The trick was to make him believe he was always in charge. Sometimes, of course, I'd guess wrong, and then there'd be hell to pay.

Mrs. Kennedy never seemed to learn.

It was plain to just about everybody that Mr. Kennedy did not want his wife in his room. There were occasions when he would tolerate her—again depending on his mood— but when he wanted her out, he would start with those long nos. You could hear him bellowing at her through the big house, and sometimes there were screams that made my blood run cold. But we got used to the way he could shout that long, loud nnnnoooooo! A stranger in the house, though, would have thought there was a murder going on upstairs.

He'd keep screaming at her.

She'd make a smile. "I'm going, dear. I'm going!" she'd say.

And the more she'd tell him, the louder he'd yell no.

And the more he'd yell no, the more she'd stay and try to explain.

It became a routine with them.

I never came right out and said it to her, but oh how I wanted to: Why don't you just stay the hell out of his room, Mrs. Kennedy, when he's like that?

I was upstairs one day when he threw one of these fits of yelling and Mrs. Kennedy came running out of his bedroom with tears in her eyes. I wished that I was someplace else as soon as I saw her.

The shouting that afternoon brought Rita out of the nursing station, as we called the spare bedroom down the hallway that was used by the various nurses, and when Mrs. Kennedy saw the nurse she explained that it was the stroke that made her husband that way. Naturally Rita said something to console Mrs. Kennedy.

After Mrs. Kennedy retired to her own room, Rita explained to me that it was the Ambassador's inability to communicate that frustrated him so. He didn't want Mrs. Kennedy in his room because he couldn't talk to her. She clicked off other psychological and medical explanations for Mr. Kennedy's manner, and I nodded back to her, not really giving a damn. I knew differently.

After all, what did Rita know of the way it was between them before the Ambassador had had his attack? I never bothered telling her of what little time Mr. and Mrs. Kennedy had spent together before his stroke. I don't think they ever communicated with each other about running the house. Mrs. Kennedy would tell me to do something, and then Mr. Kennedy would repeat the exact same instruction. Other times both of them would tell me something entirely different.

But Rita was sympathetic to Mrs. Kennedy, believing that she understood her suffering better than anyone. I heard the nurse tell Mrs. Kennedy more than once that at least Mrs. Kennedy had her husband alive, and while he lived there was always hope. Rita was a widow and would never let one forget how hard that was on her. But I don't think Rita's own sorrows consoled Mrs. Kennedy much.

It was hard on Mrs. Kennedy, no doubt. Her husband had always made the decisions. It was that way even with me. He had hired the chauffeur, though knowing all along that I was going to be his wife's driver and not once seeking her approval of me. The Park Avenue office took care of all the bills, as it always did. She never had to worry about bills. He'd seen to that, as he'd seen to everything. He'd left her nothing to worry about, nothing to do.

20

My daily routine that second summer was a good deal fuller than it had been the first. I woke before dawn to get ready to take Mrs. Kennedy to mass. I'd always been an early riser, so that didn't bother me. I took her to mass and brought her home. Then I went up to the post office, said hello to the O'Neils, got the newspapers, and carried the mail, including the president's, back to the secret service trailer. I helped the agents go through it.

Sometimes there'd be death threats against Mr. Kennedy. Whenever I'd spot one, I would put the letter aside for the agents. All the Kennedys received threatening letters, but some of them were more frightening than others. The president and the attorney general got most of them. Some threats came from people you knew right off were stark-raving mad. You could tell from the handwriting and the misspellings and the weird things they'd put in the letters. The secret service were more concerned by the calm, clear promises of death than by wild rantings and ravings scrawled by some nut. Yet they had to examine all of them, and they chased down a lot of leads.

The people who hated Mr. Kennedy because he was a Catholic liked to quote the Bible a lot. And then there were those who wrote him that he had been struck down by God because he was an evil man.

Reading the mail was a hell of a way to start the morning, but it had to be done. You can imagine how much mail the Kennedys got at Hyannis Port. Boxes of it every day. Some mornings I'd fill the Chrysler with it. Letters and packages and statues and paintings and gifts. Once I opened a box and found it filled with dead spiders. People wrote the family with moneymaking schemes. All the Kennedys had to do was send them $50,000. There were others who asked for outright loans. Religious items were big. Then there was the time I cut open a thin square cardboard package and uncovered a hideous religious painting. Sewn all around the edges were garlic cloves. There must have been one hundred garlic cloves. The agents had to toss the thing out of the trailer, it smelled so awful.

Mr. Kennedy was never told about the threats. Most of the junk that was sent to the family had to be thrown away. President Kennedy wasn't informed either about all the crazy and cruel things people wrote to his father, figuring it would only upset him. But Robert Kennedy, as the attorney general, was told about the threats, and there were a few that were taken seriously.

After the mail had been screened, I'd take the Chief's mail to him together with the morning papers. We'd spend about an hour together, most of it going over the sports news, and then I'd go down to clean the pool.

After the pool was done, I'd wash the cars. Maybe Mrs. Kennedy would have a few errands then, or I'd have to do the food shopping. There might be supplies and medicines the nurses needed. If Mr. Kennedy wanted to exercise in the morning, we'd have to take him down and work with him in the pool.

There was a lull at lunchtime.

Then there would be the Chief's afternoon movie, followed by maybe another session with him in the pool.

There was always painting to be done, or shoes to polish (George Thomas, the president's valet, shined John Kennedy's shoes; I took care of most everyone else's), and Wilbert could use a hand. And often in the afternoon Mrs. Kennedy wanted to go up Main Street to shop. Or to the hairdresser's. Someone might be coming in to visit, and I'd have to pick them up. There'd be an airport run, maybe. Or one of the daughters needed a ride.

145

And there was always the unexpected. One of the dogs was missing. Or the grandchildren's goats were loose again and were eating a neighbor's flowers.

I was exclusively in charge of the Kennedy movies that summer, and there were always films to pick up at the Hyannis theater and others to return. And of course after supper I'd show the nightly movie.

One of my great moments that summer came the first time I showed a movie on the new overhead projectors. A cheer went up when I did. Johnny Ford had realized how bad the arc-light projectors were getting and he okayed fixing them. The dual projectors were rebuilt so that they were as modern as any in a commercial movie house. Now I didn't have to be a nervous wreck in the booth waiting for the film to jump out of sync, and Judy Garland didn't have anything to complain about.

One of my more frequent and enjoyable jobs was as engineer of the Toonerville Trolley. The trolley was a minitrain—boxy, open, rubber-wheeled carts with flat roofs, pulled by a cart with a motor and controls—and it had become a familiar sight on the narrow Hyannis Port streets. The Kennedy trolley looked more like golf carts hitched together than a real train with a locomotive, but it was a big hit with the grandchildren. In fact, everyone got a kick out of it. We used it to shuttle guests and visitors from the motel a few miles away, and for jaunts to Squaw Island. And it was just plain fun for the kids to ride up and down the long driveway that had been paved that summer.

Even the secret service rode the trolley, and a few times we took it up to Luigi's for my weekly chicken barbecue. One night someone drove the trolley into the woods near Luigi's and blew the transmission. We had some wild parties at Luigi's.

Mrs. Kennedy never had a set schedule. She wouldn't tell me what she was planning, because I don't think she knew herself. Nor did her secretary know what was going on much of the time.

The one thing you could stake your life on with Mrs. Kennedy was mass. In the eight years I drove her to morning mass I can count on my fingers the times I had to go into the house and wake her up.

After mass she might swim. She'd spend time answering her mail and working with her secretary. She might read or try on dresses or go down to the doll room.

She'd have lunch with her husband. The nurse would bring him down, then take him back again for his nap before the afternoon movie. Mrs. Kennedy would have that same white-meat chicken sandwich, a glass of milk, and a piece of angel-food cake with the frosting taken off. Day after day. She had a touchy stomach, Matilda said.

After a nap she would go off to play golf. With the golf course only a few miles from the house, she would usually hop in her little white Valiant and drive herself. A few times I drove her. Once I watched her play the same hole over and over. She'd hit the ball up the fairway, then get on the green, putt the ball in, and hit the ball back toward the tee she'd just come from. Then she'd turn around and start all over. Other golfers had to play through her.

After golf she might swim. If it was a warm day and the tide suited her, she'd swim off the beach in front of the house. If I happened to be around I would watch her.

Then she'd have Fritz massage her. And because Mrs. Kennedy hated to think of herself as ever wasting time, she would listen to her French records on the phonograph and practice during the massage. Her French sounded pretty good to me. She took it seriously.

Sometimes I'd see her at dusk walking along the beach, just before dinner. And right after dinner, Mrs. Kennedy would retire to her bedroom, where she would either watch television or read. The maids told me she was usually asleep by nine. Even if there was to be a party downstairs, she would excuse herself, making it a point to tell everyone that she was an early riser.

"Stop the movie!"

Her shout was ear-piercing. But there was no swearing this time. Judy Garland wasn't yelling.

This time it was Rose Kennedy.

"Stop that movie!" she repeated, at the top of her lungs.

147

I shut down the projectors and started out the projection booth to see what was the matter.

"Out, children! Out! I won't have you watching this trash. I don't want them watching this junk, Frank," she said, ushering them out.

A crew of her grandchildren had been in the theater when she appeared suddenly and halted the film. For the life of me I can't remember what it was that upset her so. I can't even recall the movie.

There were a couple of little groans of protest, but they obeyed their grandmother. She marched them out of the cellar. Well, I thought, good for you.

She was always interested in what her grandchildren were up to and, later, as they got a bit older, loved to hear about projects they might be working on. She seemed to me to be more at ease with them when they were babies, and then much later after they reached their teens. Those in-between years tried her patience.

Mrs. Kennedy never stood for any nonsense when her grandchildren were around. She was a disciplinarian and made them toe the mark.

The younger children jumped into the bushes when they spied her coming. Hiding from Grandma was a great game, and they'd give me the sshhhh sign so I wouldn't tell on them.

"Where are your rubbers?" she'd quiz them if it had been raining. Or, if it was a chilly day, she'd corner a bunch of them and order: "Now run on home and tell your mother to put a sweater on you. You shouldn't be out without a sweater in this weather because you'll catch a chill."

The way most grandmothers are.

"I want the flag down. Take that flag down now. It's making such a racket I can't sleep."

Through Mrs. Kennedy's bedroom window I watched the blue flag with the white and gold presidential seal flapping straight out in the wind, angling at us nearly head-on. The flag was off to the right about eye level at the top of the pole in the driveway turn-around, less than one hundred feet away.

"You mean the president's flag?" I asked.

What a gorgeous view, I thought. What a pretty day.

"That flag staring you in the face. Listen to it! It's disturbing me. Can't you hear it?"

I listened. Her window was shut because there was such a stiff breeze, yet you could still hear the flag rippling. It was a noise almost like a small engine running at high rpm, but very faint, as though it was far away. A distant, steady purring.

I had an urge to stand there and watch the waves. "Sounds like a big lion snoring out there, doesn't it?" I said.

"I don't care what it sounds like. I want you to go down and take the flag down so I can take a nap in peace."

"I don't know if I have the authorization," I said, to test her and maybe have some fun. "That's the president's flag after all. I just can't take down the flag of the president of the United States without authorization."

She smiled. She was playing along. She had one big frownie stuck to each cheek and the bandages stopped her from having a real smile. It wasn't even a half smile.

"I'm all the authorization you need, Frank," she said.

"But that's the president's flag," I said.

"And this is my house. And that is my flagpole. And I am his mother. And I order you to take it down!"

Now she smiled so wide that the frownies creased. I nodded and went downstairs.

Outside the wind died to a brisk summer breeze. But you wouldn't want to go swimming on a day like this, not with the breeze this strong, I thought as I began hauling the flag down. I could feel the force of the wind throbbing in the halyards, as strong as a giant fish tugging to get away on the end of a line.

When I had the flag coming down I looked up and noticed Mrs. Kennedy standing at her bedroom window, supervising.

21

Somebody must have stolen that summer. One day it was gone. Suddenly the leaves turned gold in the high elm on Irving Avenue in front of the president's house. The hot days and muggy nights disappeared so fast it was as if a thief slipped in to tear the picture-pretty summer scene off the Hyannis Port calendar so that the next time you looked it was fall. Mrs. Kennedy, reminding me that fall was her favorite time of year, took me up to the attic for another inventory. That year, in fact, more of the family stayed on longer in Hyannis Port than during the previous year, with more of the normal comings and goings, the usual Kennedy summer life, continuing into the fall months.

"Yes, Mrs. Kennedy," I said reluctantly. "I'll do it this afternoon." I had a hint of what I was letting myself in for.

"As you wish, Frank," she said.

The brown paper bag she had handed me was very light, and the things in it were very soft. Fluffy almost. It was simple, she said. Just take them back to the store and tell them that since Mrs. Kennedy did not want them, the Kennedys would not pay for them. So she instructed.

I had taken her shopping at that Hyannis store many times.

"Well, you understand, don't you?" she asked. I could tell she was impatient for me to leave the room.

"Yes, but . . ."

"But what!" she snapped in a way that made me feel like a child.

I opened the bag. There was lingerie inside.

"Merely take it back to them, Frank!" she said.

I pulled the girdle partly out of the bag.

"But these have been worn, Mrs. Kennedy."

"Take them back, I said!"

I dropped the girdle into the big bag and looked at her.

"They know who we are, Frank."

I could see more underwear inside the bag. Bras.

"Do you have the slip?" I asked.

"There's no slip in there," she snarled.

"Not that kind of slip. The receipt, I mean."

She snatched the bag in both hands and stuffed the lingerie down in it, then folded the top of the bag over and over. She threw the bag back into my hands. "Take it back to them and tell the store manager to give us a credit. The items do not suit me," she said. Abruptly she turned away to stare out her bedroom window. She had on her ratty old bathrobe, and her face was covered with those damn frownies.

"Mrs. Kennedy?" I asked.

Turning, she said, "Oh what, Frank?" her eyes half closed as she spoke.

"Do you want me to get another girdle?"

"No, no," she snapped.

I returned the garments, and left the store thinking how much easier it would be on everyone if Mrs. Kennedy would only make up her mind and stick to her decisions.

Mrs. Kennedy did have one difficult choice to make. She had to decide what they would do about Mr. Kennedy's care. She had to choose whether he would stay away under therapy or at home. And she had to settle the fighting that went on between Rita and her niece over who should be in charge.

There had been a blowup between Rita and Ann at Horizon House, a country extension of the rehabilitation center in Pennsylvania. Ann left, according to Rita, because the doctors wanted her out of the way. Ann had been treating her uncle like a baby, the nurse said, and the doctors wanted him to apply himself and realize that it was hard work they expected from him. Just because he was the president's father, they were not going to coddle him. Ann had actually left to visit her relatives in Detroit, and on her return she told me how Rita complained to the doctors behind her back. Rita wanted to be boss, Ann said.

Anyway, Ann returned to Horizon House, and by the time they all arrived back at Hyannis Port there was no doubt that Ann was in charge. Mrs. Kennedy had made the decision.

There had been another smaller crisis at Horizon House. Mr. Kennedy did not like the food. So Matilda had been summoned, and Dora went with the cook. After their return, Matilda was especially glad to be back in her own kitchen. The one in Mr. Kennedy's cottage at Horizon House had been the size of a closet. From what Rita and Ann told me, filling me in on Horizon House, it sounded like a madhouse. They'd even had the Chief's phone tapped. Robert Kennedy ordered it, Rita said, because the attorney general didn't want some nut calling up his father.

I didn't have to ask what the feuding was about. Rita and Ann had been at each other's throats in New York, and they kept at it back in Hyannis Port. Only now more skillfully and quietly.

There had been honest disagreements about what was best for Mr. Kennedy, but in one case there were serious consequences. The doctors had clamped a special brace on Mr. Kennedy's right wrist to keep it from locking. If it should lock on him, Rita maintained, his muscles would atrophy, and his wrist would never straighten. Then, supposedly behind Rita's back, Ann took the wrist brace off. It was too late, Rita said, when they discovered it. Mr. Kennedy's wrist was frozen and twisted forever now, Rita said. On her side, Ann maintained she had taken off the brace because it was so annoying and painful for Uncle Joe, and she thought he should be allowed to enjoy his last years as much as possible.

I could see Rita's side and I could see Ann's side. Rita saw it as a medical problem, while Ann acted out of dedication and love for her uncle. Rita told me Ann was spoiling her uncle by making things too easy for him. As a nurse with experience caring for stroke victims, Rita said, she knew that patients with brain damage had to be made to do what was best even though they often did not want to. Ann told me that she knew her uncle better than Rita did, and that she understood what he wanted. Mr. Kennedy needed love more than anything else, Ann said.

The last thing I wanted was to get caught in a catfight between Ann and Rita. I had to listen to each of them because I was around Mr. Kennedy so often, but I knew I'd be a fool to get tangled up in it. So I just heard the two of them out and kept my own counsel.

There were times that first year after his stroke when Mr. Kennedy's children became dissatisfied with the care he was getting. Well, not the care so much as his lack of progress. They seemed to expect he would improve as a result of the therapy. But whenever they expressed their frustration to their mother, Mrs. Kennedy would ask if any of them wanted to take over the care of their father. None ever said they would.

Bringing him home had been a big decision. It meant there was only a slight chance for any marked improvement now. At first we thought that he would be returning to Horizon House from time to time, but he never went back. Instead the doctors came to the Cape to check on his progress.

The damage had been done at Palm Beach. So much time had elapsed before the doctors got to him that it seemed crazy to me how anyone could expect this seventy-three-year-old man to recover. I always believed that if the doctors had had him sooner it might have been different.

So Ann was put in charge. When it came down to it, Mrs. Kennedy never had a real choice. Ann was family, and Mr. Kennedy loved Ann.

Rita would be the day nurse and had charge of all the prescription medicine. She was smart enough not to live at the house. She rented a little house within walking distance for herself and her son. Ann stayed in her upstairs bedroom where she could be near her Uncle Joe day and night.

Other nurses were hired for the night shift. I was their backup in case of an emergency. If Mr. Kennedy should have an attack, the night nurse had instructions to press the button to set off the alarm in the garage apartment. When the alarm sounded it was my job to run over and help with the oxygen. During the day there was also a male aide to help the nurses move Mr. Kennedy and wheel him around. When the aide had his day off, usually a Sunday, then I would be his stand-in.

That year they also hired a young girl to be his therapist. She was not only a good therapist, she was beautiful. She didn't last long. She drew too big a crowd poolside.

There was another addition to the staff that summer. Mrs. Kennedy hired a new maid. But not for long.

None of us believed she needed another maid, but this one was supposed to be special. A very fancy maid, house gossip claimed. She had been in the employ of a wealthy socialite, and supposedly it was a coup for Mrs. Kennedy to get her. Dora and Evelyn Jones's feelings were a bit hurt, especially as Mrs. Kennedy kept boasting about her new maid and acting very smug toward them.

She was indeed a fancy maid. She looked and acted as if she had a maid of her *own*.

The new maid happened to arrive on a day when one of the laundresses was either out sick or had quit, I can't remember which. The Kennedys always had trouble with laundry at Hyannis Port—either the help or the machines, sometimes both at once—and this time the laundry had really piled up. They were running out of bed linen for Mr. Kennedy, and the grandchildren's dirty clothes kept getting deposited at the house. The dirty laundry was stacked up in the cellar as high as a snow drift. So Mrs. Kennedy asked her new special maid to do it, and the woman turned up her nose and refused. I wasn't there at the time, but Dora did an imitation of the maid refusing Mrs. Kennedy. "I don't dooooo laundereeeeee, *Ma-darm*,"

Dora mimicked. "I am accustomed to having laundry *done!*"

Dora figured that now this maid was "done" herself, but Mrs. Kennedy wasn't about to fire her, not after what she'd evidently gone through to lure her to their employ.

The laundry crisis had taken precedence over settling the new maid in, so now Mrs. Kennedy showed the woman her living quarters. One look at the room and the maid quit. And she demanded that the Kennedy chauffeur whisk her away in that big Chrysler. She couldn't wait to leave. I felt a small degree of sympathy for the maid, remembering how it had been with me and the chauffeur's quarters.

As we drove away, the maid told me, "I should have known better than to accept a position with shanty Irish!" The woman was still screaming.

"You're wrong," I said, suddenly feeling a certain pride at being in the Kennedys' employ. "They are lace-curtain Irish."

Dora was beside herself. She ran into the kitchen with tears in her eyes.

I put down my cup of coffee. Matilda and I had been talking.

"She's driving me crazy. I can't take it anymore. I can't," Dora sobbed.

"Calm down, Dora," Matilda said.

"She's doing it on purpose. I know she is."

"What's the matter?" the cook asked.

"Every time I go into her room her dresses are all over the floor. She keeps on taking dresses out of the closet and trying them on and dropping them right on the floor. I must have picked up two dozen dresses already today. Some of them twice!"

"Tell her," I said.

"I have. It makes no difference, she keeps doing it. I'm the maid, you know. I have to pick up after her."

It was the ten-best-dressed-women list. Mrs. Kennedy was determined to be named to the list. Jacqueline was on it, and Mrs. Kennedy would not rest until she was on the list with her daughter-in-law. And so, more and more, she would have these spells of having to review her wardrobe, agonizing over her hundreds and hundreds of dresses while Dora agonized after her, picking up dress after dress.

The washing machines were breaking down again.

"Mrs. Kennedy, I think you should get a new washer," I said.

"It should be fixed," she said.

"The machine needs to be replaced. It's worn out," I said.

"Well, can't it be fixed?"

I told her how much a new washing machine would cost and explained that it would cost *more* to keep having the repairman fix the old machine. "It will be cheaper in the long run," I said. "Do you want me to get you a new machine?"

"I must discuss this with the boys," she said, meaning the president, the attorney general, and Ted. "I don't want to go off and buy a new machine without talking to them first."

"And in the meantime?"

"The maids will just have to do the best they can."

Cardinal Cushing from Boston, an old friend of the family, visited the Ambassador. You could hear his singsong pulpit voice throughout the house. Even when he was in a small room, the Cardinal talked as if he were delivering a sermon in a big cathedral.

Cardinal Cushing's chauffeur had me smiling. The man was always two sheets to the wind. I was sure he kept a bottle in the glove compartment.

When the Cardinal was at the house and Morton Downey was there singing his Irish songs, Mr. Kennedy was in seventh heaven.

The new pool made Mr. Kennedy happy. It had a ramp so that he could be wheeled in and pushed out in his chair.

I can't remember Mrs. Kennedy spending much time with her husband when he was exercising in the pool. She liked to swim alone, and she preferred the ocean because the chlorine irritated her. But the Chief's children went out of their way to be with their father in the pool. The president, the attorney general, and Ted would cheer him on, and Mr. Kennedy responded to their applause.

When he was in the pool he moved fairly well, holding on to the special rails. The doctors wanted him to walk in the water to strengthen his paralyzed right leg. Just being out of the wheelchair and able to stand was great for his spirit. His daughters also took turns working with him in the pool.

The Kennedys' love for competition sometimes backfired as his children occasionally expected too much of their father. They'd forget, seeing him moving and playing in the pool, that he couldn't do all they hoped he could. If one of them challenged him and he wasn't up to it, he'd lose his temper.

Once I was walking around in the pool with my trick that made him think he was using his bad leg. I would stand right behind the Chief, helping hold him up with my arms under his chest. Then I'd kick his paralyzed right leg from behind him, so that his leg would move ahead in the water. And we'd walk around the side of the pool like that. Mr. Kennedy thought it was great. But Bobby didn't know my leg trick. This day, Bobby wanted to walk with his father and I let the attorney general take over. It didn't take Mr. Kennedy long to get impatient with his son and he motioned for me to come back, pushing Bobby away. I could clearly see from Bobby's face that his feelings had been hurt. But most of the time everyone had fun in the pool.

When it came time to take the Chief out, though, the mood would really change. You could feel it. It would get quiet, and sometimes whatever children might be there would leave, because nobody wanted to watch us take the Chief out of the pool. The wheelchair was rolled down the ramp into the water, and Mr. Kennedy was put in at the shallow end of the pool. Then we fixed the straps so he couldn't fall out going up the ramp. His children grew silent as they watched their father get strapped into the wheelchair.

Robert Kennedy especially showed his feelings about

157

his father. I couldn't tell if it was water from swimming or if it was tears in Bobby's eyes, but he'd watch his dad being strapped into the wheelchair with an awful pained look as though we were strapping Mr. Kennedy into the electric chair.

22

It struck me, now that I knew the family, that I could walk up to John Kennedy and talk with him without it entering my mind that he was the president. It certainly struck me that way when he questioned me about his father.

"Do you think he's getting the best of care, Frank?" the president asked.

"Yes I do."

"How did it happen? You knew how he was. Now look at him. I talk with him and I wonder if he really understands."

"He understands."

"But I don't understand *him*." John Kennedy smiled. "I just had a talk with him. I couldn't understand a single thing he said. And he didn't seem to know that he wasn't making one damn bit of sense."

Then the president shook his head, still bewildered by his father's stroke. "Frank, if you ever think that he's not getting the attention he should, I want you to come right to me with it. Understand?"

"Yes sir."

"I miss him, Frank," he said.

"What's the story with the washing machines?" Robert Kennedy asked.

"Didn't your mother explain?"

"Yes," he said. "She explained." He made a thin smile.

"Explain it to me again," he said. The smile had left his lips, but there was still a sparkle in his blue eyes. He, more than any of them, had his father's blue eyes.

"It's really very simple," I began.

"No, it isn't, Frank," he interrupted. "You know these things are never simple with Mother."

I nodded, then laughed. Robert Kennedy knew the game; we'd played it before.

"One of the machines is worn out," I said. "To keep fixing it will cost more than getting a new one. And every time it breaks down the girls doing the laundry go crazy. Now, I got a price for her on a new machine—"

"Get it," he ordered.

"Right now?"

"No. I'll tell Mother that I've spoken with you, I'll tell her what I suggest. Wait for *her* to tell you."

"Will you see her today?"

"I will," he said, and now he was grinning.

"Oh, hi, Frank," Jacqueline said.

I had put Mr. Kennedy back in his room after running a movie for him and was walking down the hallway when the First Lady turned the corner at the top of the stairs.

"How's Grandpa?" she whispered.

"Great! I showed him an Elvis Presley movie and he loves Elvis's movies."

She pressed by me in the narrow hall and headed for Mr. Kennedy's room. "Oh, that's wonderful," she whispered back to me.

A few minutes later I returned upstairs. I needed to ask Rita about picking up some supplies at the drugstore. A trace of Jacqueline's perfume lingered in the hallway.

There was laughter flooding from Mr. Kennedy's room.

Jacqueline was laughing loudly and I could hear Mr. Kennedy making loud gasps as if he was trying to catch his breath.

"Frank, I've discussed the problem about the washing machine with my son," Mrs. Kennedy announced.

"Yes. What does he recommend?"

"Bobby says that we should go ahead and purchase a

new machine because, you see, it will cost more to keep repairing the old one.''

"All right," I said. "That makes sense."

"So you see to it, Frank. I don't want any more problems in the laundry." She paused then said, "Can we get, ah, you know, a trade-in on the old one?"

"I doubt it. It's pretty shot," I said.

"Oh, well, do the best you can, Frank. And have them send the bill to Tom Walsh." Whenever Mrs. Kennedy told me to send the bill to Mr. Walsh, who ran her husband's Park Avenue office, I knew it would always be taken care of right away. She would have been lost without Tom Walsh.

"We're hitting him hard, Dad! Really slamming him! It's a great campaign. A really terrific one! We're going to win big. Big!"

You could hear Ted throughout the house. Often when he was in his father's room, Ted shouted and cheered as though he was the Harvard coach giving the football team a half-time pep talk.

Mr. Kennedy loved it.

"We were driving the other day and Jack Crimmins says to me, 'This guy Lodge is as soft as a sneaker full of shit!'" Ted roared the last words, and from below I could hear the loud thumping in the upstairs bedroom signaling his father's response. Ted had his father rollicking with him.

" 'Jack,' I said," Ted went on, finishing the story, "we'd better not step on him then!' "

Through the lulls in the yelling I could hear Mr. Kennedy's loud wheezing laugh. Ahhhhh. Ahhhhh. Ahhhhh.

Everyone was confident that fall that Ted would defeat George Lodge, his Republican opponent. What would make the win especially sweet for the Kennedys was the fact that the opponent was a Lodge, one of the old Yankee family that had been political enemies of the Kennedys since the days of Honey Fitz.

If there was anything sad about the prospect of Ted's victory, it was that Mr. Kennedy's dream of high political

161

office for all his sons was coming true with him sitting speechless in his wheelchair, watching from the sidelines.

"Nooooo! NnnnnnnnOOOOO!" the Chief grunted.

Eunice looked confused. "What's wrong, Dad?"

"Noooooooooo. Nooooooooooo." He waved his left hand in front of his face, as if he were shooing a fly.

"It's your cigar, Mrs. Shriver," I said.

"Right, Frank! I'd completely forgotten," she said, a look of relief in her eyes now that she knew what was bothering her father. "I'll get rid of it right away, Dad."

All the family was familiar to me now. I felt comfortable around every one of them. I wouldn't bat an eye at Eunice and her cigar, and whether Robert Kennedy was in a good mood or not didn't bother me any longer. I'd learned to roll with his moods, and the squabbles he and Ethel might get in when I was driving them in Mr. Kennedy's Chrysler no longer upset me, maybe because they always fought over some petty thing, usually when Bobby was in one of his sulks. They were only lovers' quarrels, I realized. Sometimes Bobby and Ethel reminded me more of brother and sister than husband and wife. You know the way couples have that special kind of relationship, something very deep; and even when they are having an argument and the sparks fly you just know it's because they have such deep feelings for each other, something of blood as well as love.

After Bobby's death, it never surprised me that Ethel didn't marry again. Those two had a very special love.

So, I *knew* them now, every one of them. Jacqueline always talking softly, those big brown doe eyes unable to hide her mischief. Pat Lawford bounding up the stairs to her father's room two steps at a time. Joan's smile, Joan's kindness. And then there was the realization that the Chief wanted me around him, that he felt at ease with me because I had been there before the stroke. I was familiar to him. I felt we had a bond.

The year before there had been the threat of a fall hurricane hitting the Cape. We were evacuated to Otis Air Force Base and stayed there for a few days. The hurricane never came, but there at Otis they had a sign on the door of my room: FRANK SAUNDERS. My name was lettered on my door the same as all the Kennedys. That's when I had begun to feel like I was part of them. And now, a year later, I felt I belonged.

23

Ted's Senate campaign was a tonic for Mrs. Kennedy too. It got her out of the house. It helped take her mind off her husband's situation. And it provided perfect opportunities for her to parade her Paris dresses in public in that never-mentioned, continual competition with her daughter-in-law.

Mrs. Kennedy spent hours in front of the full-length mirror on the closet door deciding which dresses she liked best. But while her fitting sessions might be hard on Dora, the time she spent in her room was time I didn't have to worry about her tracking me down with yet another list of errands. (At the end of that year Mrs. Kennedy did make the ten-best-dressed list. All the staff cheered, no one louder than Dora.)

I went on the road with Mrs. Kennedy—day trips and, when there was politicking to do in the western part of the state, overnighters. But I never got the royal treatment that Ted's driver Jack Crimmins gave me that time in Worcester. When we had to stay overnight, Mrs. Kennedy made it a point to get the least expensive room for her chauffeur.

Driving late at night, she'd slip a black mask over her eyes whenever she felt tired. She had trouble keeping her eyes closed in the car when she wanted to nap.

The first time I looked for her in the rearview mirror and saw that black sleeping mask on her face I had to fight hard to keep from laughing. But then I got used to her in it, and one night I said: "You look like the Lone Ranger back there, Mrs. Kennedy." And added under my breath, "And that must make me Tonto."

Sometimes, of course, people we passed would get a glimpse of this lady riding alone in the backseat with the black mask over her eyes and, wanting to get another look, would speed up and pass us.

If there were kids in the curious car, they might start laughing and pointing fingers and make crazy faces. But I stayed professional about it and never smiled back. Of course, with her face covered like that, no one recognized the lady riding alone in the backseat as the mother of the president of the United States.

Rose Kennedy was really very shy then. She liked the applause, but she dreaded large crowds and people pawing her.

On the campaign trail she lit up whenever someone would come up to her and tell her how young she looked. And if she was asked how she did it, she'd give them tips about keeping fit and trim and how important physical activity is as you get older. Frownies she kept as her secret.

She also had some funny political stories about her father, Honey Fitz, and the old-time Boston Irish pols she remembered from her youth. She called them Dearos because they always referred to women as "dear" so-and-so.

Many women who flocked to hear Mrs. Kennedy's spiel for her son Ted were more fascinated with the president's mother's personal life than with her son's politics. *Lifestyle* wasn't a word that was in use then, but that's what many of the women who came to see and hear Mrs. Kennedy were interested in: Her faith . . . Keeping active . . . Keeping busy . . . Staying interested in other people. And, most of all, her family. Mrs. Kennedy had answers for all of them, and quickly it turned into another spiel. I heard it so often I had it all memorized.

Once she got over her initial nervousness with a strange crowd, she'd loosen up, and before long I could tell that she enjoyed the campaigning. It energized her. And she was very generous with her time.

Then I got a bonus.

Riding in the car one day Mrs. Kennedy said that I

didn't have to wear the chauffeur suit if I didn't want to. It was my choice, she said. (Previously she'd given me a dispensation for the cap. ''That hat must be awfully hot on you, Frank,'' she'd said. I hardly ever wore the cap after that.)

With that I went up to Puritan's in Hyannis and bought two dark business suits and sent the bill to Park Avenue. Johnny Ford had said it was all right with him. So I put the chauffeur suits in my closet with the cap and never wore them again. I still wore the narrow black ties though, and stashed extra ties in the trunk, as I'd done with my old numbers tickets.

24

The new nurse said that Mr. Kennedy was balkier than a mule and refusing to budge. "He needs a bath, but I can't get him out of his chair," she said. "He needs a bath, a sponge bath anyway. See if you can get him up. He really does need one," she told me.

Rita had the day off and Ann wasn't around.

There was a chance that the Chief did not feel at ease yet with this nurse, I decided.

That stony look was on his face, and even though I'd been in his room for a few minutes he refused to look at me. "How you feeling?" I tried.

He continued to stare out the window, perfectly still.

"Did you say you wanted the Yankees today, Chief?" I asked.

You're in a good one today, I thought. His gaze was so fixed that I wondered if there might be something going on outside that had him fascinated.

But I couldn't see anything, except a few boats.

"So you've got the Yankees today then. That's what I thought. That's great because—"

"Nooooo," Mr. Kennedy said softly, interrupting me.

"You can't change your mind now. That's cheating, boss. You picked New York," I said.

"Noo!" he said.

"You had the Sox then?"

"Ahhh. Ahhhh."

"You wouldn't lie to me, would you, Mr. Kennedy?"

"Ahhhh! Ahhhhh!" He was looking straight at me now and the glaze was no longer in his eyes.

"You'd lie to your chauffeur over a lousy ball game?"

He laughed pretty good.

"You're sure you've got the Red Sox now?"

"Noooo. Noo. No."

"All right. You got Boston then."

"Yaaa!"

"You want me to have the nurse turn the game on for you later?"

He nodded.

"Well, look. Why don't you let me help you take a bath now, Chief, and that way the nurse won't have to give you one later. You'll have it out of the way then. Unless you'd rather go in the shower with the nurse?"

That got a smile. Then his face got thoughtful. He seemed to be considering my offer. Suddenly he made a fast nod yes and gestured with his left hand. I helped him onto the bed and he sat on the edge while I undressed him. He did need a bath for sure.

When the shower water was right I got him up, and as he draped his left arm around my neck I grabbed him with my right around his waist, and that way we made it to the shower. We must have looked like two kids in a potato-sack race.

The shower had rails and handles for him to hold with his left hand. And a seat. I started soaping him, but I could see that it wasn't going to work this way; I was getting soaked. So I told him to hold on for a second, and then I stripped naked and stepped in the shower with him.

He was laughing so hard now that I was afraid he might let go and fall. I was a bit short with him, telling him to stop laughing.

But he couldn't, and then neither could I.

"I hope this new nurse doesn't come in and find us like this, Chief. Or if she does I hope she sure has a good sense of humor and doesn't think something peculiar is going on."

As I dried him with the towel he was still making those short gasping ahhh, ahhh noises that were his laughs now.

The "Kennedy Compound" at Hyannis Port. Joseph Kennedy's house is in the center foreground, Robert Kennedy's at left center, and John F. Kennedy's at top center. *AP Wirephoto*.

Joseph and Rose Kennedy and their children gathered at the compound in Hyannis Port, shortly after the election of John F. Kennedy as President. Seated (Left to Right) are Eunice Kennedy Shriver; Rose; Joe; Jacqueline Kennedy; Edward Kennedy. Standing (Left to Right) are Ethel Kennedy; Stephen Smith; Jean Kennedy Smith; JFK; Robert Kennedy; Pat Kennedy Lawford; R. Sargent Shriver; Joan Kennedy; and Peter Lawford. *UPI Photo*

Frank Saunders driving Ted and Joan Kennedy and their children from the Hyannis airport. *AP Wirephoto*.

Joseph Kennedy is helped out of the New England Baptist Hospital in Boston by Frank Saunders after visiting his son, Senator Edward Kennedy, August 31, 1964. Senator Kennedy was recuperating from a broken back suffered in a plane crash in June. At right is Ann Gargan. *UPI Telephoto*.

The president's wife waterskies with astronaut John Glenn, a frequent guest at Hyannis Port. *AP Wirephoto*.

The Rose Doll from Mrs. Kennedy's collection. *Southwood/Saunders, 1981*.

Aerial, waterfront view of the Kennedy home at Palm Beach. Photograph was taken December 19, 1961, the day Joseph Kennedy was stricken on the golf course. *Telephoto*.

The boat cruise described in Chapter 29: JFK's last outing with his father on the family yacht *Marlin*. Ann Gargan is on the right. *AP Wirephoto*.

President Lyndon Johnson calls on the Kennedy family in Palm Beach, in February of 1964. Frank Saunders stands behind the car. *Photograph by Bob Davidoff.*

Mrs. Kennedy is escorted by Frank Saunders from the plane that brought her from Washington to Hyannis following the funeral of Senator Robert Kennedy, June 9, 1968. *AP Wirephoto.*

Joseph Kennedy and seventeen of his grandchildren gather to wish him a belated "happy birthday," September 9, 1961. *UPI Telephoto*.

November 18, 1969—After attending mass, just hours before the death of Joseph Kennedy, a saddened Mrs. Kennedy is helped down the steps of St. Francis Xavier Church in Hyannis, Massachusetts, by Frank Saunders. *UPI Telephoto*.

Then I realized he was trying to tell me something. He had a wild look in his eyes.

"Oh, you son of a bitch," I laughed. "You like this one?"

In the shower he'd seen my navy tattoos.

He was looking right at the hula girl on my leg and pointing at her. All those times in the pool with him he evidently had never discovered my hula girl.

"Want me to make her shake for you, Chief?"

"Ahhhh. Ahhhhh. Ahhhhhhhhh."

So I moved the muscle that made the hula girl twitch, and the president's father laughed so hard that I suddenly was afraid he would have another stroke.

After he calmed down and I had him on the bed, I asked; "What would Mrs. Kennedy say if she knew there was a hula girl with a grass skirt riding in the car with her, boss?"

That really sent him into hysterics.

Outside his bedroom the nurse asked, "What in the world is going on in there?"

"Nothing," I said. "Nothing that you would understand."

25

President Kennedy was concerned enough about his father as it was, but there was one time that fall when he lost his temper about the way his father was being looked after. Even those on the staff who had known him since he was a young boy said they'd never seen or heard John Kennedy that mad before.

It happened right after the Chief had what Rita called a "seizure." He had had a few attacks already that summer, with a couple coming at night when my alarm had rung and I had run over and given him oxygen. But this daytime attack was something different. Rita believed that it came as the result of Mrs. Kennedy coming in his room and showing off her dresses to him.

There had been an incident I have only a hazy recollection of that had to do with a fancy ball some famous writer had invited the president's mother to, and she was trying to get her husband's approval of the gown she had chosen to wear to it. It sounded to me as though Mrs. Kennedy was only trying to let the Chief know that she still valued his opinion and wanted him to know what she was doing.

Anyway, he had started in with the long nos and she fled from his room, so then he had this little seizure. Somehow President Kennedy, up for the weekend, learned about it. He ordered one of his own doctors over to see his father, then went up to his father's room himself. When he found no doctor or nurse or anyone else there, John Kennedy went wild. The staff heard him shouting all over the house.

His point was that he was the president of the United States and his father was a wealthy man and if they could not get doctors and nurses to look after Mr. Kennedy properly, why he was just not going to put up with it.

I never noticed anything different about Mr. Kennedy after that attack, but Rita maintained that he'd had a bad emotional reaction, not only from the seizure but also from his son's subsequent anger.

Mr. Kennedy did seem to get moodier the deeper we got into fall. There was more wind off the bay now, and the afternoons grayed earlier.

Ann decided to cheer her uncle up by driving him to New York, where he could visit his office in the Pan Am building. Only Ann did not let anyone else in on her plans.

She borrowed the Chrysler and, with Mr. Kennedy up front, she took off. Because of those threats against his life, an agent always had to be with him. Agent Ham Brown chased after them in his car, with Rita riding right along.

Well, Ham and Rita thought it was going to be a pleasant little chase over some back roads. But Ann left them flat and headed for New York. Ham had a little foreign car and had to drive like hell to keep up with that big Chrysler, which could really fly.

Rita said later the whole escapade was right out of the Keystone Kops.

Somewhere in Connecticut Ham was pulled over by a state trooper. While the trooper was trying to write the secret service man a ticket, Ham was trying to tell him that he was assigned to the president of the United States and was at this very moment in hot pursuit of the president's father and that the trooper had better telephone the attorney general and give him the message that Mr. Kennedy's niece had taken his father off on a jaunt to New York City without approval. If the trooper did not contact Washington, Ham told him in no uncertain terms, then the statie's fat would be in the fire.

The police got into the chase then, as Ham told me

later, and soon they flagged down the Chrysler somewhere in Connecticut. They all turned around, and with everything clearly communicated back to Hyannis Port, the attorney general made arrangements for an air-force plane to fly from Otis to Providence to meet the two cars. From there they flew Mr. Kennedy down to New York in a big empty cargo plane. I had to fly over to Providence with Captain Baird on the *Caroline* to get the Chrysler and drive it back to Hyannis Port.

I was glad that I didn't have to go to New York with Mr. Kennedy that trip. The last time he visited the Park Avenue office, I had driven him, and it left me feeling deeply sad. The men who worked for him at his New York office tried hard to make him think he was needed. They gave him papers and documents and financial sheets to look over, and set him in front of a desk. As I watched him try to shuffle through the papers with his left hand I felt myself choking up. I just couldn't look at him at his desk like that.

Here was a man who made millions with his brains, who bet on long-shot business deals and had never been afraid to take a chance, and now he could no longer tell anyone what he was thinking. It got in the newspapers that Mr. Kennedy had visited his Park Avenue office and was back in the swing of things, running his financial empire as he always had—stuff about Fighting Joe Kennedy battling back from a crippling stroke.

But I had seen it with my own eyes. He had sat there with the office papers falling on the floor and tears filling the corners of his eyes.

There were two big victories for the Kennedys that fall, and both cheered up Mr. Kennedy. The president came out on top of the Russians in the Cuban missile crisis, and a few weeks later Mr. Kennedy's youngest son handed the Yankee Republican George Lodge one hell of a beating.

The newspaper columnists really started writing about a Kennedy political dynasty now. After Jack served his second term, then Robert Kennedy might be president. Then it would be Senator Edward Kennedy's turn.

No bookmaker I knew, myself included, would have bet against the Kennedys winning it all. And I was sure that even the old man would bet his dime on it coming true.

PART TWO

26

Christmas Eve in Palm Beach, and just as on that same night a year ago, the telephone rang in my room. Again it was a request for me to come over to the house as soon as I could. No reason; just come over, Frank.

I was certain I knew why they wanted me. As I strolled into the living room, I was wondering how big my Christmas bonus would be.

Instead they wanted me to put a few toys together, so the grandchildren could play with them under the tree the next morning.

What the hell, I thought, so now you're the Kennedy toymaker too. How many trips had I made these last few weeks down to FAO Schwarz and Abercrombie's? How many hundreds had John-John's teddy bear cost? I'd forgotten, there were so many toys.

The living room was full of celebrating Kennedys.

The tree lights were on and the tall evergreen looked even better at night with the lights glowing. I was proud of the way I'd decorated it. It's even nicer than last year's, I thought.

In the big fireplace the fire I'd started earlier had burned down and needed more logs, but I was too busy putting toys together to worry about the fire. A sheet of instructions was missing from one of the toys.

Then someone was offering me a drink. I think it was Sargent Shriver. But I didn't feel like a drink. Well, I did feel like one all right, but I didn't feel like having one in their living room. I didn't want to be there longer than I had to be. I had to keep reminding myself that I was working for the Kennedys, but I wasn't a Christmas Eve guest, somebody they'd invited.

I went for a walk, down by the beach. My mind wandered. It felt like a spring night in Connecticut, not Christmas. I'll never get used to Christmas in Palm Beach, I thought.

I remembered my seventh-grade teacher back at the Willard School and those cutouts and drawings Miss Gorington had us do at Christmas time. She said I was a very good artist. She had encouraged me to draw and paint, and she had put my drawings and Christmas decorations on the window so people going by outside could see them. Oh, had Miss Gorington made me proud!

Mrs. Kennedy hadn't even thanked me for the time I'd spent decorating their tree.

Whatever happened to Miss Gorington? I wondered. I hoped she was happy. And I wondered what Miss Gorington might think, now, if she knew that Curly Saunders had put that artistic talent she'd encouraged to good use by decorating the Christmas tree of the famous Kennedy family. But then, I wondered finally, would she be able to explain to me why I was feeling so sad?

Right after Christmas I had to take the toys the grandchildren did not want back to FAO Schwarz and Abercrombie's and get refunds. The store clerks hated to see the Kennedy chauffeur coming.

Mrs. Kennedy had me drive her to Miami for a speech. She insisted that the hotel put me in a penthouse suite, and it was wonderful. She was wonderful.

"This is on the city of Miami," the president's mother said. "They are picking up the bill."

After she told me that I headed for the bar and spent a few hours drinking, telling the bartender to charge it to Mrs. Kennedy's bill.

* * *

Her husband's stroke was Mrs. Kennedy's excuse for not attending fancy parties with the Palm Beach jet set. But she had never gone to many in past seasons when he was well. Now it was just easier to refuse.

The few times she did attend a big party or charity ball, she had me take her down to Worth Avenue, to Van Cleef and Arpels, so she could pick out jewelry to rent for the evening.

I thought, Why does the wife of a millionaire have to rent jewelry?

She answered my question unasked. "I think it is foolish to spend money on expensive jewelry when I don't use it that often anyway," she said. "Besides, everyone is always getting their jewelry stolen, and it's such a bother!"

The more I thought about her reasoning, the more it made sense. I was always hearing about jewel thieves knocking off a Palm Beach mansion—the European princesses and baronesses there were forever getting robbed. The big scores never got in the newspapers—it seemed nothing bad ever got in the Palm Beach newspapers, certainly not "the Shiny Sheet," as the *Palm Beach Times* was called. But I figured the jewel thieves got their leads in "the Shiny Sheet"—like where the good parties would be and who was in town. That society paper had to be a goldmine for a jewel thief.

Mrs. Kennedy did not rent fancy jewels for quiet dinner parties alone with her old friends Lowell and Gloria Guinness at their waterfront mansion in Manalapan, south of Palm Beach. The first time Mrs. Kennedy had me take her to the Guinnesses' she said her friends always dined by candlelight. It was candlelight all right! The dining room must have had one hundred candles burning, and there were more candles all through the house.

I'd figured it would be another one of those "pick me up later" nights and was pleasantly surprised when I was also invited to stay and dine. The Guinnesses had a separate dining room for their help, with the same menu; and it was high cuisine. Of course, at home with the Kennedys the help never ate the same food as the family because more often than not they all would be eating white chicken sandwiches and oatmeal. But as good as Matilda's meals were—roasts and steaks and chops—they were not fancy. A night out at the Guinnesses', however, was as good as getting a free meal at one of Palm Beach's best French restaurants. If they were having twelve courses, then we would have twelve courses. And we had the same table setting they did, the same silver and crystal and best china. Mrs. Kennedy went down to Manalapan a few times each season, and it was always a night I looked forward to. Mrs. Kennedy would dress up and she would have her hair done at Elizabeth Arden's, though she knew she didn't have to for the Guinnesses.

Maybe she had the Guinnesses up to her house once or twice a season, and I remember thinking how seldom it was that she'd invite friends over for a quiet evening. I think one of the reasons she turned down invitations was so she would not be obligated to return them. Another was that she did not have many friends.

So her husband's condition became the perfect excuse. She used it not only to decline invitations but also to leave early the few formal affairs she had to attend.

"I really must be leaving now," she'd say. "My husband needs me."

It wasn't the truth, but it was polite, and it got her sympathy.

Still, she liked to talk every now and then when we were on long drives about how wonderful it was when Mr. Kennedy was the ambassador to the Court of Saint James's and all the gala affairs and parties they'd attended. And when the president asked his mother to come to the White House to help him entertain at affairs of state because Jacqueline was away, Mrs. Kennedy relished the chance.

It always puzzled me how she loved to reminisce about her social life twenty-five years ago, and could get so excited about standing next to the president to greet visiting heads of state, but hardly ever entertained at her own house. It couldn't have been the furniture, which looked to me like it belonged in a Victorian museum—big, old stuffy chairs and sofas and dark, ornate wood furniture—because she could have bought any kind of furniture her heart desired and sent the bill to Park Avenue. No, I think the main reason—same for Hyannis Port as for Palm Beach—was that Joe Kennedy had established the family there, and Rose Kennedy did not mix well with her husband's friends.

And now I couldn't help noticing how few of his old friends visited Mr. Kennedy. The faithful were Carroll Rosenbloom, the philanthropist and sportsman and all-around good guy; fun-lover Morton Downey, the Irish tenor whose renditions of "Sweet Adeline" and "My Wild Irish Rose" were the Chief's favorites; and Joe E. Lewis, the comic. Up on the Cape there was Joe Timilty, the bachelor and former Boston police commissioner, and Cardinal Cushing visited quite often. Another of Joe Kennedy's favorites was Francis X. Morrissey, a Boston Irishman who could always make the boss laugh. Later the family's friendship with F. X. became a source of embarrassment when the Kennedy brothers, in particular Ted, recommended him for a federal judgeship and it came out that Morrissey had attended a law school in the South—by mail.

For me F. X. was a Dearo. He had me in stitches once telling stories about John Kennedy in the campaign. "We were in Worcester I think it was, and we were stopped for some good reason that escapes me now—I think it was at a railroad crossing—and Jack's in the car and turns to me and asks, 'Do you have any money with you?' Now of course he's always borrowing money and all like that; so I said, 'I do,' and I'm reaching in my pocket to get it for him, when he says to me, 'Good, because you're going to need it to take the bus back to Boston.' So I ask him, 'And why am I going to take the bus back to Boston?' and Jack says to me, 'Because you're getting out of this car right now, because you're driving me crazy.' "

Then F.X. Morrissey smiled. "Wasn't that thoughtful of him, though, making sure I had money in my pocket before he tossed me out on the street?"

But these were Joe Kennedy's cronies, not Rose Kennedy's friends. Her own closest friend was Mary Moore, the widow of Mr. Kennedy's personal secretary Eddie Moore. Mrs. Moore lived on the Cape and I chauffeured

181

her to the Kennedys' many times. She was a nice lady. But who else had I driven to the big house or the Palm Beach house who were friends of Mrs. Kennedy? I couldn't think of any. Mary Moore said that the president's mother liked to reminisce and talk about old times when they got together, and I guess you could say—and certainly it seemed to me—that Mrs. Kennedy was living in the past, back in the thirties.

She was certainly still in the thirties when it came to the price of things.

There was the time she walked into Green's drugstore across the street from the church directly after mass one morning. I had parked the Chrysler in the back and was having a cup of coffee at the counter.

She'd decided that she would also have a cup of coffee— Sanka, as usual, because of her queasy stomach. She told me to go ahead and have another coffee while she sipped hers. But then she didn't drink all her Sanka, and soon got up and went over to the newsstand. I watched her pick up a copy of *Life* magazine.

The lady at the cash register had a peculiar look on her face as Mrs. Kennedy left, calling back to me, "I'll be out in the car," and taking her *Life* with her.

When I got to the cash register, the lady asked me, "What am I supposed to do with this?" She held up the dime Mrs. Kennedy had given her for the *Life*. I ended up paying the remaining forty cents.

Mrs. Kennedy didn't stop in Green's for coffee that often, because of a counter waitress there who'd always ask cheerfully, "What can I get for you today, Rose?"

Mrs. Kennedy didn't like that one bit, though she never said a word about it to the waitress. The president's mother just glared at her whenever the girl called her Rose.

The front of her dress was covered with those pinned-on notes. She stepped out of the little office her secretary used, glanced down, yanked off a note, read it, and told me she wanted to see me for a minute.

"Frank, what about all these telephone calls to Boston? I'm not going to have us pay for all these calls."

"What calls, Mrs. Kennedy?"

"The calls you made that time we were in Miami."

"I thought you said that the city of Miami was going to pick up the tab."

"Apparently they didn't. The Kennedys are going to have to pay for it. But these calls are personal and I don't think the Kennedys should pay for them."

"Then write Mr. Walsh a note and tell him to deduct it from my pay, Mrs. Kennedy."

"Yes. Fine," she said. "I will."

After I left and had calmed down, I thought: Now that's strange. She wants me to pay for the calls, but she didn't mention the bar tab. The bar tab had to be much more than the phone calls. Yet not one word from her.

The more I thought about it, the more it puzzled me. I finally decided that she preferred to think her chauffeur did not drink. She believed what she wanted to believe. It made me recall the time someone told her that her daughter Pat drank a bottle of wine in the morning, and Mrs. Kennedy replied that that was impossible because Pat didn't drink. Mrs. Kennedy had this amazing knack for shutting out anything she did not want to know or face or deal with, and conversely of actually believing whatever she wanted to believe. She had truly believed, when Mr. Kennedy was having his stroke and coughing and wasn't able to talk, that he would get better by himself. And she was still believing it two hours later when he got worse.

There was the time I was driving her back from her brother Tom's in Dorchester. Tom and I'd had a few drinks in the kitchen while Mrs. Kennedy was napping, and there in the car I was trying very hard not to let her smell my breath. She stuck a box of sticky-looking fudge over the seat and asked me if I wanted a piece.

I was concentrating on the road and only glanced at the candy box, but a quick look was enough. "No, thank you," I said.

Then she said, "Now isn't that strange. Everyone I know who doesn't drink has a real sweet tooth. I do myself. But you are the first person I've ever met who doesn't drink and doesn't have a sweet tooth."

183

"On second thought, Mrs. Kennedy," I said, "I'll have a piece."

She leaned over the top of the front seat again, and I reached into the box and felt for a piece of fudge without looking. It was pure sugar, just about. I had to force myself to swallow it.

27

Stray moments and reflections on that second winter in Palm Beach . . .

The Chief had a horrible scowl on his face as I walked into the living room and heard President Kennedy say, "Please, Dad, let us take you upstairs." I cannot recall who else was there—at least a few of the children.

"Noooooo! Noooooooo!" Mr. Kennedy screamed, and I noticed his left hand clutching the top of the left wheel of his chair to keep anyone from moving it.

"See if you can do something with him, Frank," John Kennedy said. The president didn't sound sad or angry, just tired. Apparently they'd been begging their father for a long time to let somebody take him upstairs.

The Chief had an awful expression. I'd never seen him look so angry before, sitting there glaring at his family.

I turned to face them. "The first thing you must all do," I told them, "is leave."

When I was alone with Mr. Kennedy I said, "I'm going to take you up now, boss."

He nodded. He took his hand off the wheel rim and I pushed him to the elevator. After I had him in his room I thought I noticed the start of a small smile creep across his twisted mouth.

* * *

Mrs. Kennedy insisted on driving her big new Dodge home from the car dealer's.

"Maybe you should let me drive, Mrs. Kennedy," I said. "After all, it's much bigger than the Valiant. It might take some getting used to. You know, around the parking lot at the house and down to the golf course, where there won't be much traffic."

"I am going to drive home," she said. "Now get in."

I sat up front in the passenger seat.

She pulled the seat forward as far as it would go, peered over the rim of the steering wheel, gripped the wheel tightly with both hands, and gunned the engine.

"Oh, this is a wonderful car," she said with a big smile when we were on the road. "It steers marvelously."

She drove through the first intersection without paying any attention to the overhead traffic-signal light, which happened to be red. Then she drove through another red light.

"Mrs. Kennedy, that was a red light!" I said.

"Oh, don't worry about it, Frank," she said.

It seemed to be asking too much for her to keep her eyes on the road and, at the same time, watch for the traffic signals overhead.

"We have to stop here at this intersection, Mrs. Kennedy. There's a stop sign," I warned.

Right through the stop sign.

She motored through Palm Beach blissfully unaware of lights and signs and other cars, all the while gripping the wheel with both hands as tightly as she could.

As soon as we headed up North Ocean Boulevard and there were no more intersections, I relaxed.

"Yes, that's a fine car!" she said, pulling into the driveway.

A few days later I noticed a little handwritten cardboard sign Scotch-taped to a window of Mrs. Kennedy's new Dodge. THIS IS MY CAR. DO NOT USE. ROSE KENNEDY.

I was cleaning the swimming pool.

Mrs. Kennedy had asked me that morning if I'd cleaned the pool yet, knowing full well that I hadn't because I had been with her since mass and then taken her shopping on

Worth Avenue. But as soon as we pulled into the driveway the first thing out of her mouth was, "Have you cleaned the pool yet, Frank?"

Then she started telling me what a wonderful worker Red was. I was thinking, In a pig's arse Red is a wonderful worker. Red was a Palm Beach golf caddy for Mr. Kennedy from way back, and the Chief had taken a shine to him. Red had gone on to college and acquired a bit of an education. He was a smooth-talking know-it-all, supposedly the handyman and part-time gardener.

Red was also a drunk. He drank out of a brown paper bag, hiding his bottle in the bag and himself in a little shed by the swimming pool. There he slept and drank, but always with a sixth sense about when Rose Kennedy might come by. At that moment Red would grab a paintbrush fast, dip it in a can he had ready all the time, and start to parade around the yard.

Red kept the brush up in the air as he walked, holding it like you would a torch. Whenever Mrs. Kennedy spotted Red parading with the paintbrush, she would say, "Isn't Red just a hard worker though. Every time I see him he's painting something. He is so industrious!"

It was hard for me not to tell Mrs. Kennedy the truth about Red and his drinking problem and how the Kennedy handyman never painted a damn thing I knew of except the air when he strolled around the yard with that dripping brush.

"When Mr. Kennedy has one of his attacks, Rita, just exactly what is it?"

"Cardiac arrest, Frank."

"You mean he's having a heart attack."

"In a manner of speaking, yes; his heart stops."

"Yeah, well so does mine every time that damn bell goes off. Sometimes I think the night nurse rings it when she doesn't have to, because she's afraid that if something *does* happen and she's there alone she'll get blamed for it."

"It's always better to have two persons there when he needs oxygen."

"Every time he has one of those attacks, though, it must make him weaker."

"Not necessarily, Frank. Mr. Kennedy is still very strong. You must understand that the cerebral hemorrhage caused a great deal of damage and that's one of the reasons Mr. Kennedy's heart just sometimes stops. That's why it is so important to keep exercising him, to get those nerves and muscles working. Oh, they should have kept him with Dr. Rusk at the institute!"

"You really think so?"

"Yes, I do. Most definitely."

"Why didn't they, then?"

Rita looked at me slyly. "You knew Mr. Kennedy before; maybe you can tell me," she said.

Rita's curious refusal to tell me her opinion about why Mr. Kennedy didn't stay in therapy stuck in my mind. It bothered me.

Later I had occasion to ask Frank Wirtanen about it. "Rita thinks Mr. Kennedy would have gotten better if they'd kept him with the doctors," I told Captain Frank. We were sitting on deck. It was a humid night and the beer tasted especially good.

"Does Rita think she's God?" Captain Frank asked.

"She's a damn good nurse, Frank," I told him. "She knows her stuff. It's just that I got the impression that she thinks they almost prefer to have him like that."

"Baloney," Captain Frank said.

I decided to change the subject. "What happens if the Chief dies?" I asked.

"They have a funeral and bury him," he said.

"Don't give me your Cape Cod humor, Frank. What happens to us?"

"You worry too much," he said. "The world is filled with rich men with yachts and big cars for chauffeurs to drive. You worry too much."

"You do not have a goddam alarm hooked up here to the boat, Frank," I said.

Across Lake Worth the lights of Palm Beach were coming on. It was getting dark. There was no wind, and I remember thinking the water was so smooth it looked like a sheet of ice. I remember it because that was the first time I let myself think Mr. Kennedy could die.

"François I and François II," I said. "We could set ourselves up as a package deal. Yacht captain and chauffeur."

"It is better to be the boat captain, because then you can tell them that you must stay with your boat," Frank Wirtanen said.

"Why don't you abandon ship and come with me?" I said.

"Where?"

"O'Hara's. I feel like some serious drinking."

sure did not want to walk into a
bedroom full of his family and
Henry and Jeanie rushing into

28

The First Family changed houses again that next summer. Morton Downey got his Squaw Island house back, and the president rented Brambletyde, a house with a sweeping view of Nantucket Sound on a high bluff on the ocean side of Squaw Island.

Squaw is a big sandhill and becomes a genuine island in the summer only when a high-course tide during the full moon coincides with high winds. Then the sea floods over the narrow road running between the beach on one side and a salt marsh on the other. The road that connects Squaw also floods in the winter months.

With Ted and Joan in one house and the First Family in another, I was running a regular Squaw Island ferry service. But then talk spread along the staff grapevine that this might be the last Hyannis Port summer for the First Family, as next season Jacqueline planned to take a place in Newport.

We joked among ourselves that two miles from her mother-in-law wasn't far enough for Jacqueline Kennedy.

At the same time rumors flew about the president spending the next summer in Rhode Island, there were rumors that Ted Kennedy was trying to buy the house next to brother Robert's. That would give all three of Mr. Kennedy's sons houses near his own big house, in the Kennedy compound. By now the place was "the compound" in the newspapers and on TV; even the family were calling it that. But the owner of the house Ted was eyeing apparently did not want to sell—the Kennedys thought their neighbors automatically tried to hold them up for more money—and the deal fell through.

I asked Joan about their plans. "Do you think you might be moving closer, Mrs. Kennedy?"

"I don't know," she said, smiling. "I love it right here."

I had my reasons for being interested. If Ted did move to the compound, and if the First Family went to Newport next summer, then I wouldn't have to run the Squaw Island ferry service, shuttling children back and forth for the kiddie movie; or whenever one of them wanted to come up to the compound and play with the cousins; or then, in the other direction, whenever one of them wanted to go home. Ted and Joan's daughter Kara was three now and Edward, Jr., was almost two; Caroline was five and John-John was two and a half. I'd pick them up in the VW bus.

With all the "uncles" around the place—Lem Billings, Dave Powers, and Mother Meredith the agent—plus a special physical-education instructor for the kids and the various nannies, the children were kept busy.

Joan was very protective toward and conscientious about her children, and they were usually the best-behaved. "You do what Frank tells you," she'd say to them, and then cleverly make her young son and daughter responsible for each other. "I've told Mr. Saunders that if either of you act up he is to bring *both* of you back home and you won't be able to see the movie."

Maud Shaw, the First Family's nanny, would hand over Caroline and John, Jr. "Bless you, Frank," she'd say.

Separately the children were usually well-behaved. It was only when they all got together things would start happening. And if I'd been out to Luigi's late the night before for my chicken barbecue for the secret service, which sometimes went into the early morning hours, then the kids screaming and yelling really got to me. I couldn't understand how Mother Meredith could take the kids all the time and keep smiling.

The thing that really tripped my temper with them was when they started that spoiled-brat whining about who they were. They all knew they were "Kennedys," but they'd carry on about whether it was better to be a Shriver or a Lawford. Jean Kennedy Smith and Stephen Smith's son, William, wasn't yet three, so he was too young to play the snob game.

"I don't care who you are!" I'd begin my lecture. "I'm driving this bus, you understand? And as long as I'm driving the bus you do what I say." If that didn't quiet them down, I would play my trump card. "I do not work for any of your fathers. None of your fathers is paying my salary. I work for Joseph P. Kennedy. I work for your grandfather. And this bus belongs to your grandfather. And if you don't do as I say, I will tell your grandfather."

Silence. It never failed.

The grandchildren had been taught that Mr. Kennedy was the end-all and be-all. They had been taught to revere him, to understand that they were rich because of him. More than once I overheard Sargent Shriver telling his children, "Everything we have we owe to your grandfather. Don't you ever forget it."

And who knew better? After all, Mr. Shriver had worked for Mr. Kennedy and married the boss's daughter. So had Steve Smith.

Ethel and Bobby's children could get particularly unruly at times. It wasn't that they were less disciplined than their cousins; it was just that there were more of them.

I always marveled at how Ethel's cook Ruby was always so unflappable with the young tribe. A hulking black woman with a warm heart and a friendly smile, Ruby would lean out the window of her kitchen when she saw me in the yard and ask, "Frank, have you had your breakfast? Come on in here and let Ruby fix you something." And if I happened to be in Ruby's kitchen when it was lunchtime I was always reminded what a real jewel Ethel Kennedy had in Ruby. The children would stream into the kitchen at lunch. "I want a tuna sandwich," one would say. "I want a peanut butter," another would demand. "I want a hamburger." "I want a cheeseburger." And Ruby always made what the children requested. If it was me, I thought, I'd make one kind of sandwich for lunch, and if they didn't like it—tough.

That's the way Jacqueline handled it for her two. Maud Shaw drew up the children's menu days in advance and gave it to the cook. This summer there was a new cook; Pearl was no longer with the Kennedys. The menu was posted in the kitchen. Jacqueline made them stick to it. Caroline and John ate what their nanny told them to, not what they felt like at the moment.

But there weren't many women with the wonderful temperament Ruby had.

In addition to everything else, Ruby made the picnic lunches they'd have on the *Marlin* when Mr. Kennedy went for a cruise.

The president took a few cruises on the *Marlin* that summer, but it seemed to me that he was spending more and more time on presidential business when he came up for the long weekends. And there seemed to be more official visitors. The helicopter still performed its Friday afternoon ritual, dropping down on the front lawn. And his father would be there on the veranda, waiting for his son. Mr. Kennedy had a male aide now, one the rest of the staff believed would stick with the job and not quit without notice. The man made my job easier.

The president landing in that helicopter was always something to get excited about, still something you'd go out of your way to watch. All of us did. There was a little story in the newspapers about how Mr. Kennedy's staff were obliged to line up and stand at attention whenever John Kennedy's helicopter was landing or taking off. I figured the guy who wrote that must have been one of the reporters who spent all his time at the bar at the Yachtsman, probably never came by the compound.

The reporters wrote a lot about fun and games, but they never wrote about the pain John Kennedy was in because of his back. It was getting worse and we all knew it. I was in the big house one day as the president came in the front door. As soon as he was inside he grabbed the crutches he kept at his father's house and hobbled off. From the expression on his face and the way he leaned and pulled himself, you knew he was in terrible pain.

* * *

The president was in the tub. He was soaking his bad back.

"Frank's here," George Thomas, his valet, said.

"Send him in. Hi, Frank," the president said, smiling.

"Mr. President, I wonder if you could autograph a picture for me. It's for two newlywed friends of mine," I said.

"Be glad to, Frank. You have the photo? Sure. Good. George, you have a pen? You've brought a pen with you, Frank? Good."

He winced when he sat up in the tub. George handed him a towel. "You don't mind if I do it right here, Frank?"

"Fine," I said.

He dried his hands and held the photo on the rim of the bathtub. "What're their names, Frank?"

I told him, and he did the honors. Then he handed me the photo and the pen, and smiled. "Now, Frank, you be sure to tell them the historical significance of this autographed portrait. Don't forget to tell them that it was signed by the president while he was stark naked and lying flat on his ass in the bathtub." Then he asked, "What's the movie tonight?"

I told him.

"Don't wait for me." John Kennedy laughed.

His mother knew how bad his back was. "Oh what will we do if Jack has to run for reelection in a wheelchair like FDR?" she said one day in the car. Then, after a few seconds, she added quietly, as if to herself, "There'll be two of them in wheelchairs."

Dr. Max Jacobson came to Hyannis Port, I guess to give the president injections for his back. Years later I read of Dr. Jacobson as "Dr. Feelgood" and learned that the vitamin shots he gave rich and famous patients were laced with speed. The story made it sound as though it was a big secret the way he had given President Kennedy amphetamines, but it wasn't that way at all. Anybody at the Kennedy place could have had a shot from Dr. Jacobson. The nurses even asked me, "Dr. Jacobson's here, Frank. Do you want a vitamin shot?"

* * *

"Hello," I answered.

There was a long pause, but I could hear that the line was still open.

"Is this . . . Frank?" Mrs. Kennedy said.

"Yes, Mrs. Kennedy."

"But I don't want you, Frank," she said.

Click. She'd hung up.

Mrs. Kennedy is never going to learn how to master the telephone, I told myself. She's always ringing the wrong number. She has the numbers on her night table—the garage, the laundry, the maid's room, the kitchen. All these years and she should know them by heart, I was thinking when it rang again.

"Yes, Mrs. Kennedy," I said right away.

"It's Mrs. Kennedy, Frank."

"Yes, Mrs. Kennedy."

"Dear heart, have you cleaned the pool today?"

"Yes, Mrs. Kennedy."

"Just checking. Just checking," she said lightly, and hung up.

Mrs. Kennedy's voice on the telephone jumped with urgency; she sounded a bit desperate. She apologized for bothering me at the garage and asked if I would please come right over to the kitchen.

A large dinner party, including the president and Jacqueline, had been waiting two hours for the main course and people were getting hungry, Mrs. Kennedy explained after she took me aside in the big kitchen. Matilda was on vacation, and Mrs. Kennedy had hired a fill-in chef. The chef's mother was a friend of a friend, and he came highly recommended.

"What does the chef say is the holdup, Mrs. Kennedy?"

"I don't want to ask him," she said.

"You mean you've been waiting for two hours?"

"You know the way chefs are, Frank. You were a cook in the army. . . ."

"The navy."

"Yes, well, could you talk to him and inquire if he needs assistance? I think I make him nervous every time I come in the kitchen. But, Frank, they're getting anxious out there." Then Mrs. Kennedy rejoined her guests.

I studied the chef and swapped small talk. I took an instant dislike to him. For one thing, he was sweating fiercely.

"You're having baked stuffed lobsters, huh? What's taking them so long?" I asked.

"I am cooking them slowly," he said.

"Maybe if you turn the oven on the lobsters would cook a little faster," I said. And I turned on the oven. This guy is no cook, I thought.

"Listen," I said, "I was a cook in the navy and maybe I can help you out. It's a strange kitchen and I know it's hard working in a kitchen you're not familiar with."

"I'm having trouble with this chocolate sauce. Mrs. Kennedy wants a chocolate sauce. But I'm having trouble with the sauce," he said.

I looked at his sauce. I took a taste. "You are definitely having trouble with this sauce," I agreed.

He began making excuses about being unable to find the proper ingredients.

"You stay with the lobsters," I told him. "You know what time they'll be ready, and if I'm not back by then, serve them. I'm going to get some chocolate sauce."

I drove as fast as I could to Luigi's, went right to the kitchen, and filled a big jar with some ready-made chocolate sauce. "Jeez, Frank, you got a sudden craving for chocolate sauce?" the cook asked me. "You pregnant?"

"Mrs. Kennedy wants it," I said.

"She pregnant?" he joked.

"We've got two pregnant Mrs. Kennedys," I said.

"Which ones?"

"Jacqueline and Ethel," I said.

"Take some more sauce then, Frank. Take some pickles, too."

"This is for *the* Mrs. Kennedy."

"*She* pregnant?"

"Just shut up and tell Dick that I borrowed some chocolate sauce," I said.

The lobsters were nearly ready when I got back.

I stayed with the new chef until the meal was finished.

Mrs. Kennedy thanked me for helping out. "He really is a good chef, Frank. He made this marvelous chocolate sauce," she said.

It couldn't have been more than a week later when I happened to notice in the *Cape Cod Standard-Times* a feature on the imposter chef. The paper gave his "famous" chocolate sauce recipe. The fake chef boasted that he'd served his special sauce to the president's mother and Mrs. Kennedy had raved about it. It was the best chocolate sauce she'd ever had, the newspaper quoted the chef as saying.

When Matilda returned, I told the story and she laughed all morning long.

The part-time chambermaids kept quitting through the summer. Mrs. Kennedy's personal maid Dora and house-maid Evelyn and the upstairs maid, a young Norwegian girl, were all faithful, good workers, but instead of prais-ing and depending on the regulars, Mrs. Kennedy was always in a turmoil over hiring new part-time maids. Some were college girls just trying to get a look inside the Kennedy compound. Some of them were maids who had been fired by previous employers. Mrs. Kennedy was having trouble with a new maid when she called me over to the house.

I could hear the screaming as soon as I came in the back door and was in the kitchen.

The new maid could hardly stand up, she was so drunk. A middle-aged black woman, she had wasted no time getting into the liquor. It was her first night on the job.

"Please take her away, Frank. Get her out of my sight," Mrs. Kennedy said. "The poor dear," Mrs. Kennedy added with some sympathy. "They usually wait at least a week before they start drinking on the job!"

We had a big Fourth of July. The compound was crowded. The president brought films of his trip to Ireland up to Hyannis Port and we had a special showing. This was one movie John Kennedy didn't sleep through.

It was magic for him. Watching those films taken on his triumphant visit in Ireland, John Kennedy was happier than I'd ever seen him. He was just like a kid. I guess he'd been in Ireland once or twice before, around the time he was at Harvard and Mr. Kennedy was U.S. ambassador to Great Britain. But of course this trip had been altogether different.

Had John Kennedy lived, Ireland would have seen a great deal more of him. He told a crowd of cheering Irish, "This is not the land of my birth, but it is the land for which I hold the greatest affection, and I will certainly come back in the springtime."

Ethel Kennedy had her own celebration. She gave birth to Christopher, their eighth child, on the Fourth of July.

"Ethel has her own kind of fireworks on the Fourth," Bobby Kennedy quipped. Their first child, Kathleen, named for Bobby's dead sister, had also been a Fourth of July baby.

Jacqueline was expecting sometime that fall.

"I could sneak by you guys anytime, I'm telling you."

"Frank says he could get by us anytime."

"Anytime it's dark, that is. I need it dark."

"Nobody's going to get by the U.S. secret service."

"Don't shit me," I said.

"Anytime, Frank?" another agent asked.

"Anytime it's dark."

"It's dark now, isn't it? You want to bet?"

"Yeah, I'll bet. I'll bet you drinks I could sneak right by you guys and you wouldn't even see me."

"You're on, François. Yes sir, François, you've got yourself a bet!"

We were at the bar at Luigi's. We'd been there long enough to have had a few drinks apiece. I don't know how the conversation swung around to security, but the agents had started bitching about how tough it was guarding the Kennedys when none of them wanted to inform the agents where they were going or when they were going someplace. And I sympathized with them, because I knew exactly what they had to go through, given how the Kennedys could keep me jumping. Then, after I'd mentioned what an impossible job they had and how easy it would be for

198

someone who was determined to sneak into the compound, the agents had got a bit defensive. So I challenged them.

We worked out the rules. No flashlights. When I got to the breakwater I'd light my cigarette lighter and wave it as a signal. They'd signal back. Then I'd begin my run.

I'm glad it isn't a full moon, I thought, but still I wouldn't mind it even blacker.

"Now listen," I said, "I don't want one of you guys down by the beach because you'd never be there anyway, right?"

They all agreed. But I knew damn well one of them would be guarding the beach.

I had on dark trousers and a dark shirt.

After I reached the breakwater I rested a few minutes before I signaled. They signaled right back. I figured the agent who signaled was standing near the flagpole in front of Mr. Kennedy's. What did I have, two hundred yards tops? They'd expect me to come right up the beach, thinking that would be the easiest, I decided.

I already knew how I was going to do it. I was going to crawl in the opposite direction in the sand until I reached the tall hedge wall, and that way get on the other side of them. That would be the trick. Then I'd run those hedges until the tennis court. I'd stay in the hedges all the way to the parking lot behind the big house, taking my time doing it. Then I'd have a cigarette.

I dropped down on my stomach and started crawling. I would crawl two feet, then stop, wait a few minutes, then crawl two more feet. I told myself not even to glance at the big house.

I must have spent thirty minutes just crawling that one hundred feet in the sand.

Once I got into the hedges I lost track of time. It was cool and wet in the hedges, and it felt good. Maybe I took another hour sneaking up along the hedges, a stretch you could walk in two minutes. They were big hedges and you could hide easily inside them. If you didn't move it would take a dog to sniff you out.

I hit the edge of the parking lot, strolled to a car, leaned against it, and lit a cigarette. By now I was dying for a smoke. I was still smoking when an agent spotted me.

"Frank?" he asked, walking up the driveway.

All I did was laugh.

"You son of a gun," he said.

The agents were pretty good about it. They congratulated me and asked jokingly how I did it, but I could tell they were bothered about my beating them. They took their job seriously.

Later the agents asked me if I would please not mention to Frank McDermott, the agent in charge of the Kennedy detail, how I snuck by them when he came up the next Friday night for his regular lasagna dinner at my place. The guys were all my friends, so I kept quiet. It was only a game for free drinks, anyway.

29

I heard the helicopter before I could see it. I was in the driveway behind the big house, and the midday sun blinded me as I searched the sky.

Then I caught a glimpse of a convertible shoot across the driveway into the turnaround. The car seemed to be heading for the landing pad. It looked like Jacqueline Kennedy's convertible.

Is someone coming or is someone going? I wondered as I ambled down the driveway. The copter was coming down now.

Jacqueline's convertible was waiting. An agent was at the wheel. Her secretary was with her and so was a man I recognized as Dr. Walsh. When I saw Dr. Walsh helping Mrs. Kennedy to the helicopter I figured they must be taking her to the hospital.

Two hours later she delivered her second son at the special maternity ward they had set up at Otis Air Force Base for just such an emergency.

The Otis hospital was in touch with the communications center in the big house and with the secret service trailer. Everyone was excited because the First Family had a new son with a reigning president as the new father.

All I could think of was, Well, there's another one for the kiddy matinee.

Then later that afternoon, the happy faces around the Kennedy compound saddened. The baby wasn't doing so well. They transferred mother and son to Children's Hospital in Boston. By then Louella Hennessey was with Jacqueline Kennedy. That was good news, for although Louella was labeled the Kennedy baby nurse in the newspapers, we knew she was really there to take care of the mother. So maybe the baby was all right. But later news from Boston wasn't good. The baby was having difficulty breathing, the doctors said.

Monday morning, after taking Mrs. Kennedy home from mass, I learned that during the night Patrick Bouvier Kennedy had died.

About a week later Jacqueline came home to Squaw Island.

One morning after mass, Mrs. Kennedy asked me, "How does Jacqueline seem to you, Frank?"

"I haven't seen her to talk with, Mrs. Kennedy," I said.

"She shouldn't have been doing all that water-skiing," Mrs. Kennedy said.

Mrs. Kennedy had masses said for her infant grandson.

Now there were new real-estate rumors. Jacqueline, so the talk went, wanted to build a house of her own on Squaw Island. She apparently had her eye on a piece of land that Ted, the president, and Morton Downey were going to buy, then divide three ways. The land was near the old windmill on Squaw, which Jacqueline was very fond of.

I had heard so many rumors that I asked Rose Kennedy.

"I suppose she has to do something to keep herself busy. Jacqueline loves building houses," she said. So, I thought, it is true. Then Mrs. Kennedy added, "But they'll never buy the land because the people will want too much for it."

A couple of weeks after Labor Day, Jacqueline returned to the White House. She was planning a Mediterranean cruise. I followed the First Lady's trip in the newspapers, and when I saw a photograph of Jacqueline and sister Lee and Prince Radziwill with Aristotle Onassis on his big yacht and all of them wearing sunglasses, I had to think back to my wonderful cruise that day on the *Honey Fitz*.

Mrs. Kennedy went down to Washington to spend a few

days at the White House while Jacqueline was in Greece. I picked up the paper one morning and read that Mrs. Kennedy had hosted a White House reception for Emperor Haile Selassie.

When she returned I asked her, "How'd you hit it off with Haile Selassie, Mrs. Kennedy?"

"Oh, Frank, you're such a stitch," she said.

"It's too bad Mr. Lawford didn't go with you," I said, sensing Mrs. Kennedy in a rare good mood.

"Why?" she asked.

"Because he could have introduced Lassie to Haile Selassie," I said.

I drew a total blank.

Then she blurted, "Oh, Frank, I slept on Lincoln's bed!"

I said to myself, I hope you didn't muss up the covers on Lincoln's bed on purpose just to have the White House maid make it again, the way you're always doing to Dora.

That Sunday in late October when the president came down to Hyannis Port from Boston was bright and beautiful, crisp with hardly any wind. The president had been in Cambridge the day before and watched part of the Harvard-Columbia football game. I read in the Sunday morning paper that he'd left the game and visited Patrick's grave nearby in Brookline. He'd tried to keep it a secret, but the reporters found out about it.

They took the *Marlin* for a cruise—the president, Mr. Kennedy, and Ann Gargan. Captain Frank piloted the yacht around to the sheltered side of Lewis Bay.

Ann said later it was one of the best rides she'd had with the president and his father. It was dead calm for one thing, Ann said, and Mr. Kennedy was exceptionally alert. She just knew that John Kennedy was cheered up by that leisurely cruise.

Monday morning dawned gray. It was blowing rain; not a heavy rain but a constant drizzle. I was in the kitchen having a cup of coffee when I heard the helicopter start revving. The president was leaving for Washington. I went to the front of the house. They had not brought Mr.

Kennedy down to the veranda to watch his son leave, because of the bad weather.

I went out on the veranda.

I saw the president wave, then look toward his father's bedroom window and wave again, this time just for his father. The big blades whirred and the spinning blades blew the rain as far as the veranda so that I had to shield my face with my arm.

In a few seconds the helicopter was out of sight.

"We won't see him again until Thanksgiving," Matilda said when I came back into the kitchen.

Mr. Kennedy did not look as if he was breathing when I got to his bedroom. The night nurse had the oxygen out and was working on him. His eyes were still open but had rolled back in their sockets.

He took the oxygen and slowly started to come out of it.

The next day I asked Rita if Mr. Kennedy knew what was happening when his heart stopped like that. "They say that some people whose hearts stop on them have the sensation of death coming, that they are sinking away," the nurse said. "But, when they come out of it, they come out slowly, and it is more like waking from a deep sleep than something painful or unpleasant."

After Halloween the weather worsened. It is the time of year when the storms come. There were more storms out of the northeast now. I thought, It's a good thing Mr. Kennedy's bedroom is on the south side of the house, because the way the nor'easters howl in here, it is like the banshees crying.

30

There was hard lead in the morning sky; a heavy-looking, thick sheet of grayness that shielded the dawn. Low across the horizon and level, a narrow slit in the cloud stretched ribbonlike.

It was the kind of cold gray dawn you get on Cape Cod, when November is dying, that scares the geese south. You could feel winter coming. Ahead, as we drove east toward Hyannis for mass, the sun kept seeping through and the bottom of the sky reddened. Red sky in the morning, I was thinking.

"Sailors take warning, Mrs. Kennedy," I said.

But she did not answer. It was dead quiet, so quiet that I searched in the rearview mirror to check if she'd fallen asleep. There she was, curled up like a cat against the door in the corner, slumped down, and I could make out only the top of her face. Her eyes were closed. It was her habit when she was cold. I turned up the heater. It felt good.

We'll beat the geese south yet, I said to myself. All we have to do is get through Thanksgiving. Thoughts of sunny Palm Beach warmed me along with the car's heater.

Certainly Mrs. Kennedy was anxious to get to Palm Beach. She'd been talking about arthritis again, hammering at it until I knew she was afraid of it, saying how old people's hands with swollen knuckles turned her stomach. That fear of joints swelling up on her was why she was so fanatic about always exercising. And seeing Mr. Kennedy crippled frightened her even more, I guessed.

I had something else on my mind. Moving all the cars and the household junk she always had to cart down with her to Palm Beach was a big enough pain for me—I dreaded even thinking about it—and there were just two weeks left. But now I'd heard rumors that Ambassador Henry Cabot Lodge was coming for the weekend to meet the president after his Texas trip, and that would only add to the chaos. Plus John would be three in just three days, then Caroline turned six two days later. They'd have their birthday parties with all their cousins. More kiddy movies. And on top of all that, I'd heard, too, that there was a crew of scientists coming.

I wanted to find out Mrs. Kennedy's plans so I could figure out if I'd have much driving to do for the family during the week.

"Mrs. Kennedy . . ." I began. Never mind, I decided. Let her nap.

She woke on her own as I pulled into the parking lot next to Saint Francis Xavier and let herself out without a word. I watched her flip up her collar and, shuffling in quick short steps, head toward the church door.

I went over to the doughnut shop for coffee.

By the time she came out of Saint Francis Xavier the sun had burned off the grayness. It looked like it was going to be a good day after all.

"I think I shall play golf this morning, Frank," she said on our way home. "Yes, I will! It looks like a nice day."

"Yes, Mrs. Kennedy," I said.

This was good news. She seldom played golf in the morning, and it would mean that she'd likely be so tired when she got home, she would sleep for at least an hour after lunch.

"Sounds like a good idea to me, Mrs. Kennedy," I said, so sweetly I was embarrassed.

Then I thought, Get good and tired, Mrs. Kennedy. Take a long, long nap this afternoon. Don't bother your chauffeur for two hours.

I ate a heavy noon meal.

After her lunch Mrs. Kennedy went up to her bedroom.

I wanted to sleep but couldn't. I was restless. So I dozed, listening to the radio. The music was soothing.

We interrupt our regular programming for this special news bulletin. According to UPI, shots have been fired at the president's motorcade in Dallas.

I bolted upright, rigid and waiting.

There is no report of injury. Again, minutes ago shots were fired at the president's motorcade as it traveled in Dallas.

I couldn't move. I sat frozen, waiting for more.

We will bring you further reports as we receive them.

The telephone is ringing. A sharp jolt goes right through me like an electric shock. On the second ring I flinch. My stomach churns.

Then I jump out of the chair and grab the phone.

"Frank, Frank! Did you hear the radio? . . ."

"Yes. . . ."

"Oh, God, Frank! What should we do?"

Dora is near hysterics.

"Where's Mrs. Kennedy, Dora?"

"Upstairs. Asleep. Oh, my God, Frank!"

Christ, I hope Mr. Kennedy is asleep. I hope he hasn't got the goddam TV on. My stomach tightens.

It is believed some shots hit the president's motorcade.

"Dora! Now listen! Is there an agent in the house?"

"I don't know, I don't know. Oh, Frank . . ." The maid is sobbing.

"I'll be right over."

Should I go to the secret service trailer first? No. The house, I decide. I sprint up the new macadam driveway.

Dora is inside the dayroom. She looks desperate.

"He's shot! Jack's shot! They just had it on. Oh, God, what are we going to do about Mr. Kennedy?"

Dallas. Shots rang out. The Plaza. UPI says John Kennedy was hit. Motorcade. Hospital. The radio announcer rattles on. I've heard enough. It must have happened.

"Let's go up, Dora."

The maid bolts down the back hall ahead of me.

On the stairs Dora stumbles. She falls to one knee,

sobbing and yelling, and I have to hold her so she will not slide back down underneath me.

She gets up but her foot slips and she lurches forward. Now she is screaming loudly: "The president's been shot! My God, the president's been shot!" Her shouts fill the narrow stairwell.

"Jesus, Dora," I mumble over and over. "Jesus, Dora."

Above us on the landing a woman's voice barks: "Be quiet!" Rita is poised defiantly at the top, blocking the stairway. "Be quiet!" Mr. Kennedy's nurse hisses.

"The president's been shot! Jack's shot!" Dora screams. She looks up at the nurse and, as she does, she totters for a split second. I shove her forward. She is a blocky woman, and she catapults up two more steps, scrambling up as quickly as she can, but then falls again.

I see Rita start down.

"The president's shot . . . ." I begin. "Stay there, Rita, for Chrissakes!" I'm afraid she will push Dora over and the both of us will tumble backward down the steep stairs. ". . . shot in Dallas. It's on the news."

"What are you say . . . ing?" Rita asks Dora. The nurse is breathing in the maid's face.

Then Dora slumps to her side on the stairs. She covers her face with her hands, and I try to move around her, but now Rita is in my way. The nurse is trying to pull Dora up.

I spot Ann at the top of the stairs.

"Oh, my God, the poor president," Dora wails.

Rita grabs her by the shoulders and is shaking her. "Dora, quiet. Be quiet."

I move up a step. Ann's face is twisted in a grimace. It's her standard angry look. She is glowering down at me.

"The president's been shot." I hurry the message out. "No one knows how bad it is, Ann."

Ann springs back as if she's suddenly stepped on a rattlesnake.

Dora's sobs get louder.

Ann's face whitens.

Behind me a hollow thud. A body hitting the wall. Silence.

Ann is trembling. A hand flies to her mouth and she bites one finger.

Then her screams come. One long shriek.

I hear Rita behind me. "Frank, help me with her, will you? Take her downstairs. She'll wake Mrs. Kennedy."

Ann runs away.

I want to scream myself. But my mouth is frozen.

An explosion of voices blows out of Ann's room. She's got the stupid thing on full blast—I can't tell if it's the TV or her radio blaring. Christ, Ann.

"Frank! Take Dora. She's too heavy for me," Rita pleads.

I am near the head of the stairs when I hear a door burst open, then footsteps coming.

I go back down a few steps and help Rita with Dora. But Dora seems all right now. To get out of their way, I move back up the stairs and stand aside on the landing.

Mrs. Kennedy's voice startles me from above.

"What's the matter with you two?" the president's mother snaps at Dora and Rita, who are almost up the stairs now.

I am sure Mrs. Kennedy hasn't even seen me, although I am close enough to touch her. She is cloaked in her old bathrobe and her hair is matted down on one side. Her eyes are puffy. On her forehead is a big oval frownie.

The nurse and maid are struggling up the last few steps.

"Please, can't you keep quiet?" Mrs. Kennedy pleads. "I've never heard so much commotion. Now keep still! Do you want to disturb Mr. Kennedy?"

Dora, whose face is raw from crying, is on the landing now with Rita. Mrs. Kennedy stares vacantly at them.

"You of all people should know better than this, Mrs. Dallas," Mrs. Kennedy says, then turns and leaves. After a few steps, she snaps over her shoulder: "And someone tell Ann to turn that television off!"

Dora buries her head against my chest. I feel her sobbing. Rita heads quickly for Ann's room.

Mrs. Kennedy halts in her tracks, spins, and walks back. I see confusion cloud her face. Her eyes widen.

Dora is still crying, muffling her sobs against my chest.

"Frank, what *is* the matter with her?"

209

The television in Ann's room quiets.

"Mrs. Kennedy. The president has been shot," I tell her.

Dora begins sobbing again. Now Ann is in the hallway with Rita.

Rose Kennedy staggers. Her upper body sways.

She steadies. "Is he dead?" she says evenly at me, aiming her eyes at mine.

"No."

Her eyes blink. Then blink again.

"Oh, Aunt Rose! Jack's been shot!" Ann blurts at the same instant Rose Kennedy's hands flutter up to the sides of her head. "He's been shot . . . in Dallas. It's on the news, Aunt Rose. Oh, somebody should be called. Frank heard it, didn't you, Frank? Didn't you, Frank? They all heard it. . . ." Ann chatters on like a schoolgirl.

Mrs. Kennedy turns her back to us and walks down the hallway toward her bedroom.

No one else moves.

Dora is silent. Everyone is silent.

Then Mrs. Kennedy spins around. She presses the tips of the fingers of her right hand against her right temple the way you do when you have a splitting headache. "He'll be all right," she says. "Don't worry. He'll be all right. You'll see. You'll see."

Then she leaves.

The latch on her bedroom door clicks like the hammer of a revolver falling on an empty cylinder.

Ann retreats hurriedly to her room.

I think about pushing Dora away from me, but the maid clings to me, and we stay like that for a few seconds. I am too drained to move.

Without a word Rita heads for Mr. Kennedy's room.

Dora and I wait.

In a few seconds Rita is padding back up the hallway. "He's sleeping," the nurse whispers. "I'll listen for him on my intercom. You'd better take Dora downstairs, Frank."

Quick footsteps pound behind us. Ann squeezes by and dashes into her uncle's bedroom.

Rita is going after her.

Mrs. Kennedy's door flies open. "Mrs. Dallas, Mrs.

Dallas. Don't let Ann say anything to my husband. Don't let her tell him. I just talked with my children. They're coming right up. I want them to be with him. I want them to tell him."

"Let's go, Dora," I say.

31

The agents were in the house now. Doors were banging. They were checking every room. Agent Ham Brown grabbed me. "Frank, listen. I want you to go over to the president's house. . . ."

"What's going on, Ham? What the hell is happening?"

"We don't know yet, Frank. The car was fired on. They took him to the hospital. You go over to his house and check the place out."

I'd never seen Ham like this before. He was always the jokester; everything was always a lark for good old Ham.

"Move it, Frank! Do it now. We don't know what the hell is happening."

I went quickly out the back door and stood just outside. I looked up, straight up at the sky—maybe to clear my head or because of the relief of being out of the house— and I took a deep breath. There were fat clouds tinged dark gray around the edges, scudding in off the bay low and fast, but the sun was still out.

I lowered my head and cut across Robert Kennedy's backyard. On the ground shadows were racing, and suddenly I halted. Hell, I thought, what am I doing? What has Ham Brown got me *doing?* He doesn't even have a gun himself and he's got me doing this. I was looking now at the back of the president's house. The sun was reflecting off the top-floor windows, then it was shining on the white shingles. What if there is somebody in that house? I thought. I knew fear when I tasted it, and it was fear I was swallowing as I neared John Kennedy's house, not sorrow or anger. My shadow shooting over the grass was braver about getting to the house than I was.

I glanced over at the secret service trailer, then went in the back door of the president's and into the kitchen. The house was warm. They'd left the heat on. And it was awfully quiet. I thought about taking a kitchen knife, but in a second I knew it was a crazy idea because if there was someone in this house, he would have a gun.

I stayed stock-still in the kitchen, thinking absurdly that I sure could use a couple of those frozen daiquiris now.

I went through the dining room, the living room. The wooden floor creaked as I walked.

I climbed the stairs one at a time, stopping to listen on each stair.

Upstairs now, I pushed open the bathroom door slowly, leaning through the doorway and reaching as far as I could. I kept pressing the door further and further until it swung all the way open and I knew no one could be hiding behind it.

Now the bedrooms.

The children's room. Toys. I shivered at the sight of them. It was starting to sink in now. What if he had taken one in the back? With that back of his he'd be crippled just like his father.

Then I went into their bedroom. I knew now there was nobody in the house, that this whole thing of the search and my fear was crazy. The president had been shot in Dallas, Texas, no one knew how badly, and I was standing in his bedroom looking for what? *What am I looking for, Ham?* A nice-guy secret service agent they won't even let have bullets for his gun because they're afraid he might shoot a hole in his foot has me searching the president's house?

"There's no one here!" I screamed as loudly as I could, then closed my eyes to make it all go away, and to think for a moment.

I detected a faint, familiar scent in the bedroom. Jacqueline's perfume?

Frank! Hey, Frank!

They must want me on the dock, I thought.

My mind spun back to that day two summers ago. Jacqueline is in the water, waiting, her face bobbing in the water. She is asking me to help her, putting out her hands for me to pull her out. But I cannot reach her this time.

Frank? Hey, Frank!

The yelling was not in my dream. It was an agent shouting for me. I snapped out of it.

"I'm coming," I said quietly, taking my hands down from my eyes, trying to focus. My mouth felt like there was a ball of cotton in it.

"He's dead," Ham told me.

"The president's dead? No, Ham."

"We just got the word, Frank."

"Oh sweet Christ."

"They want you upstairs."

"He's really dead then?"

"Yeah. Instantly."

"What about Mrs. Kennedy?"

"They want you upstairs."

"Not her. Jacqueline."

"It's just him, Frank."

"There's no one in his house, you know."

"Thanks for doing that, Frank. We had to come over here, you understand?"

I nodded.

"Frank, they want you upstairs."

"What for?"

"I don't know. But they are asking for you."

"I'm not going, Ham. I'm not going up there. I couldn't face the old man."

"They need you up there, Frank. Please."

"Did they say why?"

"Go see, will you?"

"What's going on anyway, Ham?"

"We don't know, Frank," the agent said. I could tell Ham was fighting to hold back tears. And then I couldn't hold mine any longer.

* * *

214

I took a few seconds outside Mr. Kennedy's room to collect myself. Then I burst in. "Hey, Chief. It's movie time!" I called out.

I stood there, certain I was going to give it away. I could see what he was doing: he was studying my face. "Movie time," I repeated quickly.

It was all part of the charade. Mrs. Kennedy and Ann and Rita had decided it would be best for Mr. Kennedy to stick to the regular routine. I thought, I'm not a good enough actor for this one.

Ted and Eunice had spoken with their mother and were coming up as soon as they could. The children would have to tell their father about the President, Mrs. Kennedy had said.

I had to get all this straight. What had happened when Ann went running into his room? Rita said Ann had blurted out something about there being a terrible accident, but had then caught herself—maybe she'd heard her aunt out in the hallway—and had told Mr. Kennedy that it was Wilbert. Ann had then made up some story and calmed him down, telling him that the gardener really hadn't been too badly hurt.

But he was on to something, Rita had said. "He is suspicious," the nurse had said just before I'd gone into his room.

The movie, they all agreed, would distract him.

One look at him now, though, and I could tell the Chief knew something was going on. You could cut the tension with a knife. Those eyes of his felt like ice picks jabbing at me.

"Today's feature film is a new Elvis Presley movie, boss! How about that! Your favorite movie actor! All set?"

Ann was waiting to take him down the elevator.

"Frank says you'll love this new Elvis movie," she said.

The president's father smiled. Okay.

Ann helped me wheel him into the elevator. As we went down I plotted how I would push him to his favorite spot, then let Ann lock the wheels so I could scoot right into the booth and, that way, would not have to show him my face.

If he did think something bad had happened to Wilbert, all he'd need was a good look at my face to think that Wilbert was really injured. And I couldn't go through having to explain that, making up lies and all—I'd crack, I just knew it. But then I figured, what the hell, if I should catch him looking at me funny I'd tell him I'd had a couple of good stiff drinks at lunch, and laugh it off. He'd go for that.

Ann talked to him as if nothing had happened; she was playing her part like a star. She made small talk in the elevator.

Earlier I had set up the projectors. The movie was set to go.

It was dim in the theater. "All right, Chief, get ready for Elvis," I told him. His wheelchair was where he wanted, and I hurried to the little projection room, my haven. The projector whirred. Through the narrow slit in the cement blocks I checked the lens focus. The reels rolled. The title flashed.

Kid Galahad

Maybe this will be a good one, I thought. The focus was perfect. Ann was sitting next to him. I had the lights down so he couldn't see too clearly around the room. Sometimes he liked to give Ann a glance to see what she might be thinking about the movie. We didn't want that.

A mountain lodge. Blue sky. Big white clouds. Pretty scenery. A sign: GROGAN'S GAELIC GARDENS.

A good beginning, I thought. An Irish angle. That green shamrock will catch his eye.

Charles Bronson inside the lodge. With him a pretty girl. Bronson talks with her. "There ain't nothing worse than a suspicious dame first thing in the morning." Bronson exits. Enter Elvis Presley wearing soldier's uniform. Presley: "Sorry to barge in like this. . . . I was wondering if I could see Mr. Grogan?" Pretty girl: "He isn't here right now." Girl looks Elvis over. Girl: "Are you a fighter?" Elvis: "No Ma'am, I just got out of the army and happened to drop by."

So far, so awful. The pace better pick up fast, I think.

I check Mr. Kennedy through the little window. He seems to be watching, all right. He seems to be staring at the screen.

Presley: "I could use a job for a few days." Girl: "Fresh out of the army and dead broke." Presley: "I'm afraid that is about the size of it. You see, I got in a crap game with my separation pay and it got separated from me."

This is really awful, I think. Spare me, please. The guy maybe can sing, but he's a terrible actor. Why does Mr. Kennedy like Elvis Presley movies in the first place?

Christ, World War III could be starting out there. What happened in Dallas? How could John Kennedy be *dead?*

All I must do is stay in this booth and show Mr. Kennedy this Elvis Presley movie, I'm telling myself. Show the movie. Then help Ann take him upstairs. Maybe Rita can give him something to make him sleep.

Grogan's Gaelic Gardens is a training camp for boxers. They are searching for a sparring partner for Joey the boxer. Elvis wants the job. Five dollars a round.

Now we're getting someplace. Action. Mr. Kennedy loves a good fight. Good. Ted and Eunice are probably on their way to Hyannis Port. What happened in Dallas? The whole world must know now. I wonder what is going on. A revolution?

Bronson tells Gig Young that a bookmaker is looking for him. The bookmaker, a tough guy, threatens him. Bookmaker promises to send two thugs after Young.

Why does Hollywood always make bookmakers look like tough guys? I don't know one bookie who looks like this movie actor.

Boxing ring scene. Two boxers sparring. Scene shifts. Gig Young calls sister for loan. Switch to dark-haired beauty on the phone. Says she can't help. Switch back to Young, pleading with her. Rose is her name.

Oh no! Why does her name have to be *Rose?* I check Mr. Kennedy. He hasn't moved. We're okay. Then it occurs to me why Mrs. Kennedy did not want to tell him. One possible reason. She's afraid her husband might not believe her, the way he gets mad at her when she goes in his room. Better if the children do it. I wonder if they will fly right in to Barnstable. Maybe they'll come by helicopter and land here. But that would tip the old man off—he knows it's not a Friday, when the president's expected home, and he'll see a helicopter land with Ted and Eunice instead.

I am watching Mr. Kennedy now, not the movie. That crippled, speechless man out there wanted his first son to be the first Catholic president, and what happened? His bomber explodes and all they can find is tiny pieces of the plane. Blown to smithereens. That man there wanted his second son to be the first Catholic president. Can a Catholic be president of the United States? Sure one can. Didn't John Fitzgerald Kennedy prove them all wrong? Don't give *me* any of that bullshit! Don't tell *me* that! Because I've got to tell you that if a Catholic is ever president and alive on the day his term ends, then, buddy, maybe you've got something. But don't give me any of that shit about America being ready for a Catholic in the White House, because they just killed the first one in that miserable lousy Texas cowtown.

And I slam the flat of my hand against the wall.

Crash. Elvis flattens one thug. Presley to Gig Young: "He doesn't know how to behave himself with a lady."

Two sons killed and he's sitting paralyzed in a wheelchair. The whole world is tuned in to Dallas, Texas, and I am in this cellar showing the president's father a stupid Elvis Presley movie!

Pretty girl to Elvis: "Thanks, Galahad." Second tough guy: "Who's Galahad?" Bronson: "Galahad was a knight in a tin suit, a hero with a halo, you understand that? And very courteous to broads, as I remember." Second tough guy: "Oh."

The screen blurs. They can't hear me crying in here, anyway. So let it go, I tell myself. Now I feel trapped in the little cement-block room.

I get control of myself and look through the slit, catching Mr. Kennedy as he turns slowly and glances back at the projection booth. I think I see a terrible wild flash in his eyes, but it is too dark to make out his face. Maybe the flickering light from the projector made his eyes flash.

Ann motions for me. I come out and she whispers, "He's getting fidgety, Frank." Then she turns to him and asks, "Do you want to go upstairs, now, Uncle Joe?"

He nods that he does. He tosses his left hand at the screen in disgust—the same look I saw on his face that night the president was late for his homecoming, the same flick of the hand.

I turn quickly and go back to the projection room and shut off the machine. It seems as though we have been in the theater forever, but from the reels I can see that we haven't watched half of *Kid Galahad*.

When he is back in his bedroom he makes sounds in his throat and points at the TV set. Ann looks at me and I look at Ann.

She distracts him. I pull the plug on the TV. Then I look away, out his window. The sun has slid toward Craigville Beach. Below on the Kennedy beach I spot a woman in a black coat, walking head-down. Mrs. Kennedy. There is a man with her.

Rita comes in the room, ready with something to make Mr. Kennedy sleep.

I stayed in the dayroom watching the news on the little set until someone told me that Ted and Eunice were on their way up to Otis on an air-force plane, and that I should go over and meet them at the air base.

It was good to be in the Chrysler, good to be away from the big house. The car radio was full of news from Dallas. So he was next to Jacqueline in an open car when it

219

happened. Who was driving for him? I wondered. Was it Bill Greer? Poor goddam Bill, if it was.

The faces in the cars coming the other way along Route 28 were all sad. They had to be listening to what I was listening to. The world had to be listening.

On the way back it was quiet in the car. I tried not to look at Ted and Eunice in the rearview mirror.

"Does he know, Frank?" Ted asked.

"No," I said. "Your mother is waiting for you."

It took us twenty minutes, and by then it was turning dark. As we headed up the driveway, Eunice whispered: "Oh, Jesus. Oh, Jesus help me."

32

I figured it was going to be a zoo outside Saint Francis Xavier the next morning.

It was. Cameramen and photographers crowded on a towerlike scaffold that had been built next to the church, and there were more of them at the door and on the steps.

Anticipation of what I was going to find when I brought Mrs. Kennedy to mass had kept me from getting much sleep. I wanted to get it over with, as did Mrs. Kennedy. There had never been a question whether she would attend morning mass.

"Oh," she squeaked when she spotted the crowd of reporters, as if she'd accidentally pricked herself with a pin.

We had extra secret service with us, in their own cars. The TV camera lights flared and we pushed through the reporters, all shouting to get her attention. There were more inside. I hadn't expected that they would invade the church like that. With me pushing ahead of her, she went down the aisle to the front pew she always used.

Suddenly a photographer stepped in front of me and stuck his camera over my shoulder, aiming it at her. I shoved him back. "Get out of the way, you son of a bitch," I said, just loud enough for him to hear. I was grappling for his camera when he snatched it back.

The church quieted. It seemed that finally the photographers realized that it wouldn't be right to sneak a picture of the president's mother's face during mass. Besides, by now the secret service were grouped around her.

She had a black mantilla draped over her head, hiding her face, and she kept her head bowed.

I kept thinking, That priest is saying a memorial mass for her second dead son in front of an altar honoring her first dead son. I kept thinking, too, of that summer twenty years ago Wilbert had told me about, when, after the priests told Mr. Kennedy that Joe, Jr., was dead, he'd retreated to his bedroom and turned on sad music and had not come out for a long time.

When she turned to leave, her face was as grim as it had been on the way to mass. She kept her head bowed, and I stepped in front of her to lead her out of the church toward the car. As I opened the door I noticed that she seemed frightened and confused. The photographers and the crowd must have rattled her, I decided, as I helped her into the car.

I floored it. In the rearview mirror I saw cars chasing us. I couldn't tell if they were more photographers or the secret service. We were speeding. I glanced again in the rearview mirror and I saw her slumped in the corner of the backseat on my side of the car. She was staring straight ahead, still grim. She never spoke even when I stopped in front of the house by the veranda steps and let her out. I watched her walk slowly up the steps, her head still bent over.

On the way to Mr. Kennedy's driveway, I glanced left down Irving Avenue. More reporters and photographers were milling outside the fence in front of the president's house.

When I got to the big house I was informed there would be a job for me. I was told to stand by. The reporters had been asking if Mr. Kennedy knew yet that his son was dead, and they wouldn't be held off much longer. Hadn't Ted and Eunice told Mr. Kennedy last night? Evidently not. Ted was going to tell him this morning, the reporters had been told.

When I got the word, I was to walk over to the president's house and let the reporters out in the street know that Mr.

Kennedy knew about the president. The signal would be to hoist the Stars and Stripes at the flagpole in the driveway to the president's house.

I don't remember who worked out this signal. Maybe it was Ann's brother Joe Gargan, who had come to the house as soon as he'd heard the news that his cousin had been shot. There were a lot of people in the compound now—close friends, extra agents.

I was anxious to have done with it, but it seemed a long time before I got the word to give the signal. As I carried the folded Stars and Stripes across the back lawn and headed for the president's house I felt the wind gusting. I took my time walking.

On the other side of the cedar stockade fence—Jacqueline's privacy fence—I could hear reporters talking.

I began raising the flag. As I watched it move slowly up the pole tears flooded my eyes. It was a raw day anyway. The wind was gusting and the Stars and Stripes flapped in the wind; then, when the wind died, the flag dropped down the pole and twisted slowly around it, then unfurled and waved straight out again when the wind caught it.

One of the reporters crawled up the fence. He stuck his head just above the top and shouted: "What did the Ambassador say when he heard about the assassination?"

I kept on with the flag.

The reporter was about a hundred feet away, both hands clutching the fence, his head sticking just above it.

What did he say? That's how much you know about Mr. Kennedy, I thought—to ask that. I was thinking, I hope you fall off that fence and break your neck, you jerk, asking a question like that at this moment.

The flag was at half-staff now. I fastened the rope. The reporter's face had disappeared. As I turned and started back, another reporter shouted from the other side: "Did the old man cry?"

Rita said that Mr. Kennedy had learned about his son's murder the night before.

"What are you telling me?" I asked, a little annoyed.

"He knew last night, Frank," she said.

"Then what was all this flag business? Something dramatic for the reporters? How do you know he knew last night? I heard he was all doped up.''

"Dora said the newspaper was in his room when she brought him his orange juice," Rita said.

"Were you in his room last night when they told him?"

"No. Not exactly. I was standing by the door when Ted and Eunice went in. Anyway, what difference does it make when he found out about it?"

"Yeah," I said, "so what," and walked away.

Ted took his father for a ride in the Chrysler that afternoon, and Rita went with them. If anybody can comfort him, I thought, Ted can. Now if only Mrs. Kennedy has sense enough to stay out of his room.

The doctors worried about what could happen if Mr. Kennedy went to his son's funeral. They advised against it. So that, it was decided, was how it was going to be. As far as I know, the Chief was not asked if he felt up to it and wanted to go.

Father John Cavanaugh, an old friend of Mr. Kennedy's who had been president of Notre Dame, had come to the house. Father Cavanaugh was with him in his bedroom during the funeral.

Mr. Kennedy did not want to watch the services on TV. Downstairs in the dayroom we heard that the president's father prayed with Father Cavanaugh and stared at the clock.

As I watched the TV I let myself believe now that it was all true. When I couldn't take it anymore I would go out and walk down to the beach. I was at the edge of the grass when a lone seagull swooped down at me. I suddenly remembered that day I first drove into the Kennedy place and stopped my Chevy convertible on the driveway to look the place over, when a seagull seemed to be attacking my car.

I watched this seagull zigzag out over the bay. It couldn't be the same gull, could it? I wondered.

None of us watching the televised funeral mass in the maid's dayroom had spoken for a long time. The mass was nearing its end when Dora spotted Rose Kennedy and said offhandedly, "That's the dress she's been saving for Mr. Kennedy's funeral, you know." She gave a quick little half sigh, half sob.

I knew Dora had only meant to make an innocent observation, but her remark stunned me. So Mrs. Kennedy had done more than merely let herself think her husband might die. She had actually prepared for it, had chosen the dress! As the camera panned the congregation, which was now leaving the church, I said to myself, She has faced what you have refused to face. The softened voice of the commentator droned on and on.

And then, I couldn't help thinking again of how the news of a son's death had come to Mr. Kennedy twice in this house. At least he had been there, on the scene, when they brought daughter Kathleen's body down off the mountain in France where her plane crashed. But for his first two sons he had been cheated out of the final good-bye. Twice now he had been unable to stand at the grave and bury his son.

Which is the worse grief for a father, I wondered. To have a son blown to pieces so that there is no body to bury? Or to be unable to speak so that you cannot beg them to let you be there while a nation pays its final tribute to its dead president, and he is your son they are burying?

33

"They had an awful time with Mr. Kennedy last night, Frank," Matilda said as soon as I entered the kitchen to wish her happy Thanksgiving. She was working feverishly and I could tell she didn't have time to go into detail. "It was terrible," she said.

"What time?" I asked.

"Oh, in the middle of the night."

"He all right?"

"I think so, ya. You ask Rita."

"Why didn't I get called?"

"Mrs. Tripp had orders to call Rita if anything at all happened. I guess she was expecting something. You ask Rita."

There were a dozen pies on the big long gray table.

"How they doing out there, Matilda?"

The cook stopped what she was doing and looked at me. "Terrible. This is not Thanksgiving. If I look at those children I will cry," she said.

I saw Rita later. "What happened with the boss last night?" I asked. Rita shut her eyes and shook her head. Then she began the story of what she'd gone through Thanksgiving Eve.

Jacqueline had arrived that night, a bit unexpectedly in that no one had been certain there would be a Thanksgiving at Hyannis Port. Matilda had even wondered if she should plan to give the turkeys away. Robert Kennedy and his wife had decided not to come up to Hyannis Port, I'm sure figuring that the big family gathering without his brother would be too painful. He had looked drained and exhausted when we saw him on the TV, and the staff was concerned that he might collapse. Anyway, Robert and Ethel had gone instead to Florida.

Rita said she was in Mr. Kennedy's bedroom when she heard shouting downstairs. Not shouting exactly, the nurse said, but voices loud enough to attract Mr. Kennedy's attention so that he wanted her to find out what was going on. Both the nurse and Mr. Kennedy had recognized Jacqueline's voice right away.

Rita said she heard Jacqueline say, "I'm here to see Grandpa. No, I'm not upset. I'll rest after I see Grandpa. Please, please leave me alone. I'm fine. I just want to see Grandpa."

The nurse went out to the hallway. She wasn't certain about the other voice. The nurse was trying to find out what was going on downstairs when Jacqueline came running up. The First Lady was alone.

Jacqueline said she had come to see Grandpa. Rita told her that he was awake in his room.

Then Rita noticed that Jacqueline was holding a folded Stars and Stripes. Just before she went into her father-in-law's room, Jacqueline told the nurse, "Mrs. Dallas, this is Grandpa's," and handed the flag to Rita. "It was Jack's," Jacqueline went on. "I want you to keep it, and when I leave, please give it to him. I can't, Mrs. Dallas, but I want him to have it. It's his. Will you give it to him for me? After I'm gone?"

Mr. Kennedy's nurse nodded to Mrs. Kennedy that she would do as Jacqueline asked, hardly able to keep from crying. Then the president's widow asked in that soft voice of hers for Rita to come into the room with her.

Jacqueline pulled a footstool next to his bed, sat down, and began telling Mr. Kennedy everything that had happened since she and the president left Washington for Texas. Rita said Jacqueline's voice never cracked and that Mr. Kennedy kept his eyes on her.

Rita said she was standing near the door at Jacqueline's request. She guessed that Jacqueline wanted her there in case what she had to tell the Chief became too much for him. When Jacqueline had apparently finished, she said, "I'm going home now, Grandpa. I'm very tired, but I'll be over tomorrow to have Thanksgiving dinner with you." Rita said Jacqueline kissed Mr. Kennedy on each eyelid. "Sleep well, dear Grandpa," Jacqueline said.

Leaving the room, the First Lady asked Rita to walk down the hallway to the head of the stairs. "Is Grandpa all right?" Jacqueline asked. Rita told her that Mr. Kennedy was doing well. "Did he see it on television?" Jacqueline asked. Rita said the Chief had not wanted to watch TV. "Did he read the papers?" Jacqueline asked. Rita told her that Mr. Kennedy had glanced at the front page of the newspaper, but she did not think Mr. Kennedy had read it.

"Then perhaps you were right," Jacqueline told the nurse. "Perhaps he was waiting to hear it from me. Oh, thank God, thank God I came."

Rita said Jacqueline appeared very tired. The last thing she said to the nurse was a request to let her know when she'd given Mr. Kennedy the flag.

Then Rita went back to Mr. Kennedy's room. He was staring at the ceiling, she said. She brought him his son's flag. "The First Lady wants you to have your son's flag," Rita said. She told him it was John Kennedy's coffin flag that Jacqueline had given his father.

She laid the triangle of folded cloth on the bed next to him and Mr. Kennedy touched it gently, then motioned Rita to put it on his little desk, which she did. Then Rita said she sat in a chair in the bedroom and waited for Mr. Kennedy to fall asleep.

She said she left her shift and Bea Tripp, the night nurse, took over. But Rita said she was so afraid that the ordeal Mr. Kennedy had just gone through might trouble him during the night, she made sure to tell Bea to call if anything went wrong. Rita didn't want to take any chances.

Rita's phone rang at two in the morning. It was Mrs. Tripp, and she needed Rita immediately.

The night nurse had heard Mr. Kennedy screaming. When she ran into his room she found him sitting up in his bed, still screaming, and the most awful look of fright in his eyes, Rita said.

Draped over him like a blanket was the Stars and Stripes that had covered John Kennedy's casket during the funeral. Rita said she yanked the coffin flag off him and hid it. Then they calmed him down.

"Can you believe it, Frank?" Rita asked.

"Who in Christ's name put that flag on him?" I asked Rita.

"Ann," Rita said.

"What!"

"Frank, I don't know why she did it. When we told her what she had done she looked confused. It took her a minute to realize what she'd done."

"But why?" I asked.

Rita shook her head. "Ann checked him before she went to bed. I guess she thought he might be cold, so she put the flag over him."

"And he didn't have an attack when he saw it over him?"

"No. He was screaming like an insane man. He was petrified," Rita said, "but evidently he didn't have an attack."

I was shaking my head now. "How could he go through something terrible like that and not have a heart attack, but then have one when he's sleeping peacefully with nothing bothering him?" I asked.

"I don't know, Frank. But Mr. Kennedy is still very strong. If he could go through all this, you know he is very strong."

"Rita, how long can he live?"

"As long as he keeps on fighting, Frank. And you know what a fighter he is," Rita Dallas said.

"Hello, Miss Shaw. How are you?" I greeted the nanny.

"Fine, Frank. And you?" the gray-haired Englishwoman asked.

"Pretty good."

"A trying time, hasn't it been?"

"Yes it has. How are the children?"

"It has been hardest for Caroline. She understands so much. John . . . well, he is younger. He thinks that now it's over his father will be . . ." Maud Shaw took a second

229

to collect herself. She bit her lip ". . . coming home now."

"Would you like me to play with him for a while?"

"Yes, Frank. I think that should be good for him," she said.

I played with John-John. He had a toy he wanted to show me. He was so intent in his playing that for a few minutes I forgot about the last seven days. I told myself, If he begins to cry and ask about his father, then you can tell him that your father left you, too. Maybe he will understand, I thought, but then caught myself. Of course he could never understand that. Not old enough yet to understand death, how could he understand a grown man telling him that, when he was a boy, he never had a father at all?

"Maybe we will have a movie later," I told the president's son.

His eyes danced. "Bambi! Bambi!" little John Kennedy said.

"We'll see," I said.

Then I thought: Not *Bambi*, not that movie. Where the hunters shoot the big deer.

Then the mail started coming. America was sending condolences to the Kennedys.

"Mrs. Kennedy, there is quite a bit of mail coming now. People are sending, you know, condolences," I said.

She winced.

"What should I do with it?"

"Give it to my secretary," she said.

"Mrs. Kennedy, I think you should understand that there is a lot of mail. Thousands and thousands of letters a day. The O'Neils are swamped."

"Oh, my," she said. "How will I ever be able to answer each letter? Oh, Frank, we will just have to put it all in boxes for the time being."

"All right."

"They loved Jack, didn't they?" she said. She tried to smile.

The weekend after Thanksgiving Richard Cardinal Cushing visited the big house. He had come to read Mr.

Kennedy the eulogy he had delivered for his old friend's son. I was not in the house for the reading, but the maids said it sounded like a chainsaw in Mr. Kennedy's room as Cardinal Cushing gave the eulogy.

Someone had hung the Stars and Stripes in the living room.

"What's that flag doing there?" I asked Dora.

"Don't ask me," she said.

"Is that the . . . ?"

"That's his flag."

"Who the hell hung it?"

"Don't ask me, Frank."

President Kennedy's coffin flag hung on a wall in the room for a few days until Mrs. Kennedy ordered it down because she could not bear the sight of it any longer. It was folded and wrapped, then put away, up in the attic on Mrs. Kennedy's orders, with the rest of her keepsakes. And it stayed hidden there, another soft package wrapped in brown paper.

34

"If my husband should die, we wouldn't be able to keep you on, Frank."

I was driving her to morning mass at Palm Beach in the Chrysler when she said it. Said it for the first time.

If she'd stabbed me in the back with a knife I would not have been more surprised, or hurt.

I kept quiet.

"We just could not afford your salary," she said, more slowly than before.

She is waiting for you to say something, I told myself. But do not give her the satisfaction.

I stayed silent.

Nor did Mrs. Kennedy say anything more.

She let herself out of the car. I watched her walk toward the church. I thought, I hope that made you feel real good.

Instead of coffee at Green's drugstore I went over to O'Hara's. I could get a drink in O'Hara's, even at seven in the morning. I could get a drink in O'Hara's anytime. O'Hara's was my kind of church.

I asked for a Scotch and water.

I drank slowly. I kept thinking about what Rose Kennedy had said, repeating her words over and over. I got madder and madder.

Could not afford your salary? How many thousands a week were they spending on Mr. Kennedy, with all the nurses, the medicine, the expensive specialists, another

232

male aide when they could get one who'd stick with the job? How much?

They pay me $100 a week, and she's telling me that the Kennedys can not *afford* to pay for a chauffeur?

"Give me a double Scotch. No ice," I said.

"What's a chauffeur do?" I asked the bartender as he put the drink in front of me. We were alone. He had been washing glasses.

"Drive a car, Frank. Right?"

"Right," I said.

"Right," he said

"Bet your ass," I said. "Now is a chauffeur also supposed to be a projectionist, as good as a professional one? Or a part-time gardener? A baby-sitter? A goddam bus driver who has to listen to kids whine about how goddamn wonderful they are because they are Kennedys?"

"Hey, Frank," the bartender said, "take it easy."

"Or the pool cleaner? The mailman? Errand boy? And do the food shopping like a maid?" I was counting the jobs with my fingers. "Huh?" I was running out of fingers. "I ask you," I said.

"Ask for a damn raise," he said.

"Oh, I will! I'll ask for a big goddam raise," I said, "And another thing. Is it supposed to include waking up in the middle of the fucking night and running over to save her husband?"

"Now that should be extra," he said. The bartender was playing the game bartenders are so good at. "You don't need them, Frank. There's plenty of decent people in Palm Beach always looking for help," he said.

"Don't give me your bartender sympathy bit. These are the Kennedys. These aren't some rich bastards with a shirt factory in Chicago and a big mansion in Palm Beach to show off. This is the president's family I'm talking about here."

"Not anymore it isn't," he said.

"I would like very much another Scotch but this time skip the water," I said.

"You want water on the side?"

"There is plenty of ice cubes left in the glass," I said.

"It's getting late, isn't it, Frank?"

I had an ice cube in my mouth, sucking it. I let it slide down my tongue into the glass. I thought about what time it must be as I took the glass from my lips. "She can stand on that sidewalk all day, far as I'm concerned. The way I feel now she can hitchhike her ass home."

"Be kind to Rose now," he said.

"You don't understand one bit," I said.

Then I wondered if I understood anything myself.

"She's been through hell, hasn't she?" he said.

"The whole country's been through hell," I said.

We stopped talking. He kept on washing glasses and I sucked down an ice cube until it felt like a cold Lifesaver. She must be in agony. She's torturing herself over him, I told myself. Still, is that an excuse for her to talk to me like that? Why couldn't she simply tell me that when Mr. Kennedy dies, then she will not want a chauffeur anymore and that she will give me a good recommendation and maybe even help me find a new job? Why does she have to hand me that line? The Kennedys do not have enough money to have a chauffeur! What kind of chickenshit excuse is that?

I was at the car when she came out of church. She got in and smiled. Already she had forgotten, I was sure. I gave her a quick look in the rearview mirror. I was talking to myself now, in my mind. I figured if she said it again I was going to jump down her throat. I thought, The next time the alarm goes off in the night, go in and wake her up and tell her that you forgot how to run the oxygen and she'd better do it because if she didn't her husband would be dead in two minutes.

No, you had not better tell her that. Just let it be. Let it slide. You are not the only one she has said something hurtful to. And did not mean it. You know the way she says what's on her tongue and then regrets it later. Like the time she ranted on about how people with swollen joints and knuckles made her ill; how grotesque it was. Then she caught herself, but it was too late because Mr. Kennedy was yelling at her to get out of his bedroom and hitting his good hand against the side of his wheelchair, he was so angry at her. Sure, he thought she was saying it in front of him on purpose. She'd almost cried later she was so sorry, but it was too late then.

But I could not put what she'd said and the way she'd said it out of my mind. It festered inside me for the rest of the day.

At dusk I hopped on Captain Frank's Lambretta and drove to the yacht club on the other side of the Intercoastal. The cool air felt good as I steered the motor scooter, and the ride helped clear my head.

The Lambretta had been parked in the lot, which meant Captain Frank was on the *Marlin*. The *Marlin* was a good refuge. No one would ever come looking for you on the *Marlin*. Besides, I liked to think that all Captain Frank had to do was start the engine and we could escape. But it was enough of an escape that night to sit on the boat and listen to the water lap the hull.

"You know, François," I said, "I never saw her cry when the president was killed. Or afterward, for that matter."

"She never will, François," he said.

"Why?"

"Because she is afraid to," he said.

"Maybe she cried in her bedroom. She went in there, and maybe she cried when the door was closed."

"Maybe," Captain Frank said.

"You know, I felt a bit foolish crying when she wasn't crying."

"Is she bothering you?" he said.

"No. Just something she let slip on the way to mass."

"Did you ever think that maybe she might need someone to bother? You are there, so she bothers you."

"No, I never thought that. I don't believe it either."

"When some women get old and the children are not around anymore, and they can't bother their children, sometimes they have to find someone else to bother. Yup, they do. She's a mother. She's a good woman."

"Have you ever thought about what might happen when he dies?" I asked. "Do you think the family will keep *Marlin*?"

"Nope," he said. "Haven't we been over this before?"

"What will you do then?"

"You worry too much."

"You are sure they will not keep his boat?"

"Yup. She never uses it. She's not much for boats."

"How many times has she been on it with him?"

"I could count them on one hand," he said.

"But boats are not like cars. You came with the boat, so you'll have a home with the *Marlin* no matter what."

"This is just a boat. My home's in West Barnstable, you know that."

"I never had a home. Well, I never owned a home. You think it might be time for me to get a home someplace?"

"Maybe she'll give the *Marlin* to you," he said.

We laughed at that.

Then I asked him, "Why do you think she will not cry for the president?"

"She keeps it bottled up. If she started crying she is afraid she could never stop. So she won't start."

"I think I will ask for a raise," I said.

"Good luck," he said.

"I'll ask for a raise and that will straighten everything out. Either I'll get it or I won't, and, either way, it will fix things."

"What have you been doing today?" he asked.

"Painting the house. It never ends, you know that."

"They should tear the damn thing down. It's more trouble than it's worth. That old damp rot. It's like gangrene eating away. When a boat gets it, she's done. It's in that ark of a house. Every year it gets worse," the yacht captain said.

That winter's move to Palm Beach had made me realize how tough the Kennedy job was on my wife and son. Neither liked having to move back and forth, and each seasonal move seemed worse than the one before. They had come actually to dread moving to Palm Beach. For my son Bruce it meant switching grammar schools in the middle of the year. After Bruce protested that the Palm Beach public school was two years behind his school on Cape Cod, I checked with the Palm Beach school principal. He claimed it was impossible for another public school to have done two years earlier the grade-level work Bruce

236

was doing in his school now. Then I talked again with Bruce. Then I went back to the principal. My son was right.

The Palm Beach school wasn't sure what to do about the problem. One solution was for us to keep Bruce in the school on the Cape, but that meant my wife would have to stay in Hyannis Port.

One day Mrs. Kennedy happened to ask how Bruce liked school. It sounded as if she was trying to make small talk—as if she wasn't genuinely interested—nevertheless I appreciated her asking. Her politeness gave me my opportunity.

"He doesn't like it, Mrs. Kennedy. His school back on the Cape is two years ahead of the one here. Besides, he's thirteen now, and he's got friends and hates leaving them. My wife isn't too keen about the whole thing either."

"Oh, well. We had to transfer Ted a great deal when he was a boy. When Mr. Kennedy was ambassador. One school right after another. I think it helps a young boy learn to develop friendships quickly," she said. "I believe it strengthens character."

"I think it stinks," I said, close to telling her that it was an uncertain future that made the kids back at the foster home cry at night.

"Of course, they could stay on the Cape. If you want to pay for the heat in the garage apartment, Frank."

"Maybe that's what it will come to," I said.

I was telling myself it might come to an end if she didn't give me the raise I was going to ask for. I had decided to wait until we were back on Cape Cod, figuring that wherever and whenever I told her she would protest, forcing me to quit then and there, and I didn't want to be stranded in Palm Beach.

"Won't be long now, Chief. The teams will be starting spring training in a few days," I said.

His eyes caught fire at that.

"Chief, do you think I should leave?"

He squinted at me.

"Leave. You know, quit the Kennedys and get another job?"

"No."

"You're certain?"

"Naaaah. Gaaaaaah."

"Mrs. Kennedy doesn't really need a chauffeur."

"Noooooooo! Nooooooooooo!"

I could see him getting angry now. He was glowering.

"You're afraid she'll get in another accident if she drives herself?"

He said no quietly. I thought I saw a smirk on his lips.

"Oh, you mean you just want somebody around for her to bother, huh?"

"Ahhhhhhhhhhhhhh. Ahhhhhhhh." That got a big smile from him.

"Okay, Chief. I'll stick around," I said. "I won't leave. Unless you ask me to."

35

Those Palm Beach days had a deadening sameness about them, so that now, trying to remember, much remains vague and remote to me, as forgotten as one of those old movies I showed the Kennedys a long time ago. Somehow the warm, bright sunny days did not help. Maybe I needed a real tough winter to be sad in.

And I did not want to spy on their sadness. What was there to see anyway? The deep creases furrowing the Chief's face and the persistent wetness at the corners of his eyes as though troublesome sties plagued him. Mrs. Kennedy accepted the medical explanation that the water in her husband's eyes was a condition of his stroke, a matter of muscle control.

Bullshit. He was weeping for his dead son. It was not that Mrs. Kennedy denied her husband's sorrow, it was that she would not admit to anyone that Joseph P. Kennedy would allow himself to cry that long, even for a son. He was supposed to have been too strong for that once, so now it was an uncontrollable reflex that caused him to cry. At least that's what she told anybody who asked after Mr. Kennedy.

I had turned her off after she handed me her threat about my future, that she planned to fire me when Mr. Kennedy died. I despised her for the way she'd done it—from the backseat of the car.

She had her own style of suffering, and she did it

silently. And when silence wouldn't work, she tried to recapture in brief conversations in the back of the Chrysler on trips to mass the great fun the family had had back in the thirties.

We were all plain numb. The days drifted. I let myself listen for the clatter of a helicopter I knew would never come. Sometimes I'd head for the secret service trailer, but it was gone.

John Kennedy's death left his family very empty. And beyond the loss of a son, a brother, a husband, there was something else. The excitement was gone. There was no blue presidential flag flying in the wind. What they had had, the newspapers and the television reporters and the new historians reminded the Kennedys, was Camelot. Now there was a Broadway musical of the same name. The audiences cheered, laughed, cried, applauded when the curtain came down. But what did the actors do when it was over? The Kennedys kept on pretending, and the reason, as I think on it now, was to distract them from the other, certain truth, which was that they were on their own. The old man could not be their strength now. He was crippled and speechless and suffering. But he was not dying.

Yet they had been given time to accept that he would die. Hadn't Mrs. Kennedy picked out the dress for his funeral, with the terrible irony then of having to wear it to her son's funeral first? That winter I learned that just minutes before Dora and I came up the stairs with the news of the shooting in Dallas, Ann had handed Rita an envelope of instructions about what to do if Mr. Kennedy died—what undertaker to call. (Ann was getting ready to leave for a Thanksgiving visit with her relatives in Detroit.)

If there was to have been a Kennedy funeral, it was supposed to have been Mr. Kennedy's.

A wild scene in the driveway. Confusion. The Palm Beach police have come to the Kennedys' and there are secret service agents with them. They have caught an intruder. He has been searched. Shackled at the ankles, the intruder stands expressionless. And while the police prepare to haul him away, I steer the Chrysler through the maze of parked police cars on my way to the golf course with Mrs.

Kennedy. They want her out of the house in case there's a bomb in it.

Rita said she discovered the intruder sneaking through the house. Is it true? What's going on here anyway?

"Do they know anything about the guy, Mrs. Kennedy?" I ask.

"Not a thing," she says dryly. I knew she didn't wish to talk about it, but I was curious.

"Where did Rita see him, anyway?"

"The nurse said she saw the man sneak across the patio and then enter the house. When she asked him what he was doing in the house, he told her he was a repairman. Evidently the nurse did not believe him, because she called the police. I was napping of course when the ruckus was going on. I'm certain that it will prove to be a mistake of some kind. Perhaps the fellow did not have the proper identification.

"It frightened Ann," she went on. She was silent for a minute, then said, "But the nurse was correct to call the police." Mrs. Kennedy still could not bring herself to call her husband's nurse by her real name, the name of the city where her son was killed.

"But we can't let these things upset us, Frank. We mustn't let things such as this distract us," she said.

I never found out the identity of the intruder Rita caught in the Kennedy house, and so far as I know Rita never did either. Nothing ever appeared in the papers, and little was said around the house. Rita claimed that one of the security men told her later the man had "connections in Dallas." I always thought if he was a Palm Beach jewel thief, as some speculated, he sure picked the wrong house when he came to 1095 North Ocean Boulevard.

Rita's intruder had been discovered not long after we arrived at Palm Beach. It is one of those scenes I have only a hazy recollection of, and it seems so bizarre now that I wonder why it is not more vivid in my memory. Looking back, I recall that there was a tacit understanding among the staff to play the whole thing down, even to it being a figment of Rita's imagination. It was better to block it out. What you have to understand is that, in those first weeks after Dallas, the Kennedys knew what the

241

world was thinking—that maybe Lee Harvey Oswald had not been alone. The family sensed that if they let themselves think it, if they heard any of that kind of talk coming from the staff, then it could drive them stark raving mad wondering if the next gunman might be after one of them.

And of course now the Kennedys were no longer entitled to all those secret service men guarding, as it were, a dead president's relatives. Mr. Kennedy's personal agent, Ham Brown, was reassigned, and we all missed the likable, good-humored agent, no one more than the Chief.

It was not long after the intruder incident that Mrs. Kennedy came to me and asked if I would watch her whenever she swam in the ocean. I did not tell her that I had been doing just that all along because Mr. Kennedy had ordered me to that first summer. Then I learned that she had also asked her secretary to watch her when I was not around.

Rita claimed that Mrs. Kennedy expressed concern that, if she suddenly disappeared, her children would never know what had happened to her, and would worry.

Newspapers were scattered all over Mr. Kennedy's bedroom floor. A tightly crumpled ball of newspaper lay at his feet. He sat motionless in his wheelchair as I walked into the room, and did not turn around to see who had entered.

"What's the matter, Chief?" I began. "Some of your stocks take a tumble?"

"Nooooooo. Ahhhhhhh. Noooooooooo! Nooooooo! Noo-ooo!" He was trying to kick the ball of newspaper with his good foot. I figured I'd hit a raw nerve about the stock-market report. Then he suddenly became quiet, tightened his lips, and stared blankly at the wall.

I figured that the best thing was to leave.

"What's the hair across his ass for today?" I asked Rita.

"It's Bobby again," the nurse said. "Every time he sees mention in the papers or sees it on the news about him climbing Mount Kennedy he just goes wild. He's furious at him about this mountain-climbing thing."

"This mountain-climbing thing" was Bobby's well-publicized attempt to be the first to climb the fourteen-thousand-foot Yukon peak recently renamed after his brother.

"You think he doesn't want the attorney general doing it?" I asked.

"Of course not," Rita said.

"Maybe the old man thinks Bobby will get hurt. It's a good way to kill yourself, isn't it?" I said.

"It is something much deeper than that, I think," Rita said.

Rita was right. Mr. Kennedy stayed in a blue funk for days. And when Robert Kennedy came to his father's house, the attorney general looked absolutely exhausted. He seemed to be in pain. Bobby had never had the best posture in the first place, but now he walked slumped over like an old man. Part of his agony, Rita said, was the way his father was treating him over the Mount Kennedy climb.

Bobby brought back a small rock sealed in Lucite from the top of Mount Kennedy, as a gift for his father. But the Chief tossed it across his bedroom.

Rita had a talk with the boss about that. I don't know what she told him, but most likely it was something about how Mr. Kennedy should be proud of his son for being brave enough to climb Mount Kennedy as a tribute to his brother. Whatever Rita said, it worked. After their talk the Chief kept the piece of Mount Kennedy in his room, and now there was a sliver of happiness in Robert Kennedy's blue eyes.

This time Mrs. Kennedy wanted the Christmas tree taken down Christmas morning, while she was at mass. She did not want to see the big tree in the room when she returned, she said. What was there to celebrate this Christmas? Actually, everyone seemed just as glad to get it over with, so that they could be numb again. Once more the big tree was hauled, decorations and all, out of the house and left on the tennis court, where it could be stripped of its decorations on a sunny day.

* * *

"I want you to take these old books and these other things down to the charity store and donate them on behalf of the Kennedy family," Rose Kennedy instructed me.

Old books is right, I thought. And the rest of the stuff was worthless too, just old Florida junk.

I rated the charity donation assignment just below the toy refund trips to Worth Avenue and what had to be first on my list of unpleasant tasks: having to take clothes or lingerie back to an expensive shop for a refund.

The charity store manager inspected the Kennedy offering. "I can't use any of this junk," he said. "The books are mildewed and look how the bindings are all broken. The other stuff is kindling."

"Look," I said, "understand my problem. I cannot tell Rose Kennedy that she couldn't even give the stuff away, because she is not going to believe me. Now tell me what it would be worth if it was in decent shape?"

"If that knicknack shelf wasn't all busted I could get five for it. Total? Maybe twelve bucks, if the books were good," he said.

"Fine," I said. "Now you give me an official receipt for twelve dollars and put the Kennedy name on it," I said.

He was beginning to protest and started shaking his head.

"Because if you do not give me the receipt," I continued, "I will leave all this stuff here and just might come back with even more stuff worse than this. But if you give me the receipt, I will take this junk with me," I said.

"You got your receipt," he said. "Just get it out of here."

I waited for Mrs. Kennedy to ask how it went at the charity place. "Did you go there, Frank?" she finally asked. I told her I did. "Did you get a receipt for the value?" she asked. I said yes. "Then please give it to me, Frank, because Mr. Walsh needs it for our tax deductions."

"What am I supposed to do when I open the door for him, Ann, whistle 'Hail to the Chief'?"

"Now cut that out, Frank," Mr. Kennedy's niece said.

I laughed. Everyone was taking the visit of President Lyndon B. and Lady Bird Johnson too seriously, I thought.

Mrs. Kennedy was tense, and that made everyone else in the house tense. I found the whole thing pretty funny.

It was difficult to tell whether Mrs. Kennedy was nervous about greeting the new president in her house, knowing Lyndon Johnson and his wife were coming to pay their official respects to the family and that everyone would be uncomfortable, or because she was afraid that Mr. Kennedy might start screaming at the tall Texan.

Mr. Kennedy had refused to get out of bed that morning. He was in his stubborn mood, and I told both Ann and Rita that if they tried to force him to get dressed they were in for a long battle. "If he doesn't want to meet Lyndon Johnson then what's the big deal?" I said. I could tell from the looks I got back that Mr. Kennedy's nurse and niece did not share my opinion. It seemed simple to me. All Mrs. Kennedy had to do was excuse Mr. Kennedy by telling the Johnsons that her husband wasn't feeling well. It wouldn't be a lie, either. Mr. Kennedy couldn't stomach Lyndon Johnson.

When I opened the door for President Lyndon B. Johnson, Lady Bird flashed a smile, but the president looked to me like he'd rather be anywhere else except 1095 North Ocean. He had Pierre Salinger with him, and the reporters were waiting outside in the driveway.

Mrs. Kennedy greeted the Johnsons graciously.

"Your house here reminds me of a nice big ol' Mexican ranchero, Mrs. Kennedy," Lyndon Johnson drawled.

"Actually it is Spanish colonial. The house was designed by Addison Mizner," I heard Mrs. Kennedy reply as I began to withdraw. I had decided I didn't want to be in the house in case there was a scene with Mr. Kennedy.

President and Mrs. Johnson visited for about thirty minutes. Mrs. Kennedy seemed in very good spirits after her guests left.

"How'd it go with the Chief?" I asked Rita.

"Mr. Kennedy refused to even look at him," the nurse said.

"You mean Mrs. Kennedy brought the Johnsons to him?"

"Yes."

"Why did she do that? She's lucky he didn't start yelling at him. Why didn't she just let it slide?"

Rita shrugged.

Then I smiled. "So he wouldn't even look at Johnson, huh? What did he do, just stare at the wall?"

Rita nodded.

"I would have liked to see that. Good for the Chief."

I thought about President Johnson's visit quite often in the following days. Mrs. Kennedy had to know there was no love lost between her husband and Lyndon Johnson. At the 1960 convention Johnson had called Joseph P. Kennedy "vicious." It had been in all the newspapers. And certainly Mrs. Kennedy must have known that there was a feud going on right now between her son the attorney general and the new president. If it had been up to me I would have told Lyndon Johnson that Mr. Kennedy wasn't feeling very well. President Johnson would have gotten the message.

President Johnson's visit got in the newspapers and on TV, and turned out to be the big event of that season at 1095 North Ocean. After late February, following the visit, the days flew by. Pat Lawford came and spent a lot of time with her parents, which was better medicine for her father's spirits than anything the doctors could prescribe. And with Peter Lawford at Palm Beach so often late that winter, I had my own good medicine. It just didn't seem right to me that the actor should have to drink alone in the morning, so after I took Mrs. Kennedy home I'd drive over to the McMachos' and wake up Peter Lawford and go with him for a Bloody Mary. Back on the Cape the previous summer, the waitresses at Luigi's had begged me to bring Peter Lawford in—the girls were dying to meet him—so I had asked the movie star if he'd do me the favor of dropping by the place sometime, just so I could get those college girls off my back. He had gone right over to Luigi's with me, and of course as soon as he'd walked in the waitresses had gone into ecstasy.

Rose Kennedy flew to Paris in the spring. Before leaving, she went up to Boston to visit her mother, whose eyesight was failing. Mrs. Fitzgerald was ninety-eight, and her daughter knew there would not be many more visits.

246

The French had fallen in love with John and Jacqueline Kennedy when they'd visited, and there were memorials to be dedicated there for the dead American president. Mrs. Kennedy went to participate.

Jean Smith came to Palm Beach. The youngest daughter, Jean was less flamboyant than Pat and Eunice. She and her husband, Steve, did not like being in the limelight as much as some of the other Kennedys, but Jean Kennedy Smith had a quiet strength about her and, like her sister Pat, was a tonic for her father that winter.

I made plans to move all the cars. It would be easier moving back to the Cape this spring because Mrs. Kennedy wouldn't be around with her last-minute errands.

I'd be ready to ask for a raise at Hyannis when she returned from her trip to France.

36

I waited until Mrs. Kennedy was alone in her little office at the Hyannis Port house. I knew exactly what I was going to say. For weeks I had been rehearsing my lines. My first notion had been to ask for the raise when we were in the car, but I'd decided against that, remembering how trapped I had felt when she stung me with that warning about my job. This was going to be straight business, I decided, and her office was the proper place to conduct it.

"Mrs. Kennedy, I've been with the family now for three years and I am requesting an increase in my salary," I said in one breath. I knew that if I didn't come right out with it and she got a hint of what I was after, she'd change the subject.

She fluttered her eyelids at first, but I kept on, because I knew that if I even paused for a second I might never finish. "When Mr. Ford hired me as chauffeur he did not explain all the other things I was expected to do. Since I began working for you my duties have increased. If you want me to stay on I will need to earn more."

I handed her a piece of paper with the amount written on it. "It's all here on this paper, Mrs. Kennedy."

She took the paper but did not look at it. "Oh, well, my, this comes as a surprise. How much are we paying you now, Frank?" she asked.

"One hundred dollars a week."

"And that's not adequate? Your accommodations are taken care of, still that is not adequate?"

"Not for what I do, no."

"And how much do you think would be adequate?"

"One hundred and sixty-nine dollars a week." I wanted to take home $150, which before withholding and taxes required $169.

She smiled. "I see you have it figured out. How did you arrive at that figure?"

"I know what I need to clear. It's on the paper, Mrs. Kennedy."

"I think that is far too much, Frank. You know I don't take care of salaries myself. I'll have to discuss this with Tom Walsh. But, dear heart, I think that is much too much for a chauffeur."

"I have my resignation typed out if you need it, Mrs. Kennedy," I said.

She fluttered her eyelids again.

I didn't like that dear-heart business at all. That was the tip-off. She had used it the time of her little warning about not being able to afford to keep me on. I thought, Here's your out right now, Mrs. Kennedy.

I'd met Tom Walsh and I liked him. He had replaced Johnny Ford after Johnny died (if he were alive, I knew, I'd get the raise), and we got along fine. When I put in for out-of-pocket expenses or money I'd loaned the Kennedys—ten bucks here, a twenty there—I always got a quick check from Park Avenue. But I had a feeling that Mrs. Kennedy was going to tell the Park Avenue office that she was against it. I figured it would be the same if I'd asked for an extra five dollars.

Because I was fairly certain that Mrs. Kennedy was not going to approve my raise, I had scouted other jobs. I had friends on the Cape now. A job driving a bus on the Boston-to-Hyannis run was a possibility. And a friend told me that I might be able to get a job as a guard at the Barnstable House of Correction. My wife and son wanted to stay on the Cape, and so did I, but if I could not find work on Cape Cod I knew I could always go back to the Combat Zone. Those were my kind of people, anyway. Real people you could talk to without having to hide your feelings.

The next day she accepted my resignation. I wanted too much, she said. She understood that I would need a few weeks to move and wanted to be very understanding about that. Then she surprised me. She said that Park Avenue wanted *me* to interview applicants for the chauffeur's job and pick my own replacement. I felt like telling her to tell Park Avenue that she could pick her own chauffeur, but kept it to myself. There would be no great rush, Mrs. Kennedy assured me. As soon as I found my replacement, I could leave.

That night at Luigi's I got a terrible temptation to choose a real lulu for the chauffeur's job. Maybe a cigar-smoking alcoholic.

The applicants started calling me. I didn't know where they came from, whether Park Avenue took out an ad or it was just a case of word-of-mouth, but they started flocking to the compound. Some were professional chauffeurs. Some were bums. Some were just curious.

None of them, once they got the full description, wanted the job.

I'd go into my spiel about what the Kennedy chauffeur's responsibilities were. You drive Mrs. Kennedy to morning mass, I'd begin. That means a six A.M. wakeup. Then you take her home. You pick up the mail. Then you wash all the main car. After you finish with that car, you wash all the other cars. How many cars depends on how many Kennedys are at the place. When the cars are done you clean the swimming pool. If the gardener needs help, you help him. If the maids have errands for you, you do them. You pick up medicine for Mr. Kennedy. You do the food shopping for the cook. If Mrs. Kennedy wants a ride to go shopping, you drop everything and drive her. She likes to be called Madame, remember that. After lunch you show Mr. Kennedy a movie. If they need help taking Mr. Kennedy down to the pool for his exercise, you help with that. And you shine shoes, you wash windows, you paint.

By the time I got to the exercise part with the Chief, the professional chauffeurs had already turned it down. It was the movie projector that squashed it for others, even though I explained that Wilbert and I had worked out a new system whereby whoever showed the film got fifteen dollars if the movie ran past midnight, and it was easy enough to run the movie over the deadline. So they could pick up extra money that way.

The job sounded like a lot of trouble, some of them said. The boldest asked, "If it is such a good job, then how come you're leaving?" I answered with a smile.

The final straw for those still interested came when I explained how they would have to be Mr. Kennedy's aide on the regular aide's day off, which was Sunday. And I told them that the aides quit quite often, so they should be prepared to be Mr. Kennedy's male nurse too, until a new aide was hired. That meant giving Mr. Kennedy a sponge bath in bed, I explained. And it meant doing what he wanted you to do. "Of course he cannot talk, but you'll learn how to understand him," I'd tell the aspiring Kennedy chauffeur.

There were no takers.

And so I informed Mr. Kennedy's New York office that none of the men I had interviewed wanted the job, not after all the duties had been explained. After all, it was only fair for the new man to have a complete understanding of the job because, otherwise, he would probably quit in a few weeks and then they'd have to start searching all over again. I also said that I did not want to spend too much more time interviewing job applicants because I had my own life to live.

I got the raise, all the way up to $169.

Things went back to normal.

I don't think Mr. Kennedy ever knew about the incident. Certainly I never told the Chief.

I decided to wait a while before springing my other surprise on Mrs. Kennedy.

The night nurse heard Mrs. Kennedy, up in the attic, pacing back and forth from one end of the house to the other. Some nights the pacing continued until early in the morning. Mrs. Kennedy must have worn shoes instead of slippers, the nurse said, because slippers would not click like that on a wooden floor.

Her back-and-forth walking was not loud and her footsteps beat an almost rhythmic tap-tap-tap so constant and

251

steady that the nurses said after a while they forgot about her, the same way you no longer hear a loud clock ticking unless you listen hard for it. It was when she stopped walking, however, then started again, then stopped, that her movements got on the nurses' nerves. The tapping came in spurts, as it does when a tree branch hits against a windowpane in a windstorm. When she moved boxes and dragged furniture, thunder rumbled in the attic, and the nurse on duty grew afraid Mrs. Kennedy might disturb her huband's sleep. Other times, when the nurses knew she was still in the attic after a long silence, they wondered if she had fallen asleep. It was a relief when she finally clomped down the stairs and they could hear her, trying to be quiet, as she shut the attic door behind her.

Althought the night walks bothered them, none of the night nurses felt it was her place to mention it to Mrs. Kennedy.

I noticed the attic light a few times myself, and one day I mentioned it to Rita.

"I know, The duty nurse told me. She is still having trouble sleeping."

"Can't you give her something?"

"She doesn't want anything. She's afraid it will make her sleep too long and that she won't be up in time for mass."

"She should be exhausted at night, anyway—after the walks on the beach and the way she swims so hard," I said. "And then all that golf—well, you know the way she plays golf, but it is still a lot of walking. You'd think she'd be tired as hell."

"She knows she's making noise up there," Rita said. "The other day she kidded me about it. She said she was up in the attic at night looking for all that money Mr. Kennedy is supposed to have buried."

I smiled at that, and at the way Rita mimicked Mrs. Kennedy. "She's looking for memories up there, Rita. She's looking at the things that remind her of when she was young and when the children were young and when they were all together. She's looking for the good times to remember. She's told me in the car, 'There are so many good times to rememeber, I do not want to think about the bad times.' "

*   *   *

252

"Frank."

"Yes, Mrs. Kennedy."

"Frank, I just happened to notice that there are far too many lights on in the garage. You are wasting electricity, Frank. You do not need all those lights on now, do you?"

"No, Mrs. Kennedy." Then the line went dead.

"I am buying a little house, Mrs. Kennedy."

She was so silent that I nearly began explaining why I was going to buy the house. But I waited. She is more surprised by this, I was thinking, than she was by the pay-raise.

Finally she said, "I don't think you can do that, Frank."

"I am buying it, Mrs. Kennedy," I replied quietly.

"But I've never had a chauffeur before who lived off the grounds. I want the chauffeur to be close by," she said.

"The house is less than three miles from the compound. I can be there in a couple of minutes."

"I'll have to think it over, Frank."

"Fine, Mrs. Kennedy. But I am buying the house. I am doing it for my wife and son. I'm doing it for myself too," I said.

"Yes, but I'll have to think this over. This is quite a surprise. What would I do if I needed you?"

"I'll be there early in the morning waiting to take you to mass just like always, Mrs. Kennedy. And I'll be right at the house all day. I'll come over to show the movies. And if anybody needs me at night, they can call my house," I said.

My house. It sounded good. It sounded a lot better than "garage apartment." I smiled to myself as I thought, I'll keep on as many lights as I want.

37

Mrs. Kennedy swooped into the kitchen like a hawk. There was a fierce glint in her eyes as she circled around me. "Whose coffee is that, Frank?" she screeched. "Is that my coffee? Is that our coffee? Our coffee that you're drinking!"

I felt my face beginning to flush while she screamed at me. She was pounding the air with her fists. I glanced at Matilda, who was standing at the other end of the big kitchen, where she had frozen when Mrs. Kennedy flew into the room.

Then I looked back at Mrs. Kennedy. Both hands were still clenched in a fist. "Is it Kennedy coffee?" she shouted again, and in that final outburst her voice crumbled.

"Yes," I said. The cup trembled in my hand.

She opened her fists, then pressed both hands palm-down on the tabletop. She paused. "Coffee is very expensive now, you know," she said, her voice much softened. "Isn't it, Matilda? How much does coffee cost a pound now?"

"Frank does the shopping, Madame," Matilda said softly.

"Then I don't have to tell you, Frank, how expensive coffee is, do I?"

Not only was she talking in her normal voice now, she was no longer leaning her palms on the table. She had straightened to her full height and had fixed her eyes on me. "In the future, Frank, you are to bring either your own coffee in a thermos—you can leave it right here in the kitchen; all right, Matilda?—or you can pay for the coffee you drink in my house. Is that understood, Frank?''

"Yes, Mrs. Kennedy.''

"Then I'm clear on that?'' she asked.

She waited for my nod before she spun on her heels and left.

Both the cook and I stood silent. I took a couple of deep breaths to calm down.

"Do you have a dime?'' Matilda asked.

"Don't you start on me too,'' I snapped back.

She smiled. "You don't understand. Give me a dime and we will put it someplace so that if she ever catches you drinking coffee in the kitchen again, I'll point to the little dime and tell her, 'Frank has paid me.' and that will shut her up about this coffee business.''

"Here's my dime,'' I said.

"Ya. Good. We will put the dime so on the counter here, in the back, like this, so no one will know it is here, except you and Matilda.''

"How about a refill now?'' I asked.

Matilda began laughing, and was soon laughing so hard I had to steady her hand when she poured me the second cup.

"That cheap bitch,'' I said.

"Frank!'' Matilda squealed.

"Well, she is. How much is coffee? That takes the cake! You remember that day she flew in here just like that and started plucking strawberries out of the dessert dishes? I could hardly believe my eyes. She was counting every damn berry. Remember that?''

"How could I forget?'' the cook said.

"Matilda?''

"Ya, Frank?''

"Is it true about the springwater? I mean, I've never seen it with my own eyes, but I've heard the girls talk about it. Is it true?''

"Ya.'' Matilda smiled.

"She actually makes them pour the springwater back into the bottle from half-empty table glasses? It's true, then?''

"Ya."

"She's cheap."

"She is very frugal." Matilda smiled.

"She's cheap," I said.

It was about one month after I got my pay-raise when she asked, "How much are we paying you now, dear heart?"

We were riding to church.

"One hundred and sixty-nine dollars a week," I said, giving a quick look at the rearview mirror. "That's gross, Mrs. Kennedy."

"MMMmmmm. Mmmm."

I thought, You didn't have to ask me that. You know it as well as you know what day this is. But you are just not going to let me forget it, are you?

We had been leaving for mass earlier than usual these past few weeks. Mrs. Kennedy said she wanted to get to Saint Francis Xavier well ahead of mass time so she could say a couple of decades of the rosary before mass began.

"Frank, where do you go after you drop me off at mass?"

"To the coffee shop, Mrs. Kennedy."

"How far is that?"

"Around the block. You know, in the West End."

"Do you always go there?"

"Sometimes I go up to the Rotary. Sometimes Mildred's."

"How far is that?"

"Mrs. Kennedy, you know how far it is."

"In miles, how far is it?"

"A mile at the most."

"And back again?"

"Yes, and back again, of course."

"So if it is one mile up and one mile back, that is two miles?"

"Yes."

"Now, how many miles to the gallon does this car get?"

"Fifteen on a trip."

"But less in stop-and-go traffic and short trips?"

"That's right."

"How much does it cost a gallon now, Frank?"

"Thirty cents at the pump but you get it for less through the wholesaler. I always use the pump at the garage."

"I see, Frank."

She must have asked me a half-dozen times that summer how much the family was paying me. Almost always she would pop the question when we were driving to mass.

"One hundred and sixty-nine dollars salary, plus fringe benefits," I would tell her. "I clear one-fifty."

"Fringe benefits?"

"You know, when a movie runs past midnight. I get a bit extra for that. Or like when we're on the road and you buy my lunch, Mrs. Kennedy."

38

I was cleaning the glass in the doll room again. Her grandchildren must have been in here, I was thinking, because the smudged fingerprints were down low, where a small child would reach.

I gazed at the Rose Doll as I polished the glass. . . . Something different, something I couldn't quite fix on . . . what was it? My thoughts went off in different directions. If one of the kids breaks a glass window there'll be hell to pay. She'll murder them. . . . Why do women collect dolls? Maybe for the same reason men put little ships in bottles. . . . But it must be hard for a little girl to see all these beautiful dolls and not be able to touch them, to play with them.

I looked again at the Rose Doll. You have the smile of Mona Lisa, lady, I told myself. Suddenly I had the answer, and as it struck me I stared at the Rose Doll as if seeing her for the first time. Those wide eyes. The hair. That curious smile. It was hard to believe that it had escaped me before. There was a definite resemblance, all right, and I was certain that Rose Kennedy too couldn't have helped notice how much her favorite Rose Doll looked like Jacqueline, her son's widow.

I learned about the plane crash the next morning. Ted Kennedy was in critical condition, the radio said; his back was broken. The pilot of the private plane had been killed instantly, and Eddie Moss, a friend and aide, had died a few hours later. The plane had gone down in drizzle and fog a few minutes before eleven P.M. It was the lead story on the radio news . . . *The stricken senator lies . . . Another near-tragedy for the Kennedy family was apparently averted late last night . . . The twisted Aero Commander . . . Senator Birch Bayh pulled his unconscious Senate colleague from the . . . The youngest brother of slain President John F. Kennedy miraculously escaped death himself last night when the small private plane carrying Massachusetts' junior senator to a victory speech at the state democratic convention in Springfield crashed in a fog-shrouded apple orchard west of . . .*

I turned the radio off. I thought, Sweet mother of God, not again.

"Do you want me to take you up to see Ted, Mrs. Kennedy?" I asked her the moment she stepped out of the house.

"No. Not now. Bobby's there. He'll be all right," she said.

And then I took her to mass.

The Kennedy staff looked at each other in disbelief. It was only seven months ago that the oldest brother had been killed in Dallas; now the youngest had been seriously injured.

"You slept through all the excitement, Frank," Rita said.

"Was there excitement, Rita?"

"It was bedlam at the house. The phone never stopped ringing. I took a call from Secretary McNamara myself."

"How's the Chief?"

"He's fine. He slept through the night. He understands that Ted will be all right."

"Will he, though, Rita?"

"He's young."

"I hear he's got a punctured lung. I read in the newspaper that he cracked a few ribs and there was internal bleeding. What about his broken back?"

"It is not *broken*, Frank. Some vertebrae were crushed."

259

"I read where a doctor says Ted might never walk again." Reading that, I couldn't help recall Mrs. Kennedy's fear that the president's bad back might one day give out so that he would end up in a wheelchair along with his father.

"Ted's young and strong," Rita said.

That afternoon Rita told me how Captain Baird had refused to fly Ted to the convention in the *Caroline* because the Barnstable Municipal Airport was socked in, but Ted had gone ahead anyway and chartered a private plane to fly down and pick him up. Then, the nurse continued, she had been with the crew of the *Caroline* at the Candlelight, having dinner when they got an emergency call. Bobby wanted to fly up to the hospital. The first report was that Ted might not make it.

"Captain Baird drove Bobby up," Rita said.

"What do you mean, Captain Baird *drove* Bobby up?"

"He drove him to Boston because they couldn't get clearance to fly out of Hyannis." Rita said Captain Baird had driven her from the Candlelight to the big house so she could stay with Mr. Kennedy. As soon as she jumped out of the car, Bobby jumped in.

"You sure missed a lot of excitement," she told me.

"Good," I said. "I don't need that kind of excitement."

Mrs. Kennedy planned to visit Ted in the hospital, but then canceled in order to fill in for him at a speaking engagement he had scheduled. Then she made another date to visit Ted, only to learn that her closest friend, Mary Moore, had just died. Again Mrs. Kennedy canceled the hospital visit, this time to attend Mrs. Moore's funeral. "Oh, what will I do, Frank?" she sighed in the car coming home from the funeral. "I will have no one to talk with now." I knew her well enough by now to hear the sincerity in her voice, to know that she meant it. All the way home I kept thinking how sad it was that a woman with so many children and grandchildren, a woman who could have had all the company she wanted, herself a celebrity now, should be so very lonely. But I also knew that she'd keep herself busy. Now that Ted was unable to campaign for reelection, the Kennedy women were ready to do it for him.

The traffic coming out of Boston on the Southeast Expressway was murder—bumper-to-bumper all the way. Ahead, I could see the top of a tow truck and flashing lights. "There must have been an accident, Mrs. Kennedy," I said.

"Is the air-conditioner on, Frank?"

I told her it had been on since she got back in the car in Boston.

"Oh, it's *so* hot today," she said.

"There's a lot of cars on your father's road today, Mrs. Kennedy," I said.

"It's not my father's road, Frank!"

It always got her goat when I called the Southeast Expressway her father's road. And offically it was: The John F. Fitzgerald Highway.

The heat shimmered off the roofs of the cars ahead as we moved at a snail's pace. I was getting impatient to get back to the Cape. A car ahead had overheated and the traffic was squeezing into two lanes.

As soon as the lane opened I floored the Chrysler and in no time we were on 128 in Braintree and heading for Cape Cod. The traffic was still fairly heavy, but moving along at a good clip.

I saw a flash of white in the rearview mirror. What the hell is that? I wondered. Then there was another, like a big white bird flapping in the wind.

A piece of newspaper. I watched as it crumpled and disappeared in the traffic behind us.

Then I heard air rushing as Mrs. Kennedy opened the electric window on the left side of the rear seat. I cocked the rearview mirror to check what she was doing and saw her peel off another newspaper page, and let it fly out the window.

I straightened the rearview mirror just in time to see the newspaper page stick against the windshield of the car following us, then blow off.

"Mrs. Kennedy, please don't do that," I said. "There's a fine for littering."

She laughed. "Oh, Frank. They know who we are!"

"That's not the point, Mrs. Kennedy. You can cause an accident," I said.

But she continued tossing out sheets of newspaper, page by page, as soon as she'd finished reading the page. "I just hate newspapers cluttering up the car," she said.

39

The nurse's face was as white as her uniform. "He's dead," she moaned softly when she saw me standing at the bedroom door.

Mr. Kennedy was lying flat on his back. His eyes were rolled back in their sockets. His mouth gaped open. It did not look as if he was breathing. "Get the oxygen out!" I yelled. "Why in hell haven't you slapped the oxygen on him? Don't just stand there?"

The nurse was cowering by the doorway, too frightened to move.

I pulled the oxygen canister to the bed, opened it all the way, and pressed the mask over his nose and mouth. The color had drained from the Chief's face and his skin was ashen. I thought, This is the worst one yet.

"How long's he been like this?" I barked at the nurse.

The oxygen hissed as it seeped out from the corners of the face mask.

"How long!" I shouted.

"I rang the alarm as soon as I saw him," she whispered.

You rang the alarm, I said to myself, but that's all you did.

She continued to stand motionless by the door.

I kept one hand on the mask and felt his chest with the other. He was breathing. "He's not dead yet," I shouted. "Now take his pulse, will you?"

The Chief came out of it slowly. As he did, I kept

thinking how this wouldn't have happened if Rita had been on duty. Rita wouldn't have wasted time getting the oxygen; at the least she would have started mouth-to-mouth. All the nurses who worked for Mr. Kennedy were supposed to know mouth-to-mouth.

I stayed with the Chief until I was satisfied he was out of danger. Whenever he had an attack I always wondered afterward if he was aware that he had stopped breathing.

Whenever Mrs. Kennedy heard that her husband was having a cardiac arrest, she never entered the room, but rather stood outside, waiting until the nurse came out and told her that her husband was all right now. I was glad she had not been outside for this attack, because this one was too damn close.

I felt sick to my stomach. I tried walking it off. I kept asking myself about the fear I had sensed in those first few frantic seconds upstairs. I thanked God that the Chief hadn't died on me, but in the back of my mind was Mrs. Kennedy's warning to me in Palm Beach that I had a job only as long as her husband lived. I had to ask myself if I was more afraid of losing my job or losing Mr. Kennedy. And I silently cursed Rose Kennedy for making me ask that question and feel so guilty.

The Chief rallied, and with each passing day seemed to get stronger. I began noticing signs when I was with him in the pool. He had more endurance and he was in better spirits. I sensed his own awareness that he was doing better. He laughed more often. By the time fall came, the old fire was back in his eyes. There had been other rallies—he'd seemed to improve and then suddenly would slip backward—but none had lasted this long. Every time he'd had a comeback we'd hoped that this might be the one to last long enough for him to get back some of his speech.

The first times he had bounced back his children had got their hopes up. Now no one even dared to hope that this prolonged comeback might be the one that would get him talking again. Everyone was waiting for the letdown. I think it was mostly Bobby who kept Mr. Kennedy's spirits up that summer. The boss was watching to see how his third son was doing, and now it was the attorney general who

264

had to listen to those long-winded garbled sounds from his father, knowing the Chief was trying to tell him something and yet never really being sure what it was. Like all of us, Robert Kennedy had to guess what the Chief was telling him. The only thing anybody could be certain of with Mr. Kennedy was his anger. You always knew when he was mad at you.

The compound became like a rest camp, a place where the Kennedys and their friends relaxed and played a few days before they went on the road again. Mrs. Kennedy, her daughters, and Joan were on the campaign trail. Joan, who at first had said that she didn't enjoy politicking the way her sisters-in-law did, set a pace that had the rest of the Kennedys out of breath. There seemed to be little doubt that Ted would easily win reelection—Jack Crimmins said it was in the bag—but Joan Kennedy was not taking her husband's reelection for granted. And soon it was as if the Kennedy women were competing against each other instead of Ted's Republican challenger.

Joan still managed to get some time at Squaw Island, with enough sun to get a tan anyway, and there she told me one day that her feelings hadn't changed. "I hate it, Frank. It's so artificial, meeting all those people, and shaking hands and smiling like you're their friends when you've only met two seconds ago," she said. You knew she meant it. Joan Kennedy never said anything she didn't mean. But she rose to the occasion because every time I'd see her on TV she looked like she was loving every minute of it. I think the 1964 campaign taught her that she was as good a campaigner as any blood Kennedy.

Robert Kennedy's future had everyone guessing that summer, even his family. In February, right around the time Lyndon Johnson visited Mrs. Kennedy at Palm Beach, there was a trial balloon floated in the New Hampshire primary for Bobby's candidacy as President Johnson's running mate in the November election. Robert Kennedy said he was not and never would be a candidate for vice-president. Most everyone believed him, but then he and Ethel visited West

Germany and Poland and got a lot of coverage, and the vice-president thing was back in the air again.

It's my own feeling that Robert Kennedy knew what he was going to do weeks, even months before he publicly revealed his decision. And I'd give long odds that the second person to know what Bobby was up to was the Chief. I think that had something to do with Mr. Kennedy's good spirits that summer.

When Robert Kennedy announced just a few days before the Democratic convention in August that he would run for the U.S. Senate from the state of New York, where he and his wife had a home, no one in his family was a bit disappointed. And from then on the compound was virtually deserted.

In early August Rose Kennedy's mother died. She was nearly ninety-nine. I drove Mrs. Kennedy up for the wake and then the funeral. Mrs. Kennedy had resigned herself to her mother's death, and when it came she seemed very much at peace over it. One time in the car after visiting Mrs. Fitzgerald, Mrs. Kennedy had said she wasn't certain that her mother had understood that her grandson the president had been assassinated. Her mother's sight had failed, and she had become senile, but she passed away quietly and without any pain.

40

"Where are we, Frank?" Rose Kennedy asked from the backseat of the car one afternoon. She had on her black sleeping mask.

"In Milton," I said. "We're on the expressway." It was soon after her mother's death, and this time I didn't call it her father's highway.

"It is all right if you smoke," she said.

"That's all right, Mrs. Kennedy. I can wait until we get there." In less than ten minutes we'd be in downtown Boston.

"I told you I don't mind if you smoke. I know how people are about cigarettes. It's fine with me. If you want to smoke, go ahead. I won't mind," she said.

"No, that's all right, Mrs. Kennedy. I really don't want to smoke. I can wait till we get there."

She wouldn't let it go. "Well, if you don't want to, then all right. But I want you to understand, as I've told you, I don't mind your smoking in the car, if you want to smoke." The last word always had to be hers.

"I'd just as soon wait, Mrs. Kennedy," I said.

"Where are we now?" she repeated. In the rearview mirror I saw her pull off her sleeping mask. "Oh, we're almost there!" she said, and then after a while she asked, "Frank, do you happen to know a place where I could change my dress? I want to change dresses before I get there."

I pondered for a second. "I know just the place, Mrs. Kennedy."

"Oh, fine. Is it on our way?"

"Yes. But I think I should call ahead and tell them you're coming," I said.

"Yes, that is a fine idea."

When we were off the expressway I stopped at a pay phone. I called an old friend, Sal Gennaris, whose place, Soto's Lounge, I had decided would be perfect.

"Hey, Frank! How the hell are you!" Sal said, hearing my voice for the first time in years.

"Listen, I'm coming over in a few minutes . . ." I began.

"Great to see you again, Frank. Come on over," he said.

". . . and I'm bringing Rose Kennedy with me," I said.

"The president's mother?" Sal asked. He dropped his voice.

"Yes," I said.

"Cut it out, Frank," he said.

"She needs a place to change her dress."

"You're serious."

"I'll be there in a few minutes," I said.

"Pull in the side alley and I'll be waiting for you, Frank."

I got back in the car. "They'll be waiting for us, Mrs. Kennedy," I told her. "They have regular changing rooms there with big mirrors."

"Marvelous," she said.

We drove into downtown Boston and soon were in the heart of the Combat Zone, my old stomping ground. Even in the early afternoon, lights flashed gaudily on the movie marquees.

I pulled the Chrysler into an alley. Sal was standing at the side door. "Very, very pleased to meet you, Mrs. Kennedy," he said, nearly curtsying. "You look good yourself, Frank."

I carried Mrs. Kennedy's extra dress. Sal held the door open for us. He led Mrs. Kennedy down the hallway, toward the back of the nightclub. I could hear cheering and shouting and some applause coming from the front of the club. A drum roll ended. Then two tall striptease dancers dashed by us in the hallway. The girls had on G-strings and tassels pasted to their nipples, but from behind they looked naked.

Mrs. Kennedy just stared ahead. "It's a kind of theater, Mrs. Kennedy," I said.

The girls disappeared into a room.

Sal steered her into the same room, and I followed in to give Mrs. Kennedy the dress.

"Hey, no guys!" one of the dancers yelled.

"Hello, lady," the other girl said with a smile.

"He's leaving in two seconds," Sal barked over my shoulder.

"Do you want me to hang up your dress, Mrs. Kennedy?" I asked.

Two more dancers came in the dressing room. They had more elaborate customs with feathers and beads. "Aren't you the president's mother?" one of the girls squealed.

"This is Mrs. Rose Kennedy, girls," Sal said.

Rose Kennedy smiled.

"She's going to change dresses here, so be nice to her," Sal said.

"I'll be outside in the hallway, Mrs. Kennedy," I said.

Surrounded by the tall striptease dancers, Mrs. Kennedy looked like a little girl. "I'll be but a minute, Frank," she said to me with a brave smile. Then the door closed.

"Why d'ja bring the old broad here, Frank?" Sal asked. He was smiling and shaking his head back and forth. "I can't believe it. I can't believe it. Rose Kennedy in my place. I just can't believe it.!"

One of the dancers flew out of the dressing room. "Is that little old lady really Rose Kennedy?" she asked. Sal Gennaris nodded. The dancer eyed me. I nodded. "She hasn't the faintest where she is," the dancer said in a low voice. " 'And what do you girls do?' she asked us."

I was beginning to laugh now. The dancer said, "Laura says we're actresses, and then Brenda tells her, "We take it all off, Rosey.' "

Suddenly the door opened and Mrs. Kennedy marched out. She handed me the dress she had been wearing.

"Thank you," she said to Gennaris without turning to look at him.

I held my breath in the car, waiting for Mrs. Kennedy's rebuke. Surprisingly, she wasn't angry. She was curious instead. "Tell me more about that place, Frank," she said.

"Oh, it's one of the better clubs in Boston, I'd say. It's like an English men's pub, sort of. A very respectable place."

"I've never heard of it before," she said. "Very unusual. And what part of town is this, Frank?" she added.

"This is the . . . entertainment area. In fact, Mr. Kennedy's movie-theater office is just around the corner, on Tremont there. . . ."

"Of course. Trem-mont. Of course. I know where we are. We're in the theater district, then?"

"That's right, yes." I thought about swinging by the old parking lot and showing her where I had worked before I took the job with the Kennedys, but I didn't think she'd be interested.

"I feel much better with this dress on, Frank," she announced.

In minutes we were in front of the Ritz-Carlton. I parked right in front of Boston's swankiest hotel, got out, and went around to the rear door and opened it for Mrs. Kennedy like any proper chauffeur. Then I went ahead of her and said to the doorman: "Mrs. Rose Kennedy." The doorman jumped, his heels clicked, and he ushered us through the front door for Mrs. Kennedy's engagement to address a group of Beacon Hill ladies.

41

"Are you doing food shopping for Jacqueline?" Rose
Kennedy asked.

"Not really," I answered. "It's just that when her maid
asks me to pick up a few things and I'm going to the
National anyway, yes, then I pick up some food for her."

"Is it put on our bill?"

"Yes."

"Well, I want a stop put to that immediately! I don't
want Jacqueline putting her food on our bill."

"But it all goes to Tom Walsh's office, anyway," I
said.

"That's not the point, Frank. Please do as I say. We
have to keep these things separate."

"Yes, Mrs. Kennedy."

"And Jacqueline is going to have to cut back on her
personal staff. This cannot continue. Now that she doesn't
have Jack's salary to . . ." Mrs. Kennedy paused. "She's
just going to have to learn how to manage within a budget.
Mr. Kennedy's office cannot pay for every whim of
Jacqueline's, you know."

I was beginning to wonder why Mrs. Kennedy was
telling me all this. I tried to change the subject but she
continued.

"And those people are always wanting raises."

"Her help?"

"Yes, the staff. And they are putting in for overtime."

"Who?"

"Her help, Frank. Maids and her secretary. Overtime! Can you imagine?"

Just after Thanksgiving Mr. Kennedy made it known that he wanted to visit Ted at the hospital in Boston. The Chief was informed that his son, who had been elected by a landslide to his first full term in the Senate, would probably be discharged from the New England Baptist Hospital soon enough, in time to join the family in Palm Beach for Christmas. But Mr. Kennedy was insistent. He wanted to visit Ted, and that was that.

The senator was walking with a cane. For weeks now he had been out of the bed they had strapped him in so they could rotate him and relieve the pressure on his back. He was in a rehab program, like his father.

Somehow the reporters and the photographers had heard about Mr. Kennedy's visit. There wasn't a big crowd of them, but the ones who were at the hospital kept asking for a chance to snap a picture of Mr. Kennedy and Ted together. The Chief decided that he was up to it, but only after Ted talked him into it.

There was a little balcony outside Ted's room. If the photographers could get Mr. Kennedy out there on the balcony with his son, everybody agreed, it would make a nice picture. The patriarch and his youngest son on their feet together, both with their canes.

Ann helped her uncle put on his overcoat. Ted had on his long overcoat over his hospital pajamas, and he led the way outside. Constantly Ted gave his dad encouragement as we half carried Mr. Kennedy to the balcony. "Come on, Dad, you can do it. If I can do it, you can do it," he urged.

Mr. Kennedy indicated that he was fine and would be able to stand with his son.

Ann stood behind Mr. Kennedy to keep her uncle from tottering. Then the rest of us stood back and gave the photographers a clear view. The Chief smiled, but I remained ready to jump in case he started falling. Mr. Kennedy leaned on his cane just long enough for the photographers to get the picture they wanted. Then we moved in and helped him back to his wheelchair. The Chief was exhausted. But he was overjoyed that he'd done it.

When he saw the photograph of himself standing with Ted in the papers, he beamed. It was a good photograph.

When Ted arrived at Palm Beach a few weeks later, he was wearing a back brace and still needed a cane. He limped and dragged his feet when he walked. Father and son exercised together in the pool.

42

I flew down to Palm Beach with Mr. Kennedy in the *Caroline* that year, and it was an agony. I thought we'd never get there. His old Convair was the slowest plane I'd ever been on, and I told Captain Baird that in the future I'd go back to driving because at least on the ground I could break up the monotony. I think I heard the throb of those prop engines for two days after we landed at West Palm.

As in past years, Mrs. Kennedy had gone alone to Chicago to visit her eldest daughter, Rosemary. Mrs. Kennedy usually visited her mentally handicapped daughter during the times the family was moving from one house to the other, and usually she stayed a few days.

I figured that Rosemary had to be very severely retarded for the family never to bring her to Palm Beach or Hyannis Port for visits. Yet looking at the young girl in the photos on the wall back at the big house, I couldn't understand this, because in the pictures, some of them taken well after her institutionalization, Rosemary is a beautiful young woman. I knew Mrs. Kennedy did not want to talk about Rosemary, so I never asked about her daughter, even to be polite.

All the Kennedys took great interest in projects for the mentally handicapped, but Eunice especially took the cause of helping retarded or handicapped children to heart. She started the Flame of Hope Project, and encouraged her mother to become the charity's leading and most recognized advocate. The Flame of Hope Project was a traveling slide show with Rose Kennedy presenting facts about the problems of retardation. Those who wanted to donate bought Flame of Hope candles. The idea was expressed at the start of every slide show. "It is better to light one candle than curse the darkness," Mrs. Kennedy said. "Now in this slide you'll see how the children receive the loving care . . ."

Click. Mrs. Kennedy snapped the metal "cricket" she used to give me the signal to move on to the next slide.

". . . and here you can see how these unfortunate children, who have God's special love, are trained to use those abilities God has given them . . ."

Click.

". . . for a more productive life. Now in the next slide . . ."

Soon I had Mrs. Kennedy's talk nearly memorized. But she'd change it a little each time. She had more invitations to deliver her Flame of Hope slide show than she could possibly accept. Most of the shows she did were within a day's drive of Hyannis Port. She also gave Flame of Hope talks in Florida, but there seemed to be more interest and support for the project in New England. A factory in Hyannis Port made the candles for the Kennedy charity.

"Where are the candles, Frank?"

"I forgot to bring them, Mrs. Kennedy."

"You forgot to bring them!"

"Yes."

"How did you forget to bring them?"

"It just slipped my mind."

"Well, now what am I going to do? This is just terrible, Frank."

Her anger flared, then died as quickly. During the slide show she told her audience all about the candles and how the money they brought would be donated to the children and institutions that needed it. "But my chauffeur forgot the candles," she said.

She said it in a way that had the ladies in the audience laughing. "It is better to light one candle than curse the darkness, and neither does it serve any purpose to curse one's chauffeur when he's forgotten the candles.''

Everyone laughed, and I had to too. Mrs. Kennedy was grinning.

Mrs. Kennedy began working on her memoirs. She kept her secretary busy. ''I've begun working on my autobiography, Frank,'' she said in the Chrysler. ''It will take a long time to do, so I have begun digging out my old diaries. I suppose I can't think about how it will end. I have to concentrate now on the beginning. Those were the best times. You know, I will never allow my memoirs to be published while I am alive. I don't think that would be proper.''

It was after her husband had another setback and had been in a foul mood for days when she told me again, ''You understand that the family will not be able to keep you on if Mr. Kennedy dies.'' Again she'd surprised me with the sudden way she'd come out with it—from the back of the car—and again I did not reply.

As in other years, I picked out the Christmas tree and set it up in the living room, and this time the household staff helped me decorate it.

''Why don't they decorate the tree themselves, Dora?'' I asked.

''They never have, Frank.''

''You'd think such a big family would want to decorate the tree themselves.''

''It's always been this way, since I've been with them. When the children were away in school they'd get home just a few days before Christmas and they all had friends with them and other places to go, and everyone was always too busy. When you have staff to do these things for you it is easier to let them take care of all the little details. Is that what you mean?''

''Not exactly, Dora. There's something missing.''

''What's missing? They have everything you could ever want.''

''Maybe that's it: they have everything.''

''Maybe they are a bit sad at Christmas because of all

the family that are missing. Joe and Jack are dead. And Kathleen. And there's poor Rosemary. And who knows how long Mr. Kennedy will live?''

I had always felt this twinge of sadness at Christmastime with the Kennedys. At first I thought the feeling came out of being reminded of my boyhood back at the Herman house, when at Christmas all of us were confronted with the fact that we were foster children and orphans and that the few presents we received came from the state of Connecticut and not Santa Claus or our parents.

Then I thought that the white sand and palm trees and bright sun and the absence of holiday decorations in Palm Beach had something to do with the sadness I always felt at Christmastime with this family. But by that Christmas of 1964 I knew there was another reason, and one that had nothing to do with the death of the president. It puzzled me. Here was this giant living room with a high, beamed ceiling and the tall, beautiful tree and the most expensive toys money could buy—yet something was missing.

I think it was love that was missing. Maybe I have no right to say that, but that is how I feel now, looking back. It was a strained, artificial kind of happiness that I felt in their house at that season, as if all of them were making an effort to be filled with holiday joy. I guess having lived in the foster home all those years I had expected something else from a real family at Christmastime. If it weren't for all the grandchildren running around I don't think there would have been much spirit at all at 1095 North Ocean.

That year my wife and son stayed at Hyannis Port in our new little Cape Cod house, though they did come down to spend the holidays with me. My wife had never really liked living in the garage apartment at 1095 North Ocean, which is in a fairly isolated section of North Palm Beach. Besides, there is not much to do in Palm Beach if you are not wealthy and part of the international social set that winters there. Of course I never had that problem. O'Hara's and Ta-boo and Doherty's, along with new friends, were entertainment enough for me.

What was it that Mrs. Kennedy had told me? Enjoy life

while you're young. So that was what I decided to do. I began taking the Kennedy job for what it was—a job. I drove Mrs. Kennedy and I painted the clay pots in the driveway and the peeling sections of the big mansion and I ran the errands. But when there was nothing to do I left the place and enjoyed the attractions Palm Beach had to offer.

I played more golf. One day I borrowed Peter Lawford's clubs and didn't realize until I was on the first tee that the movie star was left-handed. After that I got my own clubs. And I learned somewhat to my surprise that Mrs. Kennedy never minded hearing "Frank is playing golf."

At night, if I didn't go to O'Hara's or the Ta-boo, I'd run over to West Palm Beach for dinner at Frederick's of Palm Beach, where ex-heavyweight boxing champ Rocky Marciano was the greeter. Whenever the Rock saw me walk in he made sure I got a good table without waiting, because I was "with the Kennedys." Sometimes Peter Lawford had me drive him down to Miami Beach, where I met Frank Sinatra again and the rest of the "Rat Pack." And when the baseball teams started spring training, I'd bring some of the ballplayers over to the house to meet Mr. Kennedy.

Just observing the rich and famous in Palm Beach was entertaining. And then, every so often, I'd hear about a murder, or a big robbery. But what you read about in the newspapers and what you heard were often very different. I've always believed that, at least in those days, if you were rich enough and of the proper social standing you could get away with anything in Palm Beach, even murder. All the Kennedy chauffeur had to worry about, however, was getting a parking ticket, and after I got to know some of the guys on the police department I didn't have to worry about even that.

Ted swam a lot that winter, and his recovery was noticeable. At first it was believed that he would need a cane for the rest of his life, but then the doctors were saying that he'd just have to wear a back brace, like the president. His family figured that if a back brace hadn't stopped John Kennedy, it wasn't going to stop the youngest Kennedy brother either.

Best of all was the effect on the Chief. It was as if Mr. Kennedy forgot about his own infirmity and turned his attention to Ted's recovery. And in a strange way their physical impairments, as different as they were, seemed to form a bond between father and son. As the baby in the family, Ted had always been Mr. Kennedy's favorite. Wilbert the gardener and his sister Evelyn Jones told me that Mr. Kennedy had always made sure to include Ted in the activities of the older children. His election to his brother's unexpired term had more or less been guaranteed—Mr. Kennedy, we all knew, had made sure of it. But now Teddy was doing something for himself, and it was this determination to fight his way back from his own crippling accident that caught his father's attention. The Chief was proud of Teddy. When I was with him and he'd watch Ted swimming in the pool, Mr. Kennedy would make a fist with his good left hand, give it a little shake, and smile as a sign of approval.

The Chief may have been prouder of Ted that spring of 1965 than he had ever been, but what remained of his fire and ambitions was centered on his third son, Robert.

PART THREE

43

"Oh, Rose! So good to see you again," the woman greeted Mrs. Kennedy as she came out of Saint Francis Xavier. She was a pleasant-looking elderly woman. She reminded Rose Kennedy that they had been schoolmates together at a convent school in Europe.

"Oh, yes, yes, dear. So good to see you again. How have you been? Wonderful. That is truly wonderful and marvelous. You really must excuse me now. I have to rush home. My husband needs me." And off Rose Kennedy went, smiling back at the woman.

Her school chum seemed disappointed at the brief reunion. If it had been me and I hadn't seen a school buddy for all these years, I thought, I'd invite the old chum back to my house to talk over old times. *My husband needs me.* As if Mrs. Kennedy was going to run right up to her husband's room and be his nurse.

"Did Rita tell you to pick up the prescription for Mr. Kennedy this afternoon, Frank?" Ann asked.

"Yes. Why?"

"Just curious, Frank. She mentioned to me that she would be taking an hour off this afternoon to pick up Uncle Joe's medicine."

"Well, maybe I misunderstood her, Ann."

"I don't think so at all, Frank," Ann said, and smiled thinly.

Now what the hell do I tell Rita? I asked myself. Why are these two always so suspicious of each other? I wondered.

Mrs. Kennedy's French-lesson record was blaring. Fritz was massaging her in her bedroom while she repeated phrases over and over.

In the next room Mr. Kennedy's aide was massaging him, with classical music in the background.

It was Eunice who was having an emergency this time. She was going into labor when I got the call to come quick.

She was in bed upstairs. "I don't think I can walk, Frank," Mrs. Shriver said.

"Then I'll carry you," I said.

I lifted her, and Eunice sort of draped herself over my back as I started slowly down the steep stairs. She is a tall woman, and she wasn't exactly light either. "You all right?" I gasped.

"Don't drop me," she said. "Are *you* all right, Frank?"

"This is no good," I said. "I'm going to have to shift you."

As I did so, her kimono flew open. This is no time to worry about appearances, I thought.

"Keep going, Frank," Eunice said.

Others were at the bottom of the stairs to help me, and we got her in the back of the car. Someone said that Jack Dempsey had called the troopers informing them that Mr. Kennedy's Chrysler was making an emergency run to Saint Elizabeth's Hospital in Brighton, part of Boston, and would need an escort. I checked on Eunice Shriver, and things looked serious. "I'm not going to wait for any escort," I said, and we started toward Boston.

A trooper did spot the Chrysler as we were leaving Hyannis Port, and I saw his cruiser turn to follow us. But that was the last I saw of the state police. I had the Chrysler going so fast, I doubt any cruiser could have caught us.

Eunice kept saying that we'd make it to the hospital in time, but every so often she'd let out a horrendous squeal, and then I'd start sweating again. "If you have the baby in the car and it's a boy, you can name it after me," I said, but Mrs. Shriver was beyond jokes.

It was the most nerve-racking hour I ever spent.

Almost immediately after we arrived at Saint Elizabeth's, Eunice delivered her fifth child and fourth son. Anthony Paul Shriver, born July 20, 1965, was also Eunice's last child.

Once again it was time for Louella Hennessey to return to work for the Kennedys.

"How was the ride to the hospital?" the proud grandmother asked me later.

"Very fast, Mrs. Kennedy."

I hiked my skirt and half turned to check in the full-length mirror if the seams of my nylons were straight. Then I adjusted my bra and rearranged the padding. I leaned toward the mirror and studied my makeup. A little too much powder? I smacked my lips to blot the lipstick, took one more long look, and decided that I was one dynamite blond, good enough to make money walking the streets back in the Combat Zone.

The skin on my legs still stung a bit from the depilatory, but other than that I was ready for a wild night. I figured it would take a few minutes to get used to the high heels. I hadn't bothered to hide my hula girl tattoo, figuring that she added a certain touch.

This is my best Halloween outfit yet, I thought. I had taken the time and effort to make sure everything was just right—the dress, the expensive blond wig, even the girdle.

There were a couple of hours before the party at Luigi's started. A smile crept across my face. Why not? I asked myself. Why not, indeed.

I didn't want to get in an accident dressed like that, so I took off the high heels before getting into the Chrysler and heading for the Kennedys'. It was already dark.

The big house seemed deserted. None of the neighborhood kids dared to go trick-or-treating at the Kennedys'. My high heels clicked on the wooden floor as I walked across the veranda and knocked on Mr. Kennedy's front door.

"Yes?" Father John Cavanaugh asked as he opened it. "What can I do for you?"

"You can pucker up and give me a big kiss, you sweet-heart you," I told the priest in my best falsetto. I stuck out my chest as I reached for his neck.

"Now just a m-m-minute," Father Cavanaugh stammered.

"Oh, come on, dearie," I squealed. "Just a little kiss."

"I will have to call the security guard," Mr. Kennedy's old friend said.

"Oh, that's even better. Is he young and handsome?" I minced.

"What's going on here!" Ann Gargan shouted from somewhere inside.

"Oh, Ann, this woman seems to be lost," Father Cavanaugh said, blushing hard. And then Ann was standing there.

"You'll have to leave right now or I'll call the police," she said sternly.

"This lady isn't lost, Ann," I said in my regular voice. "This lady is Frank Saunders."

Ann's eyes widened as she stared at the blond floozy standing in the Kennedy hall.

"Frank?" Father Cavanaugh asked.

"Frank!" Ann squealed.

"It's me, Ann."

Now Father Cavanaugh was roaring, holding his stomach he was laughing so hard.

"You look terrific, Frank," Ann said.

"I was on my way to a costume party and I thought I'd stop in. I hope I didn't frighten anyone," I said.

"Of course not, Frank," Father Cavanaugh said, still laughing.

"Frank," Ann said, "you've got to let Uncle Joe see you. Oh, you've just got to show Uncle Joe! Come on." She motioned and headed up the front stairs.

"It's all right, she's Frank," Ann told the night nurse when we reached the top of the stairs. The nurse didn't laugh. "Hi, dear," I said to her as I clicked by and down the hall.

We passed Mrs. Kennedy's closed bedroom door. Mr. Kennedy's room was in darkness, and Ann flicked on the switch. As soon as the light came on the Chief stirred. "Uncle Joe! You've got a visitor," Ann said.

The Chief rubbed the sleep from his eyes with his left hand. "Oh, it's such a pleasure to meet the famous Joseph P. Kennedy," I said, once again in falsetto.

Then panic came into Mr. Kennedy's eyes. He sat up in the bed. I walked closer. The Chief recoiled and grabbed for his pillow. "NNNNNaaaaaaahhhh! Nnnnnnnnnaaaahhhhhhhhhhh!" he screamed.

"Uncle Joe, it's Frank. She's Frank, Uncle Joe!" Ann said.

"It's me, Chief. It's Frank," I said.

"GGGGGaaaaaaahhh!" he screamed.

"It's only Frank. Don't be afraid," Ann said, as she reached for her uncle in the bed.

"It's me, Chief. It's your chauffeur!" I said.

Mr. Kennedy was choking. "Get the oxygen Ann!" I said, and yelled at Mr. Kennedy, "Chief! It's Frank!" He was scrambling away as I came nearer, and suddenly he let out a long gasp and collapsed, his head falling back on the pillow.

I was kneeling on the bed now. I'd never given him mouth-to-mouth before, but I knew there was no time to waste. Quickly I put my right hand behind his head, placed my mouth on his, and exhaled into his mouth.

Mr. Kennedy came around within seconds. He was pushing me away with his left hand as I lifted myself off him.

He gave a long, loud moan that changed into a laugh, and I knew that he'd finally recognized me. "It's me, Frank, Chief," I said with a grin, though still shaking, I was so relieved that my prank had not ended tragically.

And then the Chief was convulsed with laughter. Tears were streaming down his cheeks. He kept pointing at me with his good hand, and I stood at the foot of the bed roaring myself. The three of us laughed ourselves silly.

44

The Chief had turned seventy-nine that September of 1967. A sallowness began to come into his face and over the next two years it deepened. The attacks continued, and I marveled at how a man his age, who'd already suffered a major stroke, could keep having these little attacks—moments when his heart would actually stop—and still keep on living. There were no longer any false hopes. Everyone knew he'd never be able to stand again. And finally we knew he would never be able to talk again.

Physically he was still very strong for his age. I could feel the strength sometimes when I was with him in the pool. But it was his own imprisonment that was defeating him, chipping away at him. The frustration of not being able to talk with his two sons seemed to strangle him. Even his stubborn moods did not last as long now, though there was one time when he refused to be taken off the *Caroline* after it landed back on the Cape, when he sat there for hours until I came up to the airplane and talked him into going home. Some of his family lost patience with the old man when he went into one of these stubborn moods, but seeing him like that made me feel good because I knew he was doing it just to reassert himself, to remind everybody that Joseph P. Kennedy was still around. I figured that what now was an old man's crankiness had once been drive and ambition and determination.

He was less vocal now when Mrs. Kennedy came into

his bedroom, although as soon as he heard something from her that he didn't like he'd let her know it. "I'm going, dear. I'm going," she'd say. It never changed. Only now he didn't shout as loudly.

Mr. Kennedy kept track of his two senator sons. He followed their activities in the newspaper and on TV. As tired as he often got, I still had the feeling that he was waiting and watching because, while others wondered if Robert F. Kennedy would someday seek the presidency, the Chief had no doubts. He knew damn well that his third son would go for it when the time was right. He had that to cling to, and he was waiting for the moment.

It was hard to keep an aide. The job was a miserable one, as I knew from the times when I had to fill in. The nurses would not give him a bath as regularly as they should, and I would have to wash him. He hated it and I hated it, but it had to be done. All this money, all the money spent on nurses, and still, I thought, they do not give him baths often enough. It was true what they say about money not meaning very much when you are helpless.

One of those later summers, I happened to notice him sitting in his wheelchair on the sun porch outside his bedroom. He was motionless for so long I eventually went inside and up to his room to check on him. Rita was in the nurse's station. I asked him if he wanted to come in off the sun porch, but he waved me away. I told him that I'd be in the room watching the ball game on his TV. If he decided he'd like to watch with me all he had to do was give me a sign. But he stayed sitting on the porch for a long time. More than any other time I was with him, I wished that he could talk at that moment. There were so many questions I wanted to ask him, and I felt sure he would answer them.

I wanted to ask him if he had hoped to be president once. I wanted to ask him if it had all been worth it; if he'd do it again the same way. I wanted to ask him if he knew why so many tragedies had happened to his children. But most of all I wanted to ask him why he'd kept a photograph of a movie star on his night table.

45

I spent as much time away from 1095 North Ocean and the Kennedys as I could that winter—playing golf, hiding out on the *Marlin*, and in the Palm Beach bars at night. Some nights we brought the party to the Kennedys'. I remember one time when just about the whole crowd from O'Hara's decided that they needed a swim, so I took them to the Kennedys'. I drove the Chrysler across the lawn to the pool. The next morning, early, when I went to get the car to take Mrs. Kennedy to mass, I realized how close to disaster I had come. Mr Kennedy's car was parked with its front wheels less than a foot from the edge of the pool.

"Frank! Frank, wake up! She's looking for you," said John Ryan, Mr. Kennedy's current young aide, as he shook me in the bed.

John Ryan was a tall, good-looking, good-natured young guy who had taken the job as Mr. Kennedy's aide back at the Cape the summer before. He had the sense of humor you needed to work for the Kennedys, and he made my life easier, and more fun.

But that morning, I felt life was neither easy nor fun. My head was splitting. The young lady from the night before was still asleep next to me.

"She's outside," John said.

The apartment window was open.

"Frrr . . . ank! Oh, Feeeerrrrrrank!" Rose Kennedy called.

"Tell her I'm dead, John. I can't get her to mass in time. You drive her." This is not the way to wake up with a hangover, I thought.

John stuck his head out the window. "Frank's not here, Mrs. Kennedy. There's a paint sale at the hardware store and Frank wanted to be there before they opened so he could buy the paint before anyone else."

"What she say?" I asked John a moment later.

"She thinks it's wonderful that you'd be that smart, Frank."

"I owe you one, John," I said.

"Joe, is your father going to run for president?" I asked fifteen-year-old Joe Kennedy, Bobby and Ethel's oldest son.

"Beats me, Frank," young Joe said with a smile.

"Come on, you must have an idea?"

"Can't say, Frank."

"Won't say?"

"Can't say." He laughed.

"It sure would be nice to have the inside track on this one. I could make some money betting on this one," I said.

"You'll be one of the first to know," young Joe said.

"When are you going to clean this mess up? If you're going to stay with me in this apartment when you come down to Palm Beach you're going to have to help me keep it clean, understand? It's a pigpen in here."

"Tomorrow, Frank," he said.

I liked having young Joe around. He was a lot of fun. The oldest Kennedy grandson told me he liked staying at my place rather than at his parents', where he had to run interference with three younger brothers and five younger sisters.

"Red doesn't make as much of a mess in here as you do," I said, referring to the caretaker who stayed in the apartment when I was on the Cape. "And Red has all summer to do it. Do you keep your room at school like this?" I asked.

"Even worse," he said. At fifteen, young Joe had that Kennedy charm.

Everyone was wondering if Robert Kennedy would make his move for the presidency in 1968 and go against Lyndon B. Johnson, or wait it out for 1972. The smart money was on 1972. At O'Hara's and the Ta-boo, and sometimes right on the street, people would ask me: "You're with the Kennedys. Is Bobby going to run against Johnson?" I'd give them young Joe's answer.

Robert Kennedy's colleague in the Senate from New York, the Republican Jacob Javits, often stopped in at O'Hara's with his young wife Marion, for a drink before Mrs. Javits took her husband to the airport in West Palm Beach. As soon as the Javitses left, a few friends and I would bet how long it would take Mrs. Javits to get back to O'Hara's, this time alone.

That was one part of the bet we'd make on Marion Javits. The other was how long, after she got back to the Palm Beach bar, it would take her to leave with one of the suntanned young men in O'Hara's.

To win the trifecta on Marion Javits you had to come closest on the time back, the time drinking when she returned, and pick the guy she'd leave with.

The day after Martin Luther King was assassinated the secret service gave me a loaded .38 and told me to carry it because they were afraid someone might try to kill Robert Kennedy. I didn't want the revolver, but the secret service said they wanted the Kennedy chauffeur to have it, just in case.

I began carrying the revolver in a holster I had at my waist. I wore a sport jacket all the time to hide the holster, but still the gun made a bulge at my waist.

Mrs. Kennedy noticed right away that I was wearing the sport coat all the time I was with her. "You don't have to wear that jacket on my account, Frank," she said. "It's too humid for a jacket, isn't it?"

"That's all right, Mrs. Kennedy," I said.

292

"But it's awfully hot for a jacket. Take it off and be comfortable."

"I'd just as soon keep it on, Mrs. Kennedy," I said, praying that she would just drop the subject.

Every time I asked myself if somebody really might want to kill Bobby, I reminded myself of Dallas. What the hell was it with this family? I wondered. What was it that attracted these killers? I knew Bobby had enemies, and that his enemies called him ruthless. But they never saw him with his father. Any man who loved his father as deeply as Robert Kennedy did, I knew, certainly couldn't be so cold-hearted as to warant such cold-hearted enemies. And no man who felt so deeply about his family could be insensitive to the problems of the poor and the oppressed.

Bobby Kennedy was changing. I could see it in his face. There was something different in his eyes now, something I felt that went beyond the tragedy in Dallas and the frustration—the outrage, really—over what had happened to his father. I can't explain it, but I knew it was there. I was never alone with him in his father's bedroom, but I'm certain that he was telling the Chief that he was going to finish what John Kennedy had begun. I'd have bet on it.

46

In sunny Palm Beach that winter of 1967–68 all eyes were on the politicians campaigning in the New Hampshire snow. The fact that Robert Kennedy was not in New Hampshire was viewed by many as a sign that the senator from New York was not a serious candidate, and would probably not make his move until 1972. Then Eugene McCarthy made his surprisingly strong showing in the Democratic primary in New Hampshire against the incumbent President Johnson, and it was a whole new ball game. When President Johnson said he would neither seek nor accept his party's nomination for a second term, Robert F. Kennedy's time had come.

We returned to Hyannis Port full of excitement. This was going to be something to watch. The compound would be a madhouse again. There'd be more press parties on the big lawn at Hyannis Port, more touch football games. Good, I thought, another chance to have at Shelby Scott, a pert little blonde from channel four in Boston, when the Kennedy team took on the media. Shelby threw a better block than any of the male television reporters.

Bobby Kennedy's house was crowded with all the campaign advisers and workers and politicians needed to help him with the Democratic nomination. Through it all Ruby the cook stayed calm. It never flustered Ruby if she had a last-minute meal to make for two dozen unexpected guests. And she still found time to ask Mr. Kennedy's chauffeur if he'd had a good breakfast. I knew at least Ethel would never bug me about having a cup of coffee in her kitchen.

When Bobby won the Indiana primary that first week in May, all I saw on the faces at the compound were huge smiles. The California primary one month away would be the prize. If Robert Kennedy won that primary, everyone agreed, the Democratic nomination for the presidency would be his.

After Indiana, Bobby would come to Hyannis Port for a day or two of rest, then hit the campaign trail again. When he came home he was exhausted. But after a day at Hyannis Port he'd bounce right back. It was amazing to see how quickly he was able to rebound from the campaigning. Besides, with the excitement and all the workers and advisers and press at the compound, I felt the magic coming back again. I can't explain it—you would have to be there to feel it.

I stopped wearing the .38 every day at Hyannis Port. The compound was a private preserve for the Kennedys—a safe haven. It was crazy to even think that somebody might try to kill Robert Kennedy.

47

Joan Kennedy said it was time for her to go up to Saint Elizabeth's to have her baby. This time there was no panic, no race to Brighton with my foot pushing the accelerator to the floor. Joan calmly decided that it was time and I was asked to drive her up.

It was July, a hot and humid day on the Cape. Joan was feeling very uncomfortable, she said, as we headed for the hospital. Even the sea breezes didn't seem to help.

"You sure you're all right, Mrs. Kennedy?" I asked. I was still thinking about sister-in-law Eunice and the wild ride to Saint Elizabeth's the summer before last.

"I'm fine, Frank. No need to speed, believe me. How is Bruce? I don't see him very much these days."

"He's fine. He has his friends. I don't think he misses living at the garage at all."

I watched her smile in the rearview mirror.

"And how is your wife?"

"She likes having her own house. She doesn't miss living in the compound a bit," I said.

Joan laughed softly. "I think I understand, Frank," she said.

"Bruce is happier now that he doesn't have to switch schools and move back and forth from Palm Beach."

"Oh, yes, he must be. It is unsettling for children to have to always switch schools. Ted was in and out of so many schools when he was a boy, he has trouble remembering how many.''

''Well, what's it going to be, Mrs. Kennedy? Boy or a girl?''

''I think Ted would like another boy,'' she said.

''And you?''

''Whatever God decides.''

''Do you think you'll move closer to the big house?''

''I don't know, Frank. Sometimes Ted says he would like to be closer to his father. But we really are very close as it is—just a couple of minutes. I think we'll stay on Squaw Island,'' she said.

''Well, Louella will be going back to work again soon.''

''Yes, it won't be long now,'' Joan said lightly.

There was a calmness about Joan Kennedy that I always felt comfortable with. Maybe it was her voice: soft, like Jacqueline's. She seemed very real to me, and she never made me feel like a Kennedy hired hand.

I think her mother-in-law was a little jealous of Joan's musical ability. And both Joan and Sargent Shriver always seemed odd-person-out when there was a bunch of Kennedys cutting up. I could never put my finger on it exactly, but I finally decided that it was probably her beauty and quiet demeanor that made her in-laws a bit uncomfortable. That biting Kennedy sense of humor had a way of wearing you down, as I well knew. Joan did not come from a large family and seemed to have no need to be competing all the time. Yet she could hold her own on the campaign trail. In fact, I always believed that Joan Kennedy was the best campaigner in the family. The difference with Joan was that she wasn't out there for herself, she was doing it for Ted.

''Frank! Come on in! Come on in!'' Ted beamed and beckoned for me to come into his wife's hospital room.

Joan was wearing a hospital gown and I could see that she did not have a bra underneath. ''It's all right, Frank,'' Joan beamed. ''Come on in and say hello to baby Patrick.''

Ted wore a smile over his new son bigger than the one he'd had when he marched in the Saint Patrick's Day Parade in South Boston.

I drove Joan and baby Patrick home to Squaw Island a day or so later.

"He's a little redhead," Joan said. "He's got Grandpa Kennedy's coloring."

"What more could the father ask for?" I said.

"Not a thing." Joan Kennedy said.

Joan had baby Patrick all to herself for a few days. Ted was over on Martha's Vineyard at the annual Edgartown Regatta. Joan Kennedy always said that Ted wanted very much to win that race, because none of his brothers ever had.

I didn't see much of Jacqueline that summer. According to Rita Dallas, something had happened between the Kennedys and the former First Lady, something Ethel Kennedy had said to her sister-in-law. Mr. Kennedy's nurse claimed she was there when it happened.

Everyone was excited about Robert Kennedy's announcement that he would run for president, and there was this time when Jacqueline and Bobby were reeling off the results of the latest poll, which were favorable. Jacqueline was cheering, Rita said, and then the former First Lady said something like, "Won't it be wonderful when we get back in the White House again?" With which, according to the nurse, Ethel shot back: "What do you mean *we?*" Rita saw Jacqueline turn pale, as if Ethel had slapped her face. Then Jacqueline smiled, kissed her brother-in-law on the cheek, and left the room.

Ethel Kennedy, I knew from personal experience, had a sharp, fast wit, and it may well have happened as Rita said, as a typical Kennedy remark. But not something to take to heart, it seemed to me, now that I was used to the way some of the Kennedys could tongue-lash even their closest friends.

Anyway, Jacqueline seemed less in evidence at the compound now. She still had her assigned secret service agent, Clint Hill, and a few times that summer I saw them walking together on the beach. As a matter of fact, as I look back, Jacqueline walking along the beach is my most vivid recollection of her that summer.

"Oh, I hardly got any sleep at all last night, Frank," Rose Kennedy said.

"It was a hot night, not much good for sleeping," I said.

"It's not the weather. There's always a nice breeze in my room. It's that jukebox Ethel has in the garage in back of her house. It went all night. If she can't sleep I wish she'd have some consideration for the rest of us. I will drop her a note about it when I get back from mass."

"You can hear the music in your room?"

"Music!? It's a racket. It is a good thing you're not in the garage anymore, Frank, or you'd know what I'm talking about," Mrs. Kennedy said.

Rose Kennedy invited back to the compound a group of plainclothed Jesuits who had introduced themselves to her at Saint Francis Xavier. When the priests arrived I was ordered to give them a tour of the place. "Here, Frank, give them this fifty dollars as a present," Mrs. Kennedy said, handing me the amount in cash.

"Mrs. Kennedy wants you to have this," I told one of the priests.

"This is very thoughtful of her," the head Jesuit said. "I'll make sure that this donation is put to good use. Immediately. Is there a package store around here?" the priest asked.

"Prendergast's," I said. "Now here's how you get there, Father."

A change came over Rose Kennedy that summer. She seemed less tense and more philosophical. She began asking my opinion about things. Once again she took me up to the attic for the annual inventory.

"A lot of things are gone," I said, surprised at how empty the attic looked since last summer.

"Oh, yes, some of the things have gone up to Beals Street," she replied. Mrs. Kennedy was proud that the old family home in Brookline was now a national historic shrine. "It's better to have them there, where they came from, than stuck away in this big old attic."

48

What kind of life is this for a young single girl like Ann Gargan? I'd asked myself that many times in the seven years I'd worked for the Kennedys. It wasn't much of a life really, I thought. She hardly ever went out alone. Aside from relatives she visited in Detroit, Ann didn't seem to have any friends. Her brother Joe was of course at Hyannis Port all the time, but they were not particularly close as far as I could see. In one sense Ann was like all of us—myself and Rita and Dora, Matilda and Wilbert. Everyone who worked for the Kennedys. But then she was also kin. And she made sure that the family's help knew it.

I often thought that it would have been better for Ann if, after her uncle's stroke, the family had chosen to let Rita and the nurses care for the Chief and told Ann that she was free now to live her own life. But I guess Ann wanted it this way. Certainly Mr. Kennedy felt comfortable with her around. Yet sometimes I wondered if Ann was getting back at her uncle for the way he had bossed her around before the stroke. I could still hear him ordering: "Annie! Annie! Come on, Annie, let's go!" I knew she loved her uncle, but she was a bit afraid of him too.

There were times when the Chief would want something and Ann would tell her uncle that she'd be right back, but then she'd leave and not return to Mr. Kennedy for hours. I never knew where she went. She'd just disappear. Then the Chief would get furious, and those of us who were around him after Ann had taken off had to deal with his frustration and crankiness about the way she had left him alone.

There were days when Ann would be very quiet and withdrawn. She'd take her dogs for a walk along the beach and play with them and hug them, and then she'd seem to snap out of it. Ann loved animals, yet she'd grow tired of a dog after a while, give it away and get another puppy, and the new puppy would then get all her attention.

Ann was in one of her quiet spells, and I asked Rita if she knew what was bothering her. Rita claimed that Bobby had snubbed her. He had come to Hyannis Port before heading off to the West Coast to campaign in Oregon and California. Rita and Ann had taken Mr. Kennedy up to the airport to wait for Bobby to fly in on the *Caroline*. Mr. Kennedy had given his son the *Caroline* for his campaign, but for this trip back the *Caroline* had developed engine trouble, or some kind of minor mechanical problem, and it was going to take a few hours to fix it, Mr. Kennedy was told. His son's delay upset the Chief, Rita said. However, Bobby managed to catch another plane, and when Mr. Kennedy saw his son he was happy and excited. Bobby was in good spirits too, Rita said, and wanted to drive his father back to the compound. When they got back to the big house, Rita said, Bobby told them he wanted to celebrate and was going to get his mother and they were all going to dinner.

Bobby wheeled his father into the house and, Rita said, told the Chief that he'd be right back, after he found his mother. "Just the three of us are having dinner tonight, Dad. Alone. Just us," Bobby repeated to his father, according to Rita. Mr. Kennedy's nurse said that she saw Ann just walk away, as if she'd been hurt by what her cousin had said. Then, Rita said, she noticed Ann a few minutes later running her dogs across the lawn and down to the beach.

Rita's description of Ann's reaction reminded me of the time Ann cheated me out of a dinner invitation at Palm Beach. Dr. Roger Curry, a neighbor of the Kennedys', had invited me and David Crawford, who was then Mr. Kennedy's aide, to dine with him and his wife. I mentioned it to Ann and she replied that the Currys were her friends, not mine, and that I should stay with Mr. Kennedy that night, because she was going to take up the dinner invitation herself. Rather than get into an argument, I let Ann go, but it seemed very selfish of her to do something like that. So when Rita told me of how Ann responded to Bobby leaving her out, it occurred to me Ann was jealous of anyone else getting any attention that she thought might rightly be hers.

Yet Ann could also be generous. When it had become certain that the Chief would never walk again, Ann had asked me what size shoes I wore, and then, with it clear that Mr. Kennedy and I were the same size, had told me to pick out any of the expensive handmade English shoes in his closet for myself.

I always believed that I understood what Ann was going through with her relatives better than anyone else at the Kennedys'. I had, after all, felt some of the same things when I was growing up with the Hermans as my foster parents. I could never be certain of their love. I had to work for my own keep and pay the weekly room-and-board bill because by mother was always behind in the payments. It was a little like that with Ann and the Kennedys, I thought. She was family but she was also hired help. I felt sorry for her, but I never pitied her, knowing that Mr. Kennedy had ordered his office to make sure that his niece would be taken care of very handsomely when he died.

Although Ann never let any of us who worked for the Kennedys forget that she was part of the family, she used her relationship as a shield. And being by nature a shy girl, and perhaps afraid of being hurt, she never let her guard down, never showed real affection.

Yet for a girl who was that shy, it continually puzzled me how nonchalantly she'd change out of her bathing suit in front of me after a swim. It made me wonder: She must think I don't even exist as a man who might be attracted by the sight of a nude woman. Or maybe she didn't think of herself that way, as attractive to men, had given up on that idea. Whatever, I told myself, if it doesn't bother you, Ann, it sure doesn't bother me.

49

"I shall attend mass this morning," Rose Kennedy said. I could barely hear her. She sounded far away, as if she were not holding the telephone closely enough. "Yes, Mrs. Kennedy," I said. "I understand."

But I did not understand. I did not for the life of me understand why she wanted to attend mass knowing that the reporters would be waiting for her again at the church door.

And I did not understand how it could all be happening again, why Senator Robert F. Kennedy had been shot.

The news of the shooting in California was on all the stations on the car radio as I drove from my house to the Kennedy compound. He'd won the big California primary, but what good would it do him now? I wondered as I listened to the details. It didn't sound good. The assassin had been right next to him when he fired a pistol. He'd been shot in the head, and those things were always bad. But Bobby is young and strong, I told myself. And then I thought, How much more of this can the old man take?

She was not waiting for me when I pulled into the turnaround. I got out of the Chrysler and went into the house and up the stairs. Rita was in the hallway. I told the nurse that Mrs. Kennedy wanted to go to mass, and Rita also wondered about all the reporters.

"When did she find out?" I asked the nurse.

"Not long," Rita said. The night nurse had been about to knock on Mrs. Kennedy's door when she heard the TV come on—as they learned later, she had wanted to find out the results of the primary in California—and then the door flew open and Mrs. Kennedy was crying, "It's Bobby! It's Bobby!"

Ann had learned sometime earlier during the night, Rita said, but was ordered not to tell either parent, and Ann had stayed in her room agonizing over how she would tell her aunt. Mrs. Kennedy had just turned on the TV as Ann was coming down the hallway, Rita said the nurse told her. As I listened I kept thinking, Thank God I wasn't here this time.

"The Chief know yet?"

Rita shook her head and grimaced.

"Can this be all happening again, Rita?"

She did not answer. I could tell the nurse was trying hard to stay calm, knowing that there were people in the house who might need all her help, and she couldn't allow herself to break.

"Where's Ann now?" I asked.

"In her room. She's destroyed. Absolutely wrecked," Rita said.

Then Mrs. Kennedy's bedroom door opened. She nodded at us, but I averted my eyes—not daring to look at her face—and went down the stairs ahead of her.

I opened the car door for her, and as she got in I saw that her face looked very different. She looked like a stranger, like someone twenty years older.

Nor did I dare look at her in the rearview mirror. There was nothing to say, so we drove in silence, and the closer we got to the church the angrier I got. If a photographer pulls that shit again, I thought, I'll kill the bastard.

And there they were, in a moving crowd, all yelling and shouting.

This is even worse than for the president, I thought. This is terrible. We pushed through the crowd, and it wasn't until we reached the front pews that I was certain she would be safe. As the mass was being said I couldn't help wonder if Mrs. Kennedy was too hot in that black wool coat and heavy black shawl she had wrapped around her. It was very humid in the church. I became afraid she might faint.

Again, as we moved out, the photographers and reporters pressed as close as they could and followed us to the car. It was one of those movie-star scenes with the star trying to escape. The questions they were asking her, shouting at her, were incredible. "Have you talked with Bobby?" 'How do you feel?" And probably the most asinine: "Do you feel as badly as when the president was assassinated?"

It was safe and quiet in the Chrysler and Mrs. Kennedy never spoke all the way home.

I walked into the house with her. She had a handkerchief in her hands and was wringing it as she walked up the stairs to her bedroom. After she was out of sight I went over to my old garage apartment. It was a good place to wait, to hide. I did not want to be in the big house. I did not want to see Dora and Matilda or Wilbert or any of them. The alarm was still hooked up, and I knew that if they needed me on the second floor they'd ring.

"You want to take a walk on the beach?" I asked young Joe Kennedy.

"Yeah," he said.

It was warm for the beginning of June. I knew that if Joe wanted to talk he would. I asked him how school had been. All right, he said. Then he said he had been anxious for it to end, because he'd wanted to campaign with his father. I knew then that he wanted to talk about it.

"Do you think my father is going to die, Frank?" Joe asked.

"No. He won't. He'll make it. It isn't like . . ." I had to catch myself from telling Joe Kennedy that it wasn't the same as in Dallas when his uncle was dead in a second. "You know how strong your father is, Joe. He'll make it," I said.

"I wish I'd been there, Frank. I wish I'd been out there with them," he said. Some of his brothers and younger sisters had flown out to California for the victory celebration. The family all knew that, after California, there'd be no stopping Robert Kennedy.

305

"You think there's some kind of curse on us, Frank?" Joe Kennedy asked.

"Who told the Chief, Rita?"

"She did."

"She did?"

"Right after she got back from mass. She went in and shut the door behind her and was in there for, I'd guess, ten minutes. When she came out she told me to watch out for him."

"She went in alone?"

"And closed the door," Rita said.

"How is she?"

"I've never seen her alone with him before, Frank."

"Me neither," I said.

"Then she wept," Rita said.

"She cried?"

"Yes. After she came out."

"Thank God she was able to cry."

"I know, I know," the nurse said.

This time, I thought, she was crying for both of them. Now she is finally letting the tears out for Jack too.

"You'd better stay around," she said.

"How's the boss?"

"Crying. He's got the TV on and he won't let anybody shut it off. It's not at all like before."

"If you need me, Rita, ring the alarm," I said.

But this time I couldn't stay in the old apartment. I went back over to the house and into the Chief's room and sat there listening to the TV with him, waiting for the bulletin that everyone prayed would never come. He stayed in his bed with small tears at the corners of his eyes and never uttered a sound as long as I was in the room.

Twenty-four hours later, the bulletin came. Everyone in the house wept this time. It was a double grieving, perhaps a bit like Mrs. Kennedy's. All the tears that we had held back when the president died, the shock almost too great, flowed now with tears for Bobby. And none of us, including his wife and his niece, could bear to stay in Mr. Kennedy's room very long.

50

Bobby died twenty-five hours after he was shot in that Los Angeles hotel. While our hopes had lived with him in those hours, I recall that there was a deep sense of futility too; as if the very fact of Robert Kennedy being on his way to the presidency had been in itself some kind of sentence, as if there was a force destroying the old man's dreams for his son, the dreams that this now crippled father had had for all his sons. I was still enough of a Catholic to believe in penance, but this was more than any father and mother should be expected to bear.

When my invitation came to attend the funeral mass at Saint Patrick's Cathedral in New York, my tears came again. But they were thankful tears that someone had thought to invite the Kennedy chauffeur. It was an awful way to feel part of the family, but I treasured that bit of kindness.

Of course I could not attend. I stayed at Hyannis Port with the Chief. And this time it was different than it had been when they buried the president. He had the TV on all the time. He was crying all the time, quietly. The tears never stopped for days. I tried to stay with him, but when Ted Kennedy delivered the eulogy for his brother I was so overcome that I had to leave the bedroom. I went outside and stayed in the hallway. Ted doesn't need any crib notes on his sleeve for this one, I thought.

Rita had also stayed in the room with the Chief. When

I went back into the bedroom and stood next to the Chief's bed, the three of us—Mr. Kennedy, his nurse, and his chauffeur—prayed silently.

The televised coverage continued. That long funeral train ride from New York to Washington. The black night and the rain. The Chief watched all of it. There were candles flickering in the darkness at Arlington, and when John Glenn and Bobby Kennedy, Jr., folded the flag that had covered Robert Kennedy's coffin I felt suddenly anxious for it to end. The astronaut, an old Kennedy family friend, handed the folded flag to young Bobby, and he in turn handed it to his mother. Another flag for a dead Kennedy.

One by one his children came and knelt by their father's grave. Rose Kennedy was on her only son's arm. The daughters stood alongside: Pat and Eunice and Jean. As I watched the final tribute, words Mrs. Kennedy had said to me alone in the car returning from her mother's funeral came back to me. "She had six children and she outlived three of them. She outlived her husband. But there is no suffering worse than for a mother to bury a child," Rose Kennedy had said.

Ethel had been a few months pregnant when her husband was murdered, and late into the summer she didn't let it put a damper on her tennis game. She seemed to be always on the court playing with a fury even for Ethel Kennedy, a fierce competitor to begin with. It was said she used physical activity to tire herself out, so she could sleep at night.

"I'm sorry," I told the pert little blond in Robert Kennedy's house, "but I didn't get your last name."

"Ko-peck-nee." She smiled. "Mary Jo Kopechne."

We shook hands. "Glad to meet you, Mary Jo. I'm Frank Saunders, Mr. Kennedy's chauffeur."

"How long have you worked for the family?" she asked.

"Since just after John Kennedy was inaugurated president," I said.

"They're wonderful, aren't they?"

"A little hard to work for sometimes." I laughed.

"Yes, I know." She laughed back.

"Did you work for . . . ?"

"Yes, I did," she said softly. "On the campaign. Typing his speeches. He meant a great deal to me. He would have been president, Frank," Mary Jo Kopechne said.

There were a few other former campaign workers at Robert Kennedy's house that day. I don't remember their names. They had come to help pack Robert Kennedy's papers and books, and in return Ethel Kennedy wanted to give them a bit of a vacation at Hyannis Port, in appreciation of all the work they'd done for her husband. I remember asking Mary Jo Kopechne if she was staying with Joey Gargan and his wife or the Shrivers, but I don't recall her answer.

The girls needed someone to carry out the heavy boxes of books.

"This is so sad, doing this. It's hard not to cry," Mary Jo Kopechne said.

51

Joan Kennedy was standing in the kitchen of the Squaw Island house when I went in with the Sunday morning newspapers. Somewhere in the house I could hear one-year-old Patrick crying.

"More stories about whether Ted will run for the presidency, I suppose," Joan said with a thin smile.

"There's been a lot," I said.

"They have to write about something," Joan said.

Patrick had stopped crying.

"I don't want him to run, Frank," Joan Kennedy said.

"He could walk in, Mrs. Kennedy."

"Walk into what?" she said with a hint of sarcasm. "So many people want him to run for their own reasons. There aren't many who take the time to think about what would be best for Ted."

"I guess they expected a Kennedy at the convention," I said.

Joan forced a smile. "There's so much pressure on him, Frank."

"It must be hard," I said.

"He has his family—and his brothers' children—to think about, but some of these politicians don't care about any of that." For the first time I felt uncomfortable talking with Joan. She seemed frightened and a little lost. "Sometimes I wish a big storm would come and take Squaw Island out to sea so we could be alone," she said quietly.

"Maybe Eunice should run." I laughed.

Joan smiled.

"I think she'd make a good president," I said, and I meant it.

"Sometimes I wish Ted was a banker instead of a politician," Joan Kennedy said. "Can I get you a cup of coffee, Frank?"

It was the first time I refused a cup of coffee from her. "I think I'll be going, Mrs. Kennedy," I said. I left the house without any doubt that Joan Kennedy did not want Ted to run for the presidency.

"She's going for a ride on the *Marlin*," a wide-eyed Dora told me. "With Ted!"

"She's going for a ride on the *Marlin*?" I said.

Dora raised her hand. "It's true," she said.

"Then something big must be up," I said.

I knew that if Ted was taking his mother for a ride on the yacht, it had to be a very special occasion. He had something important to talk over with her, and on the *Marlin* Mrs. Kennedy would be a captive audience.

"Ted's considering running, Frank," Mrs. Kennedy said from the backseat of the Chrysler. "He feels it might be his duty."

Why is she telling me this? I wondered. Because she has no one else to talk to?

Mrs. Kennedy started talking about the family tradition. And responsibility. Public service to others. How the Kennedys never quit. She seemed all wound up.

She was still on it when I interrupted her. "What does Joan think about it, Mrs. Kennedy?"

She did not answer. "The Kennedys have a mission," she said, and then rambled on. She started talking about her gardener. "Wilbert has been loyal to us. He's been with us twenty years. This is his dedication in life. Whatever God gives a man to do, he must do it well. With the Kennedys it is public service to others. . . ."

I thought: Wilbert has been with you for twenty years! Hell, Mrs. Kennedy, Wilbert's been with you a lot longer than that! She switched from Wilbert to her father, Honey

Fitz, to Franklin Delano Roosevelt. I couldn't make any sense out of what she was saying, but by then I knew she wasn't talking to her chauffeur; she was talking out loud to herself, trying to justify the decision her last son might make about seeking the presidency.

She never shut up all the way back to the compound. I tried to close my ears, thinking all the while about the flash of fear in Joan's eyes that Sunday morning in her kitchen. For Chrissakes, I thought, she'd rather have him alive than see him sentenced to death. And as Mrs. Kennedy ranted on about the family's tradition, I thought: Your husband's as good as dead to you, and your three sons are dead, and you're pushing your last one to run and maybe die too. I couldn't keep it back any longer.

"You know, Mrs. Kennedy, I never knew my father," I said, sneaking it in when she paused for a second. "I grew up without a father. I never even knew his name. . . ." In the rearview mirror I saw confusion in Rose Kennedy's eyes. "I lived in an orphanage in Connecticut. I never even knew my father's real name. . . ." Again I looked in the mirror. I paused, waiting for her to respond. But she said nothing, and I caught a glimpse of her twitching and turning in the seat. She can't handle this, I told myself. She's so puzzled and embarrassed that she hasn't the slightest idea what to say.

She hemmed and hawed for a second. We were in the driveway now.

"What I'm saying, Mrs. Kennedy, is that a father is very important to a young boy. Girls too, I guess. It would be better for all your grandchildren if Ted spent time with them instead of running for that damn job. You know how important your father was in your life," I said.

She flashed a quick smile. We had stopped in the turnaround, and she opened the door. "Ted'll do what's best, Frank," she said, and shut the car door.

I was glad when it became official, when Ted announced that he would not be a candidate. I think nearly all his family was pleased about his choice. And when we watched the rioting in Chicago and at the Democratic convention, everyone that I talked with at the Kennedy place said Ted was right for not getting himself in the middle of that mess. Although no one came right out and said it, I knew they were all thinking what I was thinking, that out there in Chicago there had to be some nut waiting to take a shot at Ted Kennedy, ready to get the last Kennedy.

52

Joseph P. Kennedy turned eighty that September 6, and the next day Tom Fitzgerald died. I would miss Tom Fitzgerald. I'd had a lot of laughs with him when he visited at Palm Beach, and then when he stayed at Hyannis Port for a few days, living in my old garage apartment. I used to get a kick out of Mrs. Kennedy's putting him over the garage because she didn't want her husband to know that her brother was visiting. He was a good man, and he and his wife were always kind to me. So I had another funeral to take Mrs. Kennedy to in the Chrysler. Of her three sisters and two brothers, now only one brother was left.

"Why, Frank, that little television you let me borrow until mine is fixed is color," Rose Kennedy said.

"Yes it is," I said. "And you can keep it as long as you want, Mrs. Kennedy. It's an extra set."

"But color, Frank! Mine isn't color. *I* can't afford a color TV," she said.

I wanted to call her a liar right then and there. Saying that she could not afford a color television set! It was a lie in the same way as all those times she had told me that the Kennedys could not afford to keep on a chauffeur when Mr. Kennedy died.

*   *   *

When I saw the headline in that morning's *Boston Herald* about Jacqueline Kennedy's plan to marry the Greek shipping magnate Aristotle Onassis, I was stunned. I read the story while Mrs. Kennedy was at mass.

"D'you see this?" I asked her as she got back in the car. I held up the *Herald*.

"It's true," Mrs. Kennedy replied, adding, "I've known about it for some time. Ari asked my permission."

So he's Ari to you, I thought. "So you know him, Mrs. Kennedy."

"Of course, Frank. I've known him many years. We visited with him a few times when we were at the house in Antibes and he was in Monte Carlo. Oh, yes! He is a very kind and very very successful man. But I advised Jacqueline to do what she thinks is best. Cardinal Cushing has blessed the marriage. It will give her a new life, and she will be financially independent. She will no longer be totally dependent on the Kennedys for her support. She will be able to have a new life and send the children to the best schools. Yes, I think it is wonderful!" Mrs. Kennedy said.

"Will you be going, Mrs. Kennedy? The paper says she is getting married in a few days in Greece. On some island he owns over there."

"Oh, no, Frank. I daren't leave Mr. Kennedy for even a few days," she said.

When I saw Rita I asked her about Jacqueline marrying the rich Greek. "Mrs. Kennedy said she knew about it all along but I had the feeling that she is still a bit surprised. But naturally if Cardinal Cushing says it's okay with him, you know, then it's okay with her too."

"It doesn't surprise me, Frank."

"Oh sure, Rita! I suppose you've known about it for months too," I said.

"Well, I wondered what Aristotle Onassis had on his mind when he was here."

"He was here? At Hyannis Port? Come on."

"For God's sake, Frank, you drove the man."

"I never drove Aristotle Onassis," I said.

"You must have seen him. He was right here for a few days."

"When?"

"This summer, Frank. Don't you remember? That small, dark man with the sunglasses and the white sweater. He sat right out there on the veranda."

"Yeah," I said, "I think I do. You mean that was Onassis? I thought Senator Pastore was visiting again."

Rita laughed and shook her head. Senator John Pastore of Rhode Island—a small dark-haired man in his sixties—often visited the compound. "So that was Aristotle Onassis. Well I'll be damned."

In a way I had to agree with Mrs. Kennedy. It was good for Jacqueline. Now she wouldn't have to send her bills to Park Avenue. She'd found a guy with more money than the Kennedys. After Robert Kennedy's death four and a half months earlier, Jacqueline had spent a great deal of time comforting her sister-in-law Ethel. Obviously Jacqueline didn't hold any grudges—assuming that what Rita had said about Ethel snubbing Jacqueline had happened the way the nurse said it had.

The last months had been hard on Ethel. Her secretary had had to stay at her place some nights because Ethel was having trouble sleeping, Rita had reported. And then Ethel had taken a nasty toss on the tennis court and everyone was afraid for a day or two that she might lose her baby. But by the time fall came Ethel seemed to be in much better spirits. By now she had ten children to worry about and they kept her busy. Her eleventh was due after Thanksgiving.

There seemed to be a real effort to make this Thanksgiving special. The clan gathered. But the Chief was doing poorly. He had rallied a bit after recovering from Bobby's death, but then began failing. He was losing weight and always seemed to have tears at the corners of his eyes. John Ryan worked hard cheering the boss up, but Mr. Kennedy remained listless. He didn't even want to see a movie much anymore. There was talk in the house that we might not go south that winter because of Mr. Kennedy's health. But the doctors said that the Chief should be taken to Palm Beach. If he didn't go south as usual, they said,

Mr. Kennedy might think that everyone had given up on him. Besides, Cape Cod could get pretty bleak in the winter.

So we packed all the stuff, and I got all the cars down to Florida. Mr. Kennedy's airplane had been retired after Bobby's death, donated to the Smithsonian. Joan Crawford, an old Hollywood friend of Mr. Kennedy's, offered to let the family use the Pepsi-Cola company's private plane, and that was how we flew down to Palm Beach—the Chief, Rita, and I.

53

It was a miserable winter. The weather was all right but the mood in the big seaside mansion was depressing. We were giving the Chief oxygen more and more. Dora had a stroke and had to be hospitalized. Then Rita got a terrible case of flu and was on the critical list for a while. With both his maid and his nurse in the hospital at the same time, we brought Mr. Kennedy over to visit them.

Ted would spend hours in his father's room, trying to cheer up the old man. His last son was the only one now who could get a smile from Mr. Kennedy.

Mrs. Kennedy worked on her memoirs.

I found refuge at O'Hara's.

One day I got a call from Tom Walsh. He wanted me to check out Rose Kennedy's secretary, who seemed to be doing a lot of dancing at night at the Ta-boo. The Kennedy office had reports that the secretary was dancing on the table, doing a little striptease. I checked, and it wasn't all that bad, she was just letting off a little steam. Still, Mr. Walsh had said, it just wouldn't do for Rose Kennedy's personal secretary to attract that kind of notoriety.

I didn't blame the secretary. It was so depressing at the house, we all had to do something to distract ourselves.

More than once I was tempted myself to go on a bender for a few days, but I figured that I'd better stick around, because we had the feeling now that Mr. Kennedy might not last through the winter.

* * *

At first I thought it was thunder. Terrible thuds and bangs. Then as I slowly woke up, I realized someone was pounding on my door; it sounded as if they were knocking it down.

I groped for my watch, but it was pitch-black inside the apartment and just as black outside. The middle of the night, I decided, still in a daze.

A man was shouting on the other side of the door.

My mind flashed on. It might be an emergency with Mr. Kennedy over at the house. An agent yelling? I fumbled in the darkness for my trousers. then I got the light on.

My night visitor was still yelling and banging the door, but I couldn't make out what he was saying because of the awful pounding.

"It's me!" he yelled, this time clearly.

"Who the fuck is 'me'!" I shouted at the door. I was awake enough now to be mad.

"Me! It's . . . *me*! It's . . . the . . . *senator*!" Ted boomed.

I opened the door, and there he was with his fist up ready to pound again, and with the door opening so suddenly he nearly fell through the doorway. That's when I smelled him. Ted had been drinking, all right.

"You okay, Senator?" I asked.

He looked rough and was breathing heavily.

"Yeh, I'm fine. Jesus, Frank, what took you so long? Listen, Frank, I've had a little problem with the car," he said.

"I was asleep, Senator. It's the middle of the goddam night, you know."

Ted laughed. Brother, are you ever ripe, I thought.

"You alone?" I asked.

"I think so," he said with a grin.

Now I laughed.

"Car's stuck. The fucking thing's stuck down the road," he said.

"Where?"

"The road. Down the road! This road, for Chrissakes. Can you take care of it?"

"How far?"

"Just down the road." He threw out his arm. "Down there. I walked."

"Out of gas, you mean?"

"No! It's stuck. Didn't I say it was stuck?" Ted lowered his voice. "I missed the turn," he said. He gave me his college-boy chuckle.

"Where?"

"The turn up from the golf course. You know, you know."

I knew the turn, all right. "I'll take care of it," I said.

"Take care of it," he said.

"You want a ride home?"

"No. I'll walk. Just take care of it."

"You sure you don't want a ride? You all right?"

"I'm fine," he said.

I stared at him and smiled. "You look just fine."

"Oh, I'm fine all right," he said, and slapped me on the shoulder. "You take care of it for me and do it now so nobody will spot the car."

"Okay, Senator. I'll take care of it. You'd better go home."

Then I watched him walk into the night, down North Ocean in the direction he had come from. He seemed to walk fine. Ted and Joan's rented house was close by—Ted had walked by his driveway to get to me.

By the time I had the car out of the garage, Ted was gone.

I went down the road. I knew the corner. It was a bad one.

His car had crashed two-tenths of a mile from his father's house. Heading north toward Mr. Kennedy's, where the straight road takes a sharp turn to the left, Ted had missed the turn. He had plowed straight ahead, over a curb and into a tangle of shrubbery just short of a cement wall.

I aimed my headlights at his car. It looked to be bogged down in sand. Hopeless. I would need a wrecker to haul it out.

No car went by. North Ocean dead-ends past the Kennedy house; there is no through traffic. At this time of night, I figured, a car coming up the road would be either a neighbor or the police. Either way we'd have no trouble.

Careful now, I told myself. Make sure you can trust these garage men to keep their mouths shut about this.

I returned to my garage apartment and called for a wrecker. After the man heard it was for the Kennedys, the tow truck roared up right away.

Soon the car was hauled out.

The wrecker crew helped me bend back the twisted, crushed shrubs. We did the best we could to cover up the mess.

It was near dawn when I finished straightening things out. I paid the garage men out of my own pocket, giving the guys on the truck a good tip.

Driving Mrs. Kennedy home from mass a bit later, I slowed before the turn so I could take a good look at it. The road is a long straightaway before it turns. The golf course is on the left and the ocean is on the right. I didn't mention Ted's accident to his mother.

Looking at it in the daylight I knew Ted had to be going like hell to miss the turn. Maybe he'd fallen asleep, maybe he'd been too drunk, maybe it was both. I didn't see any skid marks. If he had been really flying he could have smashed into the thick cement wall. He might have been hurt.

When I saw Ted again he said nothing about his accident. He didn't even ask how much I'd had to shell out to fix everything. He never even thanked me for my trouble.

But I did get my money back. I sent the bill to Tom Walsh at the Kennedy office in New York. Ted's accident was another lesson for me in how ungrateful the Kennedys could be toward the people who worked for them. They *expected* you to do everything for them, no matter how dirty the work. If only they'd show some appreciation every so often . . . yet getting any kind of thanks from them was about as likely as getting a pay-raise.

She visited Jacqueline and Aristotle Onassis in Greece at Easter. It was, I thought, a convenient way of not having to be around when they moved Mr. Kennedy back to the Cape.

It was my job to close down the Palm Beach house. We packed all the household items—from alarm clocks to

321

silverware—and I got the spare cars moved up. Then I threw a party. It lasted for days. Even now, that party at the Kennedys' is remembered in Palm Beach—not, of course, by the socialites and rich people, but by my friends. It took two days just to clean up after, but I had plenty of help.

When she returned from her visit with Jacqueline, Mrs. Kennedy asked, at Hyannis Port, if I'd done what she asked me to when I closed the Florida house. She had a long list of questions. Yes, I'd put the lawn furniture away. And yes, I'd made sure there wasn't a dirty dish in the sink. And yes, I'd called the exterminator.

"How's Jacqueline?" I asked.

"That's a damn lie!" I said.

"The maid said you did," Mrs. Kennedy said.

"Well, I didn't," I said.

"The maid said you did," she said.

I hit the brake and the Chrysler stopped dead in the traffic on Main Street in the West End of Hyannis. I spun around in the driver's seat so I could look right at her. "I'm telling you that I didn't," I said. "You can believe her if you want, but I am telling you that I didn't."

Behind us car horns were blaring. One driver shot me a peculiar look as he squeezed by the Chrysler.

"I do not like being called a liar, Mrs. Kennedy." Then I turned back and drove off. On purpose I stomped the accelerator to make the Chrysler lurch ahead. And when we reached the rotary by the Music Tent I went around it so fast that the tires screeched.

She didn't say another word until I parked in front of the big house. After she got out of the car, she came around to my side and said, "I'm going to ask the maid right now what happened." She spun on her heels and headed toward the veranda steps.

"You bitch," I said loudly, aiming my words at her back.

I knew she'd heard me because I saw her hesitate for a split second, but she never turned around. And I was ready to say it to her face, that she was a bitch for acting that way over who had left the light on in her doll room.

54

"Mary Jo Kopechne. I met her last summer at Bobby's house," I said. "Sure. The little blond—I don't think she was much over five feet—with the long hair. And she drowned in Ted's car? Jesus, the poor kid," I said.

"The poor guy, you mean," said Jack Crimmins, Ted's chauffeur.

"Yeah, but she's *dead*, Jack," I said.

"And the thing could ruin the guy," Jack Crimmins said.

"It was an accident, right?"

"You think those guys outside give a damn if it was an accident?" He nodded in the direction of the gate, where the guards were keeping the crowd of reporters out of the compound. "They'd nail him to the cross, you know that, Frank."

"What the hell happened? He had to be shit-faced to miss a turn like that," I said. Like he was that night at Palm Beach, I thought.

"What can I tell you, Frank? I wasn't in the car." He gave me a knowing Irish look, this savvy bachelor who worked as an investigator in the Suffolk County district attorney's office in Boston when he wasn't driving Ted Kennedy. Whatever he might know, he clearly did not want to talk about what happened that night on Chappaquiddick Island. "Read what those guys say in the papers. They got all the answers," he said.

"It's too bad you weren't driving, Jack," I said. Ted's chauffeur glared at me. "All I mean is that if you were driving him he wouldn't have missed that turn and the girl would still be alive and, well, that's all I meant."

Jack Crimmins nodded and smiled painfully. "I know, Frank," he said.

"Joey Gargan looks like he got banged up worse than Ted," I said.

"What do you mean?" he asked, sounding more like a cop now than a chauffeur.

"He's got on a long-sleeve shirt and it's humid and hot, and I saw him a little while ago and he walks like he hurt himself."

"Don't tell those reporters a damn thing you see in here. But I don't have to tell you that, do I, Frank?"

At first none of us realized how bad it was. It was drizzling and overcast that mid-July Saturday when we got word that Ted's car had been in some kind of accident on Chappy, as we called Chappaquiddick, a little island on the western end of Martha's Vineyard, just off Edgartown. It was where they were having the annual Edgartown Regatta, and Ted had gone over again to sail the president's boat *Victura*.

All the Kennedys had sailed in the Edgartown Regatta, since they'd been boys. Joe, Jr., and Jack and Bobby and Ted. The summer before no Kennedy had sailed in the weekend race, because six weeks earlier Robert Kennedy had been assassinated, but Ted had returned for this 1969 regatta. In the newspaper accounts of the accident, I'd read that Mary Jo Kopechne, twenty-eight, and five other girls who had worked for Bobby had a cookout at a little cottage on Chappy that Joe Gargan had rented. The girls were called "The Boiler-Room Girls" because they had sweated in the political "boiler room" of Senator Robert Kennedy's presidential campaign. The names of a couple of the other girls who'd been on Chappaquiddick that night sounded familiar and, I thought, maybe I had also met them that day I helped the girls pack Bobby's books and papers. But I remembered little Mary Jo well from just those few hours. I remembered how she idolized the Kennedys.

I read that there were three men besides Ted and cousin Joe Gargan at the cookout on Chappy—Paul Markham, a former U.S. attorney in Boston and a friend of Joey's and Ted's; Ray La Rosa, another of Ted's friends who had worked on his 1964 campaign; and Charles Tretter, who had worked for Ted for a few years, until 1966. And of course Jack Crimmins was there to take care of all the chauffeuring.

The newspapers said Joe Gargan had organized the regatta weekend as a favor to Bobby's most dedicated campaign workers.

Ted's car, the way I heard it around the big house that Saturday morning, had been in an accident and had gone off a little wooden bridge and into a tidal pond. I guess one of the maids heard something on the local radio station. Right away I thought something must be wrong, because I knew that Jack Crimmins was too good a chauffeur to drive the big Oldsmobile 88 off a narrow bridge.

Then we heard that a girl, a Kennedy secretary, was discovered drowned in the overturned Olds.

By the time the radio had more details, and reported that Ted told the police he had been driving, Ted and Paul Markham had flown back from the Vineyard in a private plane and were at the compound.

It wasn't until late that Saturday afternoon that the radio identified Mary Jo Kopechne as the dead girl in Ted's car. Already there were reporters hanging around the entrance to the Kennedy driveway.

"I won't be going to mass in Hyannis," Mrs. Kennedy said. "A priest will come in and say mass in the house."

I nodded. I understood. She didn't want all those reporters swarming after her this time, with perhaps embarrassing questions. Having mass said at the house was the smart thing to do, she must have realized, and I had to agree.

That Sunday after the accident, I had to go up to Boston and chauffeur a carload of lawyers back to the compound. I picked them up at a downtown office in Boston. They were a somber bunch, and I remember that the faces I saw in the rearview mirror on the way home to Hyannis Port had the same kind of expressions you see on men riding in a funeral procession. Most of all I remember their silence—total silence—until one of them said, "We've got to get him in that court quickly and get it over with. Even if he has to plead to a leaving-the-scene. The longer it festers the worse it will get."

Then another lawyer mentioned that Mary Jo Kopechne's body was being flown off Martha's Vineyard that day and that there was not going to be an autopsy.

The Chief sat in his wheelchair and stared out the window at another overcast day. There was a fog on Nantucket Sound, and I had the feeling that we were in for a spell of lousy weather, a long stretch of drizzly days. I was glad that I wasn't one of those Cape Cod vacationers who had picked this week in July to spend at the beach. Mr. Kennedy was listless and uninterested in anything I talked about.

I asked his nurse what the Chief knew about the accident on Chappaquiddick. "Ted told him as soon as he came home," Rita said.

"What did you do, listen on the intercom?" I asked.

Rita glowered at me.

Mr. Kennedy was not interested in the newspapers now, and it had nothing to do with Ted being all over the front page. He had not really been interested in anything since Bobby's death. So I knew he wasn't reading about Ted's accident. Still, Mr. Kennedy continued to have an uncanny sense of what was going on in his house. He could not talk, his hearing was bad, and his eyesight was failing, but he *knew* something serious was happening around him.

Rita claimed that Ted had told his father that it was all an accident. Twice he had repeated that he was telling the truth and that no matter what the newspapers and others might say about the girl's death, Ted wanted his father to know that he was telling the truth.

Strange things happened those next few days. I saw Mrs. Kennedy talking alone with Ted by the flagpole at the turnaround in front of the house. Rita had said that whenever mother and son had something to discuss they went outside and stood by the flagpole.

Another time I noticed Ted surrounded by his mother and sisters Eunice and Pat, both of whom had come to Hyannis Port right away, along with Ethel. When I saw Ted surrounded by all those Kennedy women I felt sorry for him. This time more than perhaps any other he could have used his brothers to advise him, I thought. Really for the first time, he was on his own.

Ted would come up from Squaw Island and there'd be meetings in Mr. Kennedy's house. I made it a point to stay out of the way. A few times Joan came with him, but mostly he was alone when he came to his father's house.

55

Joan began drinking right after Chappaquiddick.

Before Ted's accident I never saw Joan with a drink in her hand. I remember that because it was a rarity to see anyone around the Kennedys without a drink sooner or later. There was always a pitcher of awful-tasting Bloody Marys somewhere, and you didn't have to search hard for a drink at the house, and of course there were parties all the time. But I never saw Joan wandering around with a glass until her husband got in all the trouble.

From then on that summer, I hardly ever saw her without a drink. When I went into the house on Squaw, either to drop off the morning newspapers or to pick up or bring home the children, Joan looked mulled. I had done enough drinking myself and had spent enough time in bars to know when someone was on the sauce. It hurt to see Joan Kennedy like that, even if it was understandable. Some people believed Ted's story of what had happened that night and some did not; but everyone wondered what he was doing alone with an unmarried blond in his car. That was the real tragedy of Chappaquiddick for Joan Kennedy.

As far as I was concerned, the key lay with Jack Crimmins. Jack never would have let Ted drive a girl back to her motel on Martha's Vineyard, he was much too smart for that. The senator already had a reputation as a bit of a womanizer, and nobody was more protective toward Ted than his chauffeur. If Ted had said that he was leaving and taking Mary Jo to the ferry and then back to the motel south of Edgartown where the girls were registered, I was certain that Jack Crimmins would have insisted on going with them. Jack might have let Ted *drive*, but he would have been in that car. Even at midnight, little Edgartown would have been humming with the yachting crowd. Jack would not have let Ted risk being seen alone that late at night with a young blond. Neither would Jack, who was in his late fifties at least, have passed up a chance to trade a night at a cramped little beach cottage with lousy beds for a nice private room in a motel. Jack Crimmins liked his creature comforts. And there was still another point, something I could appreciate professionally. Chauffeurs hate letting their cars go. A chauffeur without his car feels as naked as a gunfighter without his six-shooter.

I have no idea what really happened that night of July 18–19 over on Chappy, but I can't picture Jack Crimmins tossing Ted the keys to the Olds, or just saying, "Sure, Ted, they're in the car. Have fun."

Maybe Joan sensed it, too, this feeling that Jack wasn't the kind of guy who'd let Ted drive a girl alone back to her motel. If anything, Joan knew her husband's driver better than I did, and how protective he was toward Ted. With only thirteen months having passed since Bobby's assassination, Ted'd driver wasn't going to let the last Kennedy go *anywhere* alone, at *any time*.

So more than once that summer I saw Joan wandering across the compound lawns, glass in hand. She was still always polite to me, and tried to be warm and friendly whenever I stopped to chat with her, but I could tell it was an effort. She was very depressed.

One morning, when I was alone with her in the Squaw Island house, Joan began talking about how important family and parents are to children.

"Some friends—I guess they're friends," she said with a weak smile, "told me I should divorce my husband." She paused. She looked tired, as if she had not gotten much sleep. "They don't know how anybody can live with the Kennedys, they're so, well, overpowering sometimes. Some of them have said they don't understand politicians and I told them that they don't understand love. You've seen Ted with the children. You know how much he loves his children and I know how much he loves me. How can people get divorced so easily, so thoughtlessly? I don't understand it, Frank, do you?"

She seemed to be talking more to herself than to me, as though she wanted to say out loud what she must have been telling herself.

I shrugged, unable to come up with any helpful response.

"The worst thing that ever happened to me was when my parents were divorced," she went on. "It hurt me deeply. I could never do that to my children. I could never divorce my husband, no matter what."

And then Joan—self-conscious, I thought, for having bared her feelings to a chauffeur—made a little joke. "Perhaps Ted might want to divorce *me* but . . ."

I was glad to leave. It had been an uncomfortable few minutes. Afterward, I thought about what Joan had said every time I saw her with a glass in her hand, stumbling across the front lawn toward the beach. Anyway, I figured, Joan doesn't have to worry about Rose Kennedy taking her for a drunk, remembering all those times in the car when I had a breath on and Mrs. Kennedy had a few drinks himself every so often. One night I'd had more than a few with a priest while Mrs. Kennedy was giving a talk to the Women's Guild at Saint Francis Xavier, and it was a miracle I had been able to drive home. And still she hadn't said a thing. If she couldn't detect liquor on her chauffeur that night, she wouldn't notice Joan drinking, I was sure.

56

It was also right after Chappaquiddick that the Chief started going downhill fast. He had been failing before, but now he seemed to be getting worse day by day, it was so very noticeable.

His eyes had a film on them. Sometimes I even wondered if he recognized me. Often I had to make an effort to get his attention. His freckles had became big liver splotches, and his face was very drawn. All his meals were brought to his room now, and it was harder for him to force himself to eat. He'd lost his fight. He wasn't even interested in seeing a movie anymore. And always there were those tears in his eyes.

He had stopped wearing his glasses now and would sit in his wheelchair on those days the nurse and John Ryan could get him out of bed. He would rub the corners of his eyes with his good left hand, leaving his eyes almost constantly red.

Ted visited, and that still cheered the Chief up. But as soon as Ted left, Mr. Kennedy would sink right back. None of the rest of us could reach him.

Rita told me that almost one hundred nurses had worked for Mr. Kennedy in the seven and a half years since the stroke. She'd kept track of them, she said, even the ones who'd only worked one day before quitting. I found myself wondering if it had been worth it; what good had it been, anyway. He'd never walked again and, worse, never talked. So what had all the expensive medical care accomplished? They'd kept Mr. Kennedy alive, and in those years two sons were murdered and his last son had brought shame to him. Maybe it would have been better if he had not lived.

Mrs. Kennedy came into her husband's room now and stayed with him, alone. The Chief no longer had the strength to chase her out. The noises he could still make were too weak.

It didn't matter to me now when she reminded me that the Kennedys could not afford to keep me on when Mr. Kennedy died. It was a matter of *when* now, not *if* he died. For the life of me I don't know why she kept repeating it.

Seven years is a long time to have the dress you will wear to your husband's funeral hanging in your closet, I said to myself.

"He's blind," Rita said.

"He can't see at all?" I asked.

"He can make out shapes. And he can recognize voices."

"But he's blind then?"

"Yes. An operation would probably do no good. It's been discussed."

"It would be better if he just goes."

"Yes. He's in pain now. Have you heard him give those little sobs?"

"Yes," I said.

"Well, that is from the pain. He's having trouble breathing. I'm giving him oxygen all the time. And his throat is constricting on him so that he's having trouble swallowing. I put an ice cube in a piece of cloth and he sucks on that to loosen his throat."

"What do they want us to do?"

"They want nature to take her course. But there will be no heroic measures. They have decided against that."

"Is the oxygen out now?"

"Of course not, Frank! They just don't want him put on a machine. Mr. Kennedy will not be admitted to the hospital. He will remain here, in his own house."

*   *   *

Mary Jo Kopechne's death was in the news again that October. There had been talk of exhuming the body for an autopsy. But her parents said they did not want their daughter disturbed, and a judge in Pennsylvania, where she was buried, blocked the request by the Massachusetts county district attorney.

An inquest into the circumstances of her death was still scheduled, however, and with that to go through and Mr. Kennedy dying, the mood at the compound was somber indeed.

After Halloween it turned sour. The cold damp days bothered Mrs. Kennedy. I made sure to have the heat up high in the Chrysler when she got in the car for morning mass. We had a stretch of gray days and the wind came up at night, and when the wind blew in off the ocean the first thing it hit were the Kennedy houses. There was a terrible two-day storm, but it did not matter now because Mr. Kennedy was on his deathbed and he could not hear the banshee in the wind.

"Frank, please tell Ethel that I think it is near the time and she should begin calling everyone," Mrs. Kennedy said.

"You want me to tell her that you have requested her to call everyone?"

"Yes, I do. Tell her I said it is time."

How ironic this is, I thought. It was Ethel Kennedy who first told me that Mr. Kennedy was coming home to Hyannis Port, and now I am the one who has to tell her that she should begin calling the family because Mr. Kennedy is dying.

Jacqueline smiled and whispered, "Frank, it is so good to see you." The photographers snapped pictures as I walked with her to the waiting car. "It's good to see you, Mrs. Onassis," I said.

"Mrs. Onassis" didn't sound quite right to me, but Mrs. Kennedy had referred to her as Mrs. Onassis when she said I was to meet Jacqueline at the airport, so I called her Mrs. Onassis.

It was a cold day. I had on my hunting mackinaw and

wool cap. Jacqueline shivered and hunched her shoulders as she got in the Chrysler.

"How's Grandpa, Frank? Is he in any pain?"

"No, he's not, Mrs. Onassis. Well, some, I guess. But not so that he's suffering. They're giving him medication now, anyway."

"It has been a long ordeal for him, hasn't it?"

"I think I should tell you that he is blind now. He may not even recognize your voice," I said.

Jacqueline was silent. I could see in the rearview mirror that one of the photographers was following us.

"Well, I'll bet you don't have this kind of raw weather in Greece, Mrs. Onassis. I'll bet it's beautiful over there."

"Yes, it is. I am very happy, Frank."

"We got your house ready."

"Thank you," she said softly, then added after a pause, "What will happen to them, Frank, after Mr. Kennedy dies?" I did not answer. I did not know what to say.

"He was a magnificent man," she said.

"He was a good boss, I can tell you that."

"He was your friend, too. He was my friend," Jacqueline said.

"Mrs. Kennedy . . . I'm sorry," I said, "would you like me to take you to your house, Mrs. Onassis?"

"Please take me to Mr. Kennedy's. I want him to know that I am here," she said.

All the family were gathering. It was November 15 when Jacqueline arrived from Greece, and on that same day Dr. Russell Bowles was called. Dr. Bowles was more than Mr. Kennedy's doctor; he was an old friend.

The next morning Mrs. Kennedy said, as she got in the car, "I didn't get much sleep. I sat up with him all night." She had expected her husband's death any time for eight years, and now that she knew it was coming Mrs. Kennedy was facing it with a calmness I had not expected.

"When will he die, Rita?"

"Soon, I think," the nurse said.

"Does he know they are all here?"

334

"Yes. Mr. Shriver told him that everyone had come early for Thanksgiving."

"Did he understand?"

"I don't know. He didn't recognize Ted the other night. Oh, it was so sad. Ted was telling him, 'Dad, it's me, Teddy. Can you hear me? Please talk to me, Dad.' But Mr. Kennedy couldn't respond."

"Then I guess I'd better say good-bye to him."

"I would, Frank, yes."

I went in alone. Mr. Kennedy's eyes were open and he was staring at the ceiling. I looked at the intercom and thought about turning it off, but I didn't. I went to the bed and took his left hand in both of mine. "It's Frank, Chief," I said.

He did not move. "It's Frank, Chief. Your chauffeur."

I felt his left hand move slightly. "I did the best I could, Chief," I said.

Once again a priest came and gave him the last rites. In the late morning of November 18, my son's birthday, Mr. Kennedy died. His family was at his bedside with him. Jacqueline, Ethel, Pat, Eunice, Jean, Ted, Joan, Steve Smith, Sargent Shriver, Ann, Rita, and Louella Hennessey. Just before he died, they called Rose Kennedy into her husband's room. Rita told me thay were saying the Our Father when Mr. Kennedy died.

Mr. Kennedy was waked in the living room of his house. It was a private wake, for the family and a few close friends. The funeral mass was at Saint Francis Xavier. This time I did not drive Mrs. Kennedy. She rode in the black limousine with her family. After the mass the funeral cars headed for Boston for the burial. Wilbert drove me up. The gardener had offered to drive and I let him. It was over, and I knew that I would never drive a Kennedy car again.

Wilbert was a slow driver. We fell behind the funeral cars. By the time we got to the cemetery outside Boston the graveside services were just ending and they were lowering the Chief's casket into the ground.

* * *

335

I loaded Ann's luggage into her old, battered Willys Jeepster. "You sure you'll be all right?" I asked, because her old station wagon was always breaking down. "I'll be glad to drive you, Ann."

"I'll be fine, Frank," she said.

"Well, this is good-bye then, I guess, Ann."

"Good-bye, Frank," Ann Gargan said.

"Good luck to you, Ann," I said.

Ann smiled. Why after nine years does Ann have to be so shy with me? I wondered as I watched Mr. Kennedy's niece leave down the driveway. I thought: Maybe now at last she can make a life for herself. With the money her uncle left her she won't have to worry about earning a living. It is a luxury you do not have, I told myself.

"As I said, we cannot afford to keep you on, Frank," Rose Kennedy told me in her little office. We were alone.

She kept her eyes down at the desk while talking. "But I have told Tom Walsh that you should be paid through the end of the year."

I nodded.

"But you may leave today if you wish."

"Then I will."

"Fine, Frank." She had not yet looked me in the eye.

"Mrs. Kennedy. May I have a letter of recommendation from you?"

"See my secretary about that," she said, and began busying herself scribbling on a piece of paper.

I walked out of her little office without a further word. The kitchen was empty. It had always reminded me of a ship's kitchen. Battleship gray. In a cupboard, behind a stack of dishes, I found the dime Matilda had asked me to leave in the kitchen that day Mrs. Kennedy complained about her chauffeur getting a free cup of coffee. I put the dime in my pocket, went out the back door, and walked down the long driveway, out of the Kennedy compound.

57

And so, in the early spring of 1980, I came back to the Kennedy compound. The Chief had been dead ten years. That spring, as his last son campaigned for the Democratic nomination for the presidency, everything was coming full circle.

I'd had some bad times right after I left the Kennedys.

My marriage broke up. It was coming apart when I worked for the Kennedys. One night I came home to the little Cape Cod house on Old Stage Road and my wife had locked me out. The hell with it, I decided. I left and told my wife that was the end of it.

I tried selling cars. It didn't work out. Then one night I felt a terrible pain, as if I'd been stabbed in the stomach with a sword, and I collapsed. When I regained consciousness there was no pain, but I was on the floor in a pool of blood. My old navy ulcer had gotton worse and now it had burst.

I was lucky. I had enough strength to make it to the telephone, and the police came and rushed me to Cape Cod Hospital. They operated, and slowly I recovered.

Still in the hospital, I called Ted Kennedy's office to see if they could help me with the Veterans' Administration. I was desperate, with this big hospital bill and no job. Ted's secretary Angelique took care of everything. Then, after a while, I got a job with the town of Barnstable, next door to Hyannis Port, and my life took a turn up. I work for the town to this day, doing a bit of drafting in the engineering department of the Public Works Department, using what talents I have as an artist.

When I heard the Kennedys were looking for a weekend security guard that spring, I applied and was put back on the payroll. Once again the "Kennedy Special" checks started coming from the Park Avenue office.

I figured I could use the extra money, but the real reason I went back to work for the family was to see Rose Kennedy again, face-to-face. It was the only way I could know for certain that the bitterness I had felt toward her all these years was gone.

She was in Palm Beach and the compound was empty. As I walked through the house and roamed the compound alone, I began rounding up my memories. I'd see an old TV film of the president or a picture in the newspapers of Ted and a memory would come back. But it had all happened so long ago, and thinking about my days with the family, about Rose Kennedy and what she'd done to me, my feelings of resentment became less certain. Maybe I didn't resent her at all. That was what I needed to know as I waited for her to come home.

That spring Rose Kennedy's crocuses and daffodils bloomed without Wilbert to tend them. The gardener had retired. Matilda was gone, as was Dora. And I knew that when summer came there would be no *Marlin* and no Captain Frank Wirtanen on Nantucket Sound.

I saw Ted around some weekends, but not to talk to. He seemed preoccupied whenever I saw him. Joey Gargan was around the compound, and one weekend Jack Dempsey came in with some friends. Jack showed them the Kennedy place, boasting how close he was to the family. But other than that the compound was quiet.

It was late that spring when Mrs. Kennedy came up to Hyannis Port, the first of the family to settle in for the season.

At first I stayed out of her way, out of the big house. And I didn't see her outside. She was in and out of a wheelchair now, and the nurse, who had also worked for Mr. Kennedy, told me Rose had her good days and her bad ones. In July she would be ninety.

I knew that sooner or later Rose Kennedy and I would have our meeting, but something kept me from pushing it.

Then, one sunny day after it turned warm, I saw Jacqueline Onassis walking across the yard behind Robert Kennedy's house. She was alone. She came toward me, and I saw her smile. "Oh, Frank! How nice to see you again!" Jacqueline said. Still that hushed, girlish voice, that smile that was always a mystery to me. She looked wonderful, but then she'd always made sure that she did. She extended her hand, but instead of a handshake she crooked her pinky and I touched her finger. I felt a bit peculiar doing it.

Jacqueline had come to visit her mother-in-law. She had begun building her dream house at Gay Head on Martha's Vineyard. Finallly Jacqueline was getting her house on the sea, the one she had once thought about building on Squaw Island. She would have her own summer place away from the Kennedys now. I wondered what would become of their house on Irving Avenue.

"Have you talked with Mrs. Kennedy?" Jacqueline asked.

"Not yet," I said.

"Oh, she'll be glad to see you again," she said with a smile. I doubt it, I said to myself.

"So nice to see you again, Frank," Jacqueline said, smiled again, and walked away.

I recognized Rose Kennedy's voice right away. I was coming around the corner of the big house, at the front, when I heard her. As soon as I did, I stopped in my tracks, but then, after about a minute, I proceeded and turned the corner of the house. She was no longer talking. She was standing on the lawn, her back turned to me, and she was alone.

"Hello, Mrs. Kennedy," I said.

She turned and smiled. "Hello," she said.

"How have you been, Mrs. Kennedy?"

"Fine. Just fine," she said.

She seemed a bit puzzled, and I wondered if perhaps I had startled her. The years had been gentle on her.

"Well, it's nice seeing you again, Mrs. Kennedy," I said.

"Thank you," she said. She kept on looking at me, and I knew from the blankness on her face that she had not recognized me.

I snuck up into the old attic alone. It was nearly empty. There was a metal file cabinet and three big cardboard boxes on the floor. I knelt and began thumbing through the letters that were stuffed in the boxes, those tens of thousands of letters of condolence from America to the Kennedys on the death of the president. After a while, I felt the eeriness up there in the attic alone with those letters of sorrow, and started to leave. I took one last look around. Gone with all the rest of the heirlooms and junk and treasures and memorabilia was the brown paper package tied in hemp. So, I figured, the old torn lace curtain had been thrown away.

Mrs. Kennedy's nurse said she needed help. The elevator wasn't working. Mrs. Kennedy would have to be carried up the stairs to her bedroom, and the nurse said she didn't have the strength. "Would you do it, please, Frank?" she asked.

I lifted Rose Kennedy as gently as I could. I could tell she was a bit frightened. "Just relax now, Mrs. Kennedy, and I'll carry you up to your bedroom," I said as I started up the stairs. She felt light in my arms, and it was not hard carrying her.

Behind us on the stairs the nurse kept saying, "It's Frank, Mrs. Kennedy. It's Frank, dear. You remember Frank. Your old chauffeur." The nurse repeated it all the way up the stairs.

I carried her into her bedroom and set her down on her bed. And just as I did, as I was releasing her, Rose Kennedy kissed me on the cheek. "Oh, thank you, Frank. Thank you," she said.

I stepped back from the bed and smiled at her. It was over. It was finished between us. Finally I felt free. But I could not help but wish that she'd done it ten years ago.

"It's Frank," she said to her nurse.

"Yes. It's Frank, dear. Isn't it nice to see Frank again?"

Rose was still smiling. I turned to leave. For the last time I took in the view from her window. In my mind I pictured the blue and gold and white presidential flag on the flagpole. As I turned away I happened to notice that she had strung along the top of her little desk the funeral-mass cards of her husband and dead children. At the end of the row was a photograph of a darkly beautiful young girl, her daughter Rosemary, who was still in that home. But I knew, seeing Rosemary's picture there with the Chief and Joe, Jr., and Jack and Bobby and Kathleen, that Rosemary too was dead for Rose Kennedy.

"Good-bye, Mrs. Kennedy," I said.

But that was not my last good-bye. It was just getting dusk a few days later, the end of a beautiful summer day. I was leaving in my car, turning to drive away, when suddenly Rose Kennedy appeared at the front corner of the house, by the veranda. She was dressed all in white, a kind of hospital gown and a long white lace shawl wrapped around her head. She was sitting in the wheelchair. And there, pushing her aunt, was Ann Gargan.

Ann Gargan! I hadn't seen her since that day I packed her luggage into the old Jeep. I had heard that she'd married an airline pilot not long after leaving the Kennedys. But then Ann's husband had died suddenly, a year or so later. And now she was back for a visit, pushing a wheelchair for her aunt the way she had pushed a wheelchair for the Chief.

"Hello, Ann," I said. "It's me, Frank. Hello, Mrs. Kennedy."

They were twenty feet away, and Ann slowly pushed the wheelchair closer. "Hello, Frank," she said, then smiled.

"How have you been, Ann?"

"Fine, Frank. And you?"

"Can't complain."

"Who?" Rose said.

"It's Frank, Aunt Rose," Ann said.

"Nice seeing you again, Ann," I said.

"Yes, Frank," Ann said with that shy smile.

341

The wheelchair was just off the edge of the driveway on the grass. I drove slowly by them. "Mrs. Kennedy," I said. She looked at me and grinned, and all the way down the driveway I wondered if Rose Kennedy had in fact recognized me, or if she was smiling to be polite.